ML

ook is to be returned
ast da

92

194

5

17 MAR   JUL 1991

中国点心谱大全
DIMSUM

MARGARET LEEMING AND
MAY HUANG MAN-HUI

中
国
点
心
谱
大
全

DIMSUM

Chinese light meals, pastries and delicacies

Macdonald

FOR GILL ROWLEY

A **Macdonald** BOOK

© Margaret Leeming and May Huang Man-hui, 1985

First published in Great Britain in 1985
by Macdonald & Co (Publishers) Ltd
London & Sydney

A member of BPCC plc

British Library Cataloguing in Publication Data

Leeming, Margaret
  Dimsum.
  1. Cookery, Chinese   2. Cookery (Appetizers)
  3. Snack foods
  I. Title   II. May Huang Man-hui
  641.8912   TX724.5.C5

  ISBN 0-356-10244-0

Filmset by Flair plan Photo-typesetting Limited

Printed and bound in Spain by Printer Industria Gráfica SA,
Barcelona. D.L.B. 35126-1984

Macdonald & Co (Publishers) Ltd
Maxwell House
74 Worship Street
London EC2A 2EN

Editor: Lee Faber
Designer: Pete Pengilley
Photographer: Christine Hanscombe
Illustrator: Tessa Land

目 录
Contents

Chapter 1

'Order dish, following inclination'

点菜随心'

Dimsum are a special feature in Chinese food. Embracing both the simple and the sophisticated, they are prized and eaten by all levels of Chinese society. On Sundays whole families go to a big restaurant to eat dimsum for lunch. On weekdays the same dimsum may be the basis for a smart social gathering for the rich, or alternatively part of a quick snack for workers.

A large dimsum palace in Hong Kong or in the West may be on several floors seating a thousand people on each floor. Everywhere there are crowded tables and down the aisles between them, waiters push trolleys laden with dimsum kept warm by heaters. Each trolley carries a different style of dish, one *shaomai* and other dumplings, another deep-fried croquettes, a third sweet dimsum such as egg tarts and water chestnut jelly, and so forth. You stop the waiter and select one or two of the dimsum he has to offer, or perhaps reject his in favour of another trolley with a different range of goodies. All the time other waiters hurry between the tables refilling the tea pots; everywhere there is noise and bustle.

The idea of dimsum is not new to the Chinese community: in Tang times, around the eighth century, the words *dim sum* (*dian xin* in Mandarin) came to be accepted as meaning small snacks or 'little eats'. The literal translation of *dian xin* is 'light the heart' as in 'light a fire' (*dian huo*). These snacks eaten apart from a main meal have been part of Chinese life for over a thousand years. More to the point, as the items themselves became more elaborate and numerous the words 'order dish, following inclination' (*dian cai sui xin*), or more colloquially 'spot the dish, follow your heart', became increasingly relevant – as anyone who has chosen their dimsum from a passing trolley in a dimsum restaurant will appreciate. The normal usage in the West is the Cantonese word dimsum rather than the Mandarin form *dianxin*, because of the overwhelming preponderance of

Cantonese restaurants among those that serve dimsum in the West. The odd Chinese expression *dimsum* (or *dianxin*), which appears to be a shortened form of *dian cai sui xin*, can be illustrated by various stories and quotations from Chinese classical texts. According to one of these stories a family named Zheng travelling sometime in the eighth century stopped at an inn where their servant prepared various delicacies for their refreshment. When Madame Zheng was told that the food was prepared, she sent a message to say that she had not yet finished her toilet and was not ready to eat but that the others 'should please themselves – *dian xin*'. According to another story, a boy selling fish at the gate of the magistrate's court produced a steamed cake from his pocket as a snack (*dian xin*).

By the time the phrase dimsum came into common usage there was a wide range of different small snacks from which to choose. Accounts of Changan (modern Xian), the capital of China under the Tang during the seventh and eighth centuries, mention *wuntun* made by the Su family and sold at a particular street corner. It seems probable that these *wuntun* were what we now call *jiaozi*, or dumplings – the name *jiaozi* is of much more recent origin. Elsewhere in Changan hawkers sold cakes, both fried and steamed, some of them possibly rather like modern Western doughnuts. The city had two vast market areas where sesame cakes – 'crisp and fragrant from the oven' – were sold. Bamboo-wrapped packets of glutinous rice were made by the Yu family, and a wide variety of pastries, including cherry pastries, were on sale. *Shaobing* (unleavened buns) were a common snack. Already the relationship between small snacks and tea-drinking had been established. By the second half of the eighth century tea was drunk by all levels of society except the very poorest throughout China. The most popular variety appears to have been a green powdered tea, which was sprinkled onto boiling water and whisked in – very similar to the way it is currently done in the Japanese tea ceremony.

Over three hundred years later under the Song, when the capital of China was at Hangzhou in the east of China, dimsum and snacks were a firmly established part of life. There are long lists of the dimsum sold in the markets and by the hawkers in the contemporary twelfth century records of the city – a bewildering profusion of snacks and foods catering for both rich and poor. Many of the dimsum listed were sold in the numerous taverns and wine houses that were part of the bawdy night life of the city.

Many snacks and dimsum in the menus from Song Hangzhou are still being made and sold in China today under the same names. There is no reason to believe that the recipes for them have changed to any significant degree in the intervening six hundred years. Many of them are still standard, and recipes for them are given in this book – big *baozi*, spring rolls, mooncakes, crystallized fruits, small crab-meat *baozi*, small prawn *baozi*, bamboo and meat *baozi*, thousand layer cake, *shaobing*, bamboo leaf packets – all appear in the Song menus. Specialist dimsum, to cater for the large Buddhist and vegetarian sector of Song society, were listed separately and included false meat *baozi*, gluten and bamboo threads and sweet paste many-coloured spring rolls. There were many more buns, pies and cakes listed, but since their names are no longer in common usage they are not easy to identify. This is rather a shame since 'golden orange-juice cake' sounds very inviting and the name 'one inside the other magic peaches' is intriguing. At the gates of the city cooked-meat stall holders called their wares – venison, duck, goat and chicken – to the passing travellers. Throughout the city hundreds of noodle houses, some no more than a street stall, advertised their food with a huge soup pot, while small wine shops sold stews of various kinds including a 'hundred-flavoured' stew. In Hangzhou at this time there were several night markets where snacks and refreshments were continually on offer; one account of the city mentions hawkers carrying through the streets a sequence of foods suitable for the passing hours of day and night.

There is a clear distinction in Chinese thinking between snacks, which can be eaten standing, and primarily serve the purpose of allaying hunger, and dimsum which are always eaten seated, and are fun food – 'idle eats'. However, some items such as *jiaozi* or noodles may be used for either. Dimsum cooking for all social classes is highly skilled, often involving trained pastry cooks, while snacks involve lesser skills, not far removed from family cooking.

Dimsum are always special items. They may be used to make up a whole meal at lunchtime (particularly for well-off people or parties of women), or as an hors d'oeuvre for a snack meal, or simply alone as a titbit. Snacks without dimsum, however, form a continuum with ordinary meals at any time of day, especially for working-class people.

In modern China the lists of snacks available are generally much more limited than those of twelfth century Hangzhou. However, since 1980 throughout China there has been a tremendous increase in the number of small restaurants and street stalls selling snacks and dimsum. In modern Xian whole streets are once again devoted to eating stalls, each offering two or three dishes. Cooked meats hang at the sides of the stalls and there is an array of seasonings ready for the customer. At a street corner in the city a man cooks savoury-smelling soup noodles and around him stand a crowd of customers; elsewhere women can be seen deep-frying glutinous rice balls filled with red-bean paste or *baozi* filled with sugar and Chinese hawthorn fruits, bread twists and batter sticks. Cooked meat stalls in Guangzhou and Nanjing quickly collect queues for their chickens and bits of cooked pig, and in Guangzhou small family shops sell cool drinks and sweets. In the summer hawkers in Beijing squatting beside boxes covered by old quilts do a brisk trade in white ice creams, made from milk powder and beanflour. Restaurants selling *baozi* throughout China are always crowded, with scarcely an empty seat.

Large tea houses in China have a regular clientele; some indeed are in restaurants only open to party officials and the higher ranks of the bureaucracy. In the tea houses, people sit round big, often crowded tables each morning for a few minutes gossip and relaxation over tea and a sweet or savoury pastry before starting work. Other restaurants serving a rather different need open as early as 6 am to cater for their customers wanting a more substantial snack such as beanflower soup or noodles before work begins. They continue serving small snacks and tea until the afternoon, while yet others cater for the lunch time crowds or groups of people out to enjoy themselves after they have finished work in the early evening.

In Hong Kong and Taiwan there is a very wide clientele for all sorts of dimsum and snacks, ranging from the well-to-do to all kinds of working people. Apart from the large dimsum palaces, in Taibei nowadays there are small rather expensive restaurants which serve dimsum to customers on fancy crockery with starched tablecloths. It is this kind of dimsum house which now serves small portions of banquet dishes such as shark's fin soup to be eaten as dimsum. There are also smart cake shops that cater primarily to women, serving fruit juice and sweet cakes and pastries, which may be either of Western or traditional Chinese origin. In Hong Kong some stalls in the night market sell snacks of seafood or congee (thin rice porridge), while another has a row of small sandpots simmering on a line of gas burners ready for the late night diners who sit at wooden tables set out on the pavement – in the summer electric fans stand near the tables circulating the open air. Most Hong Kong noodle houses are very Cantonese, with cooked meats hanging near the window, and these serve a choice of noodle and congee dishes, often with *chahsiu* or other cooked meats in them, or *wuntun* noodles, whereas in Taiwan, a wider range of immigrants from all over China has created a market for more varied noodle dishes.

In mainland China there are increasing signs of the resurrection of all these styles of eating. The restaurants and street stalls of modern Hong Kong and Taiwan are likely to be the prototypes for China in the future. Many new books of dimsum recipes are being published in all regions of China, mainly for restaurant use, and we have often used materials from these books in our work.

Chapter 2

Planning a dimsum meal

如何计画点心餐

Snacks in the Chinese world can be eaten at any time of the day or night, but dimsum are only served in restaurants during the day up to 5 pm. So a dimsum meal is either lunch or – if it starts in the middle of the morning – a kind of 'brunch'. Chinese people customarily go in parties of 6, 8 or even 12 to eat a dimsum lunch. A dimsum meal is not really suitable for anyone eating alone, and you would do better to settle for a snack meal such as *wuntun* noodles and a dish of *choisam* with oyster sauce, or a plate of Singapore noodles, or rice noodles with beef and black beans if you are by yourself.

Everybody in a party eating dimsum at a restaurant chooses at least one dimsum to start the meal, or possibly two, depending on the size of the party. This is a communal business and there is often a lot of discussion over the choice, to make it as varied as possible. The range of choice lies not only in the wrappings and skins – made from several different kinds of flours, eggs, beancurd, yams, bread dough or pastry – around the various minced meat fillings and in their cooking, mainly steaming and frying, but also between other styles of unwrapped dimsum such as meat balls, spareribs, ducks' webs, firewood bundles and various sweets. Some big restaurants in the West have between 50 and 100 different dimsum from which to choose, and provide illustrated menus to help customers who are unfamiliar with the dimsum to make their choice. The trolleys in these big restaurants each contain a different style of dimsum so that after selecting from one to start a meal, later on you can choose another range of dimsum from a different trolley. Generally speaking, a party of six making a whole meal of dimsum eats between 18 and 24 portions. These are not always different, for if one kind is particularly popular, two or more portions of it may be ordered, so that everyone can have a taste. Tea, usually oolong or puer, is drunk throughout a dimsum meal; the teapot is refilled with fresh boiling water whenever it is empty. Some people like to finish a meal with a sweet dimsum, such as waterchestnut jelly or egg tarts, while others prefer a dish of noodles. The essence of dimsum eating is that you may please yourself.

In a dimsum meal served at home it is not so easy for everyone to please themselves – and basically the element of free choice has to go. However, by selecting from a wide range of different dimsum in planning the menu, you will be unlucky if there is not something for everyone in the meal. We believe that for a dimsum party eight people is the best number. This allows for a wide range of dishes without either overwhelming the diners or working yourself into the ground. Allow one recipe from the following chapters for each person, plus whatever filler, such as a rice or noodle dish, you wish. If you like, you can also add a sweet soup or other sweet dish as well. Select the recipes with an eye to different cooking styles, a range of doughs and skins, and a variety of fillings. Try to make the selection as wide as possible. All steamed dishes can create a log jam in the kitchen, but if every dish has to be made at the last minute, you may be too exhausted to enjoy the party – and it is, after all, your party.

Lay the table with chopsticks, a bowl, an empty dipping sauce dish, a small plate for bones, a teacup and/or glass for everyone. Provide a selection of soy sauce, chilli bean sauce, red vinegar, chilli oil, sesame oil and garlic paste (see page 17) in bowls in the centre of the table. The diners each mix their own dipping sauce to their own taste. If you are serving a sweet soup, have ready small soup bowls and spoons. Serve tea (and/or wine or beer) throughout the meal. Do not clear away any of the empty plates during the meal – you must avoid any suggestion of a meal divided into courses and a litter of plates is both authentic and traditional.

In the following paragraphs we suggest possible menus for both dimsum parties at home and family dimsum and snack meals. We give timetables that roughly outline the order in which the meal can be prepared and offer some guidelines to the time the preparations may take. The timetables can either be followed exactly or used as a guide for your own planning. Time for preparing stock, washing up, heating oil for deep-frying and bringing water to the boil is not specifically included. Always allow yourself plenty of time, and perhaps practise a few of the recipes on the family before attempting a full-blown dimsum party. However, the recipes are not difficult in themselves, and require very little skill, only a little practise. The quantities we give in the recipes suggested for the menus are sufficient for a meal for four or more people when they are served with other dishes (except for those *jiaozi* recipes made with ordinary flour, which are given in quantities sufficient for four people to make a whole meal of *jiaozi* only).

A DIMSUM MEAL FOR 8

Transparent prawn *jiaozi* (page 71)
Steamed spareribs (page 39)
Pork and coriander balls (page 29)
Three-flavoured steamed *jiaozi* (page 56) (serve half quantity only)
Pork rolls (page 31)
Agar-agar salad (page 47)
Curry buns (page 89)
Crabmeat small buns (page 105)
Silver wood-ears soup (page 149)
Noodles with barbecue sauce (page 127)

TIMETABLE

Several days before the meal
Make and freeze the transparent prawn *jiaozi*, crabmeat small buns, three-flavoured steamed *jiaozi*, pork rolls, curry buns, and egg noodles.

The day before
Prepare and cook the spareribs.
Cook the chicken for the salad.
Steam the silver wood-ears.
Prepare the sauce for the noodles.
Make the meat paste for the pork and coriander balls.

The day of the party
Defrost the prepared foods.
Prepare the bean sprouts and cucumber for the noodles and kiwi fruit for silver wood-ears soup.
Finish the pork and coriander balls.
Steam the spareribs and keep warm.
Assemble the salad.

Twenty minutes before serving the meal
Steam the transparent prawn *jiaozi*, the three-flavoured steamed *jiaozi* and the pork and coriander balls for 20 minutes.
Deep-fry the pork rolls for 4 minutes.
Start the meal with the agar-agar salad, steamed spareribs, transparent prawn *jiaozi*, three-flavoured steamed *jiaozi*, pork and coriander balls and the pork rolls all on the table.

During the meal
Steam the crabmeat small buns for 20 minutes.
Deep-fry the curry buns for 5 minutes
Bring these two dishes to the table together.
Serve the silver wood-ears.
Cook the noodles, heat the sauce. Mix and serve.

A SNACK MEAL FOR 4

Cut buns (page 112)
Pork and pickled mustard greens (page 112) *or*
Pork shreds with red-in-snow (page 113)
Simple cucumber salad (page 47), made fresh
Wuntun soup without noodles (page 64)

A quick snack meal can be made in approximately 20 minutes from foods previously prepared and stored in the freezer. Alternatively, this meal could be prepared on the day of the meal.

Make and freeze the cut buns, filling of your choice, *wuntun* and soup stock at your convenience. When they are required, take straight from the freezer and reheat the cut buns and filling in a steamer for 20 minutes. Bring the soup stock to the boil and drop in the *wuntun* and fresh green vegetable. Simmer for 3 to 5 minutes. Make a fresh cucumber salad and serve the meal with beer.

ANOTHER DIMSUM MEAL FOR 8

Transparent chicken pasties
(page 71)
Rice paper prawns (page 33)
Flower petal *shaomai* (page
61)
Prawn filled egg slice (page
34)
Green and silver salad (page
47)
Three-thread eyebrow buns
(page 88)
Lamb and leek small buns
(page 106)
Stuffed mushrooms (page
30)
Water chestnut jelly (page
149)
Coriander rice (page 139)

TIMETABLE

Several days before the meal
Make and freeze the transparent chicken pastries, *shaomai*, prawn filled egg slices, three-thread eyebrow buns, lamb and leek small buns.

Two days before the meal
Soak the jelly fish.

The day before
Prepare the meat and prawn pastes.
Make and cook the stuffed mushrooms.
Make the water chestnut jelly.
Prepare and cook the stir-fried meats for coriander rice.

The day of the party
Defrost the prepared foods.
Clean the prawns.
Prepare and assemble the salad.
Wash the rice.
Reheat stuffed mushrooms and keep warm.

Twenty minutes before serving the meal
Steam the transparent chicken pasties, prawn filled egg slice, and *shaomai* for 20 minutes.
Deep-fry the rice paper prawns, about 5 minutes.
Start the meal with the green and silver salad, paper wrapped prawns, transparent chicken pasties, prawn filled egg slice, *shaomai* and stuffed mushrooms all on the table.

During the meal
Steam the lamb and leek small buns for 20 minutes.
Deep fry the three-thread eyebrow buns for 5 minutes.
Bring both these dishes to the table together.
Warm the water chestnut jelly and serve.
Cook the rice
Finish cooking the coriander rice and serve.

A FAMILY DIMSUM MEAL FOR 4

Shaomai with beef and
    Chinese leaves (page 59)
Baked spareribs (page 38)
Bean sprout salad (page 48)
Fish and noodle soup (page
    122)

Simpler family dimsum meals do not need elaborate advance planning and can easily be made during the morning of the day they are to be eaten. Place all the dishes on the table at once and serve tea with the meal. Put out a chilli dipping sauce, soy sauce and red vinegar.

TIMETABLE

Three hours before the meal
Prepare and marinate the spareribs.
Make the filling for the *shaomai*.
Make *shaomai* dough.
Prepare fish, stock and other soup ingredients.
Cook spareribs

One hour before the meal
Roll out and fill *shaomai*.
Wash and trim bean sprouts. Mix dressing.

Twenty minutes before the meal
Steam *shaomai*.
Finish fish and noodle soup.
Serve.

Chapter 3 | Ingredients and Equipment

材料工具简介

There are few places more intriguing and also more incomprehensible to the Western cook than a Chinese food shop, where it often seems as if all points of reference have been lost. The Chinese eat a far wider range of foods than is common in the West; many of the foods are dried and unfamiliar in form, so it is hard for a Westerner even to begin to identify the contents of the various packets and bags on sale. Chinese groceries range from dried and salted vegetables and seafoods through the various commercially prepared dough skins and noodles to the bottled sauces that feature in most Chinese recipes. All Chinese cooks freely use prepared sauces, such as the ubiquitous soy sauce and the various regional bean sauces.

We have limited ourselves to explaining the ingredients listed in the recipes in this book. Although many of the items might seem expensive, the quantities used at any one time are often very small and many of the ingredients will keep for months if not for years. A Chinese cook builds up a store cupboard of assorted dried foods and spices, and anyone intending to cook Chinese is recommended to do the same. Items sold by Chinese grocers are not as uniform and predictable as those found in Western supermarkets, being dependent to a large extent on the vagaries of a Third World economy. They come and go, and supplies are irregular. Nor is the quality of the food always standard and there may be considerable variations among the different brands of certain foods. Labels on packets, and bottles are generally consistent in the use of Chinese names, but English translations on labels can vary widely and unpredictably.

FRUIT AND VEGETABLES

BAMBOO LEAVES The dry bayonet-shaped leaves should be washed well and then simmered gently for 5 minutes before being used. Sold in bundles at Chinese grocers.

BAMBOO SHOOTS Two grades are sold in the West in cans: winter bamboo, which are the first shoots of the year and are smaller, more delicate in flavour and texture and more expensive; and standard bamboo shoots. To keep bamboo shoots once the can is opened, boil them in sufficient fresh water to cover every 3 or 4 days, and allow to cool before storing in a clean container. They will keep in this way for up to 3 weeks.

PICKLED BAMBOO SHOOTS These preserved strips of bamboo shoot have a strong sour flavour, which is not unpleasant when they are properly prepared. Blanch several times in boiling water and rinse in cold water between each boiling to reduce the sour flavour before using.

BLACK FUNGI There are several varieties of dried Chinese fungi available in the West, among them one called 'wood-ears' (*muer*), which has a coarse texture with a grey velvety top and a black underside, and another sometimes called 'snow-ears', which is dark brown and thinner in texture. Always soak all dried fungi in warm water for 30 minutes before rinsing well and discarding any hard or gritty pieces. Sold in polythene bags at Chinese grocers often under the general name 'black fungus'.

CHINESE OR FRAGRANT LEEKS These are the *allium ordoratum* and are difficult to find in the West. They have a pungent odour somewhere between garlic and chives, and look like the flowering stalks of giant chives. Substitute garlic cloves and the inside leaves of leeks.

CHOISAM This is probably the most delicate variety of Chinese cabbage, with small bright green leaves, yellow flowers and green succulent stalks. Sold at Chinese grocers and occasionally on market stalls.

CORIANDER This fresh herb looks like a flat leafed parsley, but it has a distinctive aroma. Keep as you would a bunch of flowers – in water in full daylight. Sold in bunches at Indian grocers.

DRIED BEANS Red adzuki beans, green mung beans and white haricot beans are all used to make different coloured sweet pastes for fillings for Chinese pastries and cakes. Do not confuse red bean paste, which is used for stuffing sweet dumplings and cakes, with sweet bean sauce, which is a commercial sauce used in savoury dishes. Dried beans are sold in most Western health food shops.

DRIED MUSHROOMS The best Chinese dried mushrooms have brown caps patterned by a light-coloured crazing. They vary greatly in size and are expensive, but beware of cheaper varieties of dried mushrooms – without the crazing on their caps – which have neither taste nor texture. Soak for 30 minutes in warm water to soften the caps before discarding the hard stalks.

GARLIC SHOOTS These light green long shoots with a strong garlic smell are sold occasionally at Chinese grocers. They can be grown at home from aging garlic cloves. Substitute garlic cloves and spring onions.

GARLIC PASTE To make, crush 6 cloves of garlic and mix with 5 ml (1 teaspoon) cold water and 1.5 ml (¼ teaspoon) sesame oil into a pungent paste.

LOTUS The dry round leaves of this water lily will keep in a dry store cupboard for many months. Pour boiling water over them to soften, then pat dry and paint with oil before using. Sold at Chinese grocers, often rather battered. The seeds of the lotus lily – called lotus nuts – are sold canned in a sweet syrup. They are also made into a sweet paste, sold in cans and used as a stuffing for buns.

MUSTARD GREENS This variety of Chinese cabbage is sometimes sold fresh, but more usually salted and sold either canned – called pickled mustard green – or loose from large stone jars as 'pickled cabbage'. It has a strong sour flavour. We have found that it will keep well if immersed in a fresh solution of salt and water. Allow 600 ml (1 pint) water to 5 ml (1 teaspoon) salt.

PEA STARCH VERMICELLI: see silk noodles.

PINE KERNELS, pine nuts. These are small white nuts with a rich aromatic flesh, often included in cooked dishes to give texture. They are never eaten by themselves as nuts. Bought at Chinese grocers or health food shops.

PRESERVED AND DRIED FRUITS There is a wide range of sweet preserved fruits from China and Taiwan including crystallized winter melon, 'dehydrated' papaya and pineapple, preserved kumquats, apples, plums and red dates without stones; none of these need soaking before use. There are also dried red and black dates with stones which require soaking for several hours before using.

RED-IN-SNOW This variety of cabbage is always salted and sold in small cans labelled 'snow cabbage' or sometimes 'pickled cabbage'. It will keep opened in the refrigerator for about a week.

SESAME SEEDS Both white and black sesame seeds can be bought at Chinese grocers. White sesame seeds are sold in Indian and health food shops.

SICHUAN PRESERVED VEGETABLE The club-stalk of this variety of Chinese cabbage has a peppery flavour of its own, which is enhanced by the preserving spices. Sold only in cans in the West. Remove from the can when opened and store in a clean container in the refrigerator where it will keep for months. Rinse before using.

SILK NOODLES or transparent noodles. (Also sold as *pea starch vermicelli*.) These fine wiry transparent noodles are made from mung beans and are considered more a vegetable than a staple in Chinese terms. They need soaking in warm water for 5 minutes before using.

SILVER WOOD-EARS (*baimuer*) This creamy yellow fungus comes in small clusters of paper thin wafers. Soak in warm water for 30 minutes and rinse well, discarding any hard or discoloured pieces.

SOYA BEANS These small round beans are one of the richest sources of vegetable protein. Sold dry at Chinese grocers and Western health food shops. Many soya bean products including soy sauce and the various bean sauces are used in Chinese cuisine as well as beancurd, which is made from coagulating the milk obtained by boiling and crushing soya beans.

Beancurd is sold loose by the square – which may vary considerably in weight – or prepacked in water. Either way, turn it out into a bowl of clean water and store in a cool place changing the water every day. Beancurd kept in this manner will keep reasonably fresh for about 5 days.

Beancurd skin comes in flat brittle yellow sheets which break easily; provided it is kept in a dry place, beancurd skin will keep for between 6 to 8 months.

Fermented red beancurd has a strong savoury flavour and is made with the lees of wine. It is sold in both jars and cans. The former keeps for several years.

SWEET POTATOES There are at least two varieties of sweet potato. One has a very sweet orange flesh and a purple-red skin (sometimes called the Louisiana yam), and the other a white flesh, which is much less sweet, and a pinkish brown skin. They are both sold fresh in most West Indian markets.

WATER CHESTNUTS These can sometimes be bought fresh, but are more usually canned. If fresh, peel and use as required. If canned, once the can is opened, drain and deep-freeze in small packets until required.

WHITE RADISH This root vegetable, which looks like an overgrown white carrot, is often called by its Indian name, *mooli*. It is sold fresh in supermarkets and greengrocers.

DRIED WINTER MELON Dried strips of winter melon look like thick lengths of raffia. Sold in bundles in polythene bags, they need soaking for 10 minutes in warm water to soften.

FLOURS AND FARINACEOUS FOODS

BUCKWHEAT NOODLES These are greyish-coloured noodles made from a mixture of buckwheat flour and ordinary wheat flour. Sold in health food shops and Japanese grocers under the Japanese name *soba*.

GLUTINOUS RICE This is a matt-white round grained rice with a high gluten content. It is very sticky when cooked and is used principally for stuffings and for wine making. Always soak before cooking.

GLUTINOUS RICE FLOUR Rice flour stales easily, so always buy fresh when required. Do not substitute ordinary rice flour, which turns hard when boiled or steamed.

NOODLES Egg noodles made with wheat flour are

sold either fresh or dried, and in either a round or flat form. Use round for fried noodles and flat for soups. Other types of dried noodles include those without egg (plain noodles) and those deep-fried before they are dried (*yifu* noodles). Substitute Italian egg noodles if necessary.

POTATO FLOUR This very fine white flour makes a smooth non-sticky thickener for soups and sauces. However, care must be taken to mix it completely into the liquid at a low temperature before bringing to the boil. Sold in polythene packets at Chinese grocers.

RICE There are three varieties of rice available in the West that are eaten as staples in China: long grained rice (*Indica*), the most common southern Chinese rice; a short grained stickier rice (*Japonica*) popular in eastern China (usually a version of this rice called American Rose must be substituted); and a more expensive rice (*xiangmi*), which has a penetrating smell when cooked.

RICE NOODLES These off-white round thin dried noodles are sold in skeins, sometimes called *rice vermicelli*. Another variety called *rice sticks* are flat dry ribbons approximately 5 mm ($\frac{1}{4}$ inch) wide. Soften both varieties in warm water and use as directed. Fresh rice noodles, called *hefen*, are soft pearly-white in colour and about 1 cm ($\frac{1}{2}$ inch) wide. Always buy *hefen* fresh and use at once; they become brittle as they stale.

RICE PAPER These thin round sheets of edible rice paper can be bought in packets from Chinese grocers. They are coarser than the rice paper used in Western cake making, which cannot be substituted for them.

RICE SKINS Soft sheets of pearly-white dough used for wrapping round savoury fillings are sold from chilled cabinets of Chinese grocers. Always buy fresh and use at once. Avoid skins that look yellow or transparent.

SPRING ROLL SKINS These paper-thin sheets of pasta made with wheat flour are difficult to make at home successfully. Buy them ready-made. The best variety is sold fresh, not frozen.

WUNTUN SKINS Small squares of yellowish pasta made from wheat and egg are sold fresh in packets at Chinese grocers. These packets contain between 32 and 34 squares and will keep, sealed, in a refrigerator for only about 4 days. They can be deep-frozen *after* they have been filled, but we do not recommend freezing them as plain skins because they do not defrost satisfactorily.

WHEAT STARCH This is a very soft wheat flour from which all the gluten has been removed.

SAUCES AND FLAVOURINGS

BARBECUE SAUCE This sauce, also known as *sweet bean sauce*, is made from soya beans, sugar and salt. It is a commercial substitute for a northern speciality sauce made from fermented flour, and is frequently confused with *hoisin sauce* (see below). It is used in savoury dishes and as an accompaniment to Peking duck.

CHILLI BEAN SAUCE This fiery hot sauce made from salted soya beans, chillis and garlic is used with caution both as a table dip and in cooking, particularly in Sichuan dishes. Do not cook it over too high a heat or the flavour will become acrid. One variety from Hunan whose coarse texture includes chilli seeds is excellent for both cooking and as a table dip.

CHILLI SAUCE A hot, orange-coloured ready-made dipping sauce particularly good with noodle dishes; it is not used in cooking.

CINNAMON BARK OR STICKS Both the bark and the rolled sticks of cinnamon are milder in flavour than Western powdered cinnamon.

FENNEL The dried seeds of this herb are used in Chinese cooking to flavour stews, particularly those cooked with soy sauce.

FERMENTED BLACK BEANS The process of fermentation turns soya beans black and gives them a strong savoury flavour. It is one of the earliest recorded food processes in China, virtually unchanged in nearly two thousand years. These beans, sold dry in polythene bags, will keep for years in the refrigerator. Black bean sauce sold in bottles is not for cooking but is used as a table sauce.

FIVE SPICE POWDER or *wuxiang*. This pungent powdered spice is a blend of star anise, fennel, cinnamon, cloves and Sichuan pepper, and should be used in small quantities. Since commercially made five spice powder is good and keeps well, we do not recommend mixing it at home.

GINGER Fresh root ginger is used extensively for flavouring savoury dishes. Now easily obtainable in many supermarkets; powdered ginger is *not* an acceptable substitute.

HOISIN SAUCE This sauce is sometimes confusingly labelled *barbecue sauce*. It is a southern Chinese sauce made with vinegar, soya beans and sugar, and therefore is more a sweet and sour sauce than the northern sweet bean sauce, for which it is a substitute.

LARD The Chinese use pork dripping or lard in many of their pastry and dimsum recipes, partly for its flavour and partly for the texture it gives to pastries. We have found that on most occasions solid white fat or shortening made from vegetable oils, which is higher in polyunsaturated fats, can be substituted for the pork fat. Where this is not the case it has been noted in the text.

LIQUORICE POWDER This yellowish pungent powder is one of several spices occasionally used in Chinese stews.

LYE WATER An alkaline liquid, which when used in small amounts reduces the smell of fermented flour and gives noodles a crunchier texture.

MSG This flavour-enhancing powder – monosodium glutamate – is a common constituent in most Chinese savoury recipes. However, since some people in the West have been found to be allergic to it, we have not included it in any recipe in this book, although it was frequently included in the original Chinese versions. If used, it is particularly efficient with sour and bitter flavours, less so with sweet or spicy foods.

OILS For stir-frying or deep-frying Chinese food any oil with a high smoking point can be used. Peanut oil, although having a lower smoking point than some oils, gives a distinctive nutty flavour to foods. Oils can be filtered through coffee filter paper while still warm and then stored away from the light to be re-used. Always throw away used oils once they become even slightly discoloured or cloudy.

Chilli oil can be bought ready-made, but is easy to make at home: place 6 dry chillis in a small pan with 45 ml (3 tablespoons) fresh vegetable oil and cook until the chillis swell and darken. Leave to cool, strain off and use as required.

Sichuan pepper oil is made by frying 10 ml (2 teaspoons) Sichuan peppercorns in 45 ml (3 tablespoons) fresh vegetable oil for about 4 minutes. Leave to cool and then store with the peppercorns in the oil. Strain and use as required.

ORANGE PEEL Dried tangerine peel is used in many spiced soy cooked stews. Sold in polythene bags, store in a dry cupboard, where it will keep almost indefinitely. Thinly peeled zest of fresh orange or tangerine can be substituted.

OYSTER SAUCE A thick savoury sauce made from oysters, it is not in the least fishy, but rich and appetizing.

RICE WINE This wine is usually made from glutinous rice, but in some areas of China chestnuts are added and fermented wheat is used as a starter. Called yellow wine, it is a rather coarse wine used everywhere in China for both cooking and drinking. It is about 16° proof and the best known variety in the West is *Shaoxing* from Zhejiang. Before drinking it, stand the flask in hot water until it reaches blood heat and dissolve crystal sugar in it to taste. Substitute dry sherry or Japanese *sake* for cooking.

Ginger wine To make, take 25 g (1 oz) bruised ginger in one piece and put it into 100 ml (3½ fl oz) rice wine. Leave for at least 24 hours, strain and use as required. This wine will keep for several weeks if stored in a closed container. The ginger can be used for cooking after being soaked in the wine.

Onion wine To make, soak 30 ml (2 tablespoons) grated onion tied in a bag in 45 ml (3 tablespoons) rice wine overnight. Remove the onion and use as required. Alternately add 5 ml (1 teaspoon) Sichuan peppercorns to the onion to make *Onion and pepper wine*. These wines will also keep for several weeks if stored in a tightly closed container.

Huadiao is matured *Shaoxing* rice wine, smoother and less harsh than ordinary yellow wine;

it also should be warmed and sugared before drinking. Drunk with meals or with small fried snacks and dimsum.

Cassia flower wine (labelled *Kuei hua chen chiew*) is a very sweet wine with a low alcoholic content flavoured with cinnamon. Drunk with sweet cakes and pastries.

Chinese white wines are in fact distilled spirits. Made mainly from millet and wheat, there are many regional varieties in the north and west of China, including *Guizhou maotai* (labelled *Kweichow Moutai*) and *Fenjiu*, both potent spirits about 106° proof. *Gaoliangjiu*, from Hebei and elsewhere, is also made from millet and is about 50° proof. These are not table wines but are drunk with small fried snacks at evening drinking parties.

Meiguilujiu (labelled *Mei Kuei lu chiew*) is made in Tianjin and elsewhere from millet and rose petals distilled with rice wine. It is a pleasant but very strong drink, 96° proof, and improves with ageing in the bottle.

ROSE WATER A non-alcoholic flavouring tasting strongly of roses, best bought from Indian grocers.

SESAME OIL A delicately flavoured oil extracted from sesame seeds, it has a low smoking point so care must be taken not to overheat and spoil its flavour when using it for frying. Also frequently used to add extra flavour to savoury stuffings. Always buy Chinese sesame oil rather than Western sesame oil, because it is made with roasted sesame seeds and has a much better

flavour.

SESAME PASTE This thick oily paste, like peanut butter in consistency, has a strong sesame flavour. Substitute *tahini*.

SHACHAJIANG (Also sometimes labelled barbecue sauce.) This is a quite different sauce from either *hoisin* or sweet bean sauce and is made with fish, dried shrimps, spices and rice flour. It has a slightly fishy flavour and is not sweet.

SICHUAN PEPPERCORNS Native Chinese pepper has a flavour much more spicy than hot. The dried calyx and seed look rather like a brown clove. The flavour is improved by toasting in a dry frying pan before grinding.

SOUR PLUMS These small plums are the preserved fruit of the Japanese apricot. Sold in jars, they are preserved in brine and have a dry sour taste.

SOY SAUCE The basic Chinese savoury sauce is made from soya beans and is rich in protein. It is widely sold in Western supermarkets, but the varieties sold at Chinese grocers tend to be more reliable. *Dark soy* – called *Soy, Superior sauce* is a heavy, rich-flavoured soy particularly good for slowly cooked dishes. *Mushroom soy* is a dark soy but with the addition of mushrooms; it makes a good all-round soy. *Light soy* – called *Superior soy* is saltier and good for most general cooking and for table dips. There is also a Japanese soy sauce, which is lighter in flavour than the standard Chinese light soy sauce. It makes a good dipping sauce for those

who are not sure they like the flavour of soy.

STAR ANISE A dried star-shaped seed head with a flavour resembling fennel.

SUGAR Chinese crystal sugar, which comes either in lumps like quartz or in small lozenge shaped pieces, is not as sweet as refined Western sugars, but gives a syrupy consistency to the gravies of dishes cooked with it. Western granulated sugar can be substituted, but it tends to make the gravy sweet.

Maltose is a sugar syrup made from wheat. It has a lower crystallizing temperature than ordinary sugars and is not as sweet. Chinese honeys sold in the West are flower-flavoured and often have a slightly fermented tang.

VINEGAR Chinese vinegars, made from rice, are milder and less astringent than Western malt vinegar. *White vinegar* is colourless and very mild. *Black vinegar* is very dark and dense in colour, but surprisingly mild in flavour. *Red vinegar* (labelled *Red vinegar sauce*) has a pleasing spicy flavour and is usually brown in colour.

WUXIANG: see *Five spice powder*

YELLOW BEAN SAUCE This sauce is sold either in jars as *whole yellow beans in soy* or in cans as *Crushed yellow bean sauce*. Use either.

MEAT, FISH AND SEAFOODS

AGAR-AGAR A transparent colourless dried seaweed, which is the vegetable form of gelatin. Sold in bundles, it looks like crepe-knitting wool, and is used for making jellies and for salads. (Substitute gelatin for making jellies.) Soak in warm water for about 4 minutes before using.

CHAHSIU Cantonese roast pork can be bought ready-made from cooked meat shops in Chinese shopping areas, or make your own (see recipe on page 42).

CHICKEN'S FEET You may find it easier to buy chicken's feet fresh from a butcher or poulterer than at a Chinese grocer, in which case they will need skinning. Wash them well and dip them individually in boiling water for 15 seconds only. Do not leave them longer or the flesh will soften and tear off with the skin. Peel off the scaly skin as if removing a glove. Cut off the nails.

DRIED SHRIMPS These are used for flavouring a variety of savoury dishes. Soak in hot water for 30 minutes, or, to reduce their rather strong flavour, put into a pan of hot water and boil for 2 minutes, then leave to soak for 15 minutes.

DUCKS' WEBS The frozen ducks' feet sold at Chinese grocers are already skinned and prepared for cooking. To prepare ducks' feet at home, wash them well and follow the instructions given under *Chicken's feet.*

HAM There are many varieties of Chinese ham ranging from a sweet cured ham from Yunnan, smoked hams from Zhejiang – like English smoked bacon, and a ham very similar to French cured ham from Shanghai. Some Cantonese cured ham – slightly sweet and spicy – can be bought very expensively in the West, or substitute English smoked bacon.

JELLY FISH Salted jelly fish come in flat sheets and are flaccid to the touch. Pour boiling water over them and then leave to soak in cold water for 3 days, changing the water each day. Cut into thin shreds and use as directed.

PRAWNS Uncooked frozen prawns – often called Pacific prawns – are grey in colour with their shells intact. They are essential to the success of some dishes, where previously cooked prawns cannot be substituted. If they have been defrosted, use them on the day of purchase and do not re-freeze. Always de-vein, (remove the dark digestive cord that runs through the centre of their bodies) before use. Pink prawns sold either fresh or frozen, with or without their shells, have been boiled. Their flesh is too dry to make into successful pastes.

SALTED EGGS These preserved eggs are covered in black soot when they are sold at Chinese grocers. Wash carefully and hard boil before shelling and using in mooncakes.

SAUSAGES In China there are many varieties of sausages, some like salami, others more like German sausages, while still others are made with liver. Some are flavoured with *wuxiang*, and others with local herbs. In the West a liver sausage and a meat sausage are sold, both either in pairs joined with string or in packets. They can be kept in a cool airy place for up to 2 weeks.

SEA CUCUMBERS The best quality sea cucumbers look like hard black gherkins – the poorer quality have a powdery white coating. Small-sized sea cucumbers are cheaper than big ones. They need long and careful preparation. Soak them in cold water for 3 days, changing the water frequently and then boil them in fresh water for 20 minutes. At this stage they are dark, semi-transparent, tough gelatinous tubes. Scrub them very thoroughly with a stiff brush to remove all the hard excretions on their skins, and slit them open to clean the insides. When they are clean put them into about 1 litre (1¾ pints) of chicken stock and simmer for an hour; discard this stock and use the sea cucumbers as required. At

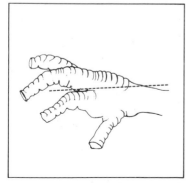

Cut skinned and trimmed chicken's feet in half along line shown.

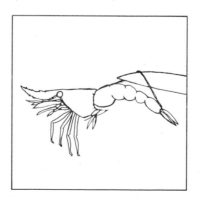

De-vein raw prawns.

Pull head and entrails from body.

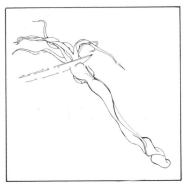

Cut off tentacles.

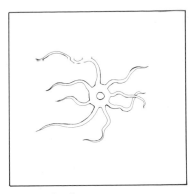

Remove beak.

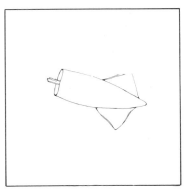

Remove 'bone' from body sac.

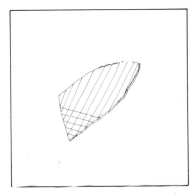

Score opened body sac on outside.

this point they can be deep-frozen.

SQUID Dried squid, which tastes quite different from fresh squid, has a slightly sweet taste and a resilient texture. They come in various sizes and qualitites. They all need soaking for 2 days in a solution of 2 litres (3½ pints) of water to 2.5 ml (½ teaspoon) bicarbonate of soda. After soaking, the transparent 'bone' should be removed and the dark skin scraped off. Then score the squid on the skin side to half its depth in a fine diamond pattern. Cut as required.

Fresh squid are sold in most good fish shops. To clean, gently pull the head, tentacles and attached entrails free from the body sac. Cut through the head of the squid just above the eyes to remove the tentacles and reserve. Discard the rest of the head and entrails. Squeeze out the 'beak' from the centre of the tentacles and discard. Remove the 'bone' from its pocket in the body and discard. Tear off the bottom flaps from the outside of the body and reserve. Split open and rinse out the body sac and peel off the dark skin. Score the outside with a fine diamond pattern.

EQUIPMENT

Almost all the equipment required to cook dimsum is already to hand in a Western kitchen. However, many people consider that using authentic Chinese equipment adds to the pleasure of cooking and serving Chinese food. Therefore the following is a list of such equipment, which may be easily bought in the West, with an explanation of its function and suggested Western alternatives.

WOK This is the Chinese all-purpose pan with a rounded base and flaring sides. It is extremely efficient at developing very high temperatures in the centre of the pan when it is used on a Chinese-type stove, in which direct heat is applied to the base and half-way up the sides of the pan. It is not so efficient on a flat Western gas ring and is inefficient on an electric ring, where so little of the pan is in direct contact with the heat source. It is now possible to buy flat-bottomed woks, which have the advantage of stability and better heat contacts on a Western hob. Woks are used in Chinese kitchens for deep-frying, stir-frying, braising and steaming. Alternatives in a Western kitchen are a deep-fat pan for deep-frying, a large frying pan for stir-frying and a saucepan or steamer for steaming.

If you use a wok for steaming or deep-frying on a Western gas hob, it is useful to have a base ring to hold it stable;

unfortunately they do not always fit electric hobs.

STEAMERS Chinese steamers are round bamboo boxes with latticed bottoms that fit one on top of another, the uppermost being covered with a domed woven bamboo lid. They are placed over a wok of boiling water. They are made in three sizes: the smallest, which is also used for serving dimsum in restaurants, is about 14 cm (5½ inches) in diameter and holds three to four small dimsum items in each box. The next size is about 19 cm (7½ inches) and the biggest at 26 cm (10½ inches) holds about 20 small *baozi* in one box. The Chinese usually put foods such as dumplings and bread buns directly onto a damp cloth laid on the bottom of the steamer, while foods with sauce are put into the steamer in small bowls or plates. They also have wood or metal racks or stands that they use in a wok covered with a domed metal lid to steam small quantities of food. Instead of a Chinese steamer, you can use a Western steamer or a rack in a Western saucepan, in which case the water level must always be 3 cm (1 inch) below the top of the rack.

ROLLING PIN A Chinese rolling pin is about one-third the diameter and only two-thirds the length of a standard Western rolling pin. It is much easier to roll out small discs of dough or pastry with a thin, short pin than with the more cumbersome Western version.

CLEAVER The Chinese use a cleaver with a sharp blade and a metal handle for all cutting and slicing operations. On the whole, we think you get the best results from using the implement you are most at home with, but for making meat pastes, there is no real alternative to a cleaver. Whatever knife or cleaver you use, it is essential to have a big solid chopping board on which to work.

SAND POTS These are small casseroles of unglazed clay, sometimes bound with wire, which are an attractive feature in serving snack or dimsum meals. However, they are very fragile and great care must be taken not to put empty sand pots onto a hot hob or hot ones onto a cold surface. Obviously, any flameproof casserole can be used as an alternative serving pot.

MEASUREMENTS

In this book we have given measurements in both metric and imperial quantities. They are not necessarily exactly equivalent and they should not be confused. Use either one form or the other in any one recipe.

Chapter 4 | Meat and fish dimsum

魚肉点心炎

Many of the dimsum we have chosen in this chapter will be familiar to you, since they appear regularly on menus in Chinese restaurants in the West. The main ingredient for most of them is a stuffing made from either meat or fish paste. These dimsum are served as individual helpings on small plates or steamers rather than as big dishes, and have little or no sauce of their own. But they are frequently accompanied by additional dipping sauces of soy, sometimes mixed with vinegar, garlic or chillis.

Texture is valued almost as much as taste in meat stuffings and pastes, and they should remain moist and slightly chewy after they are cooked. Traditional Chinese chefs create this texture by pounding the meat with two cleavers, one held in each hand, to separate the fibres rather than cut them. Cutting the fibres turns the meat into a puree with no cohesive quality. For such a process it is better to use cuts of meat where there is little gristle or connecting tissue running through the flesh. Cuts such as pork leg or pork loin (sometimes sold now as pork steaks) are ideal meats for making meat pastes without going to the expense of buying pork fillet. The quality of the fat used with the meat or fish in a paste is equally important, for it must have no layers of tough tissue in it. The fat that lies along the back of a pig, which can be trimmed from chops or a loin joint, is best for this purpose, but the fat just under the skin of a leg of pork can also be used. Belly fat and the fat lying between the layers of meat in a belly joint are not suitable. We found that we obtained the best results from putting the pork back fat through the coarse grille of a mincer before starting to pound it with the meat.

To make a satisfactory paste of prawns it is essential to use raw prawns. The flesh of the pink boiled prawns is too dry and its fibres too rigid to bind into a paste. Raw prawns, often known as King prawns, or Pacific prawns, usually have a thick dark digestive cord running through their bodies.

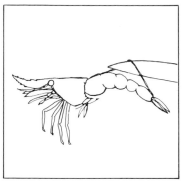

De-vein raw prawns.

Prawns are dirty feeders, and it is most important to remove this digestive cord (de-vein) before cooking them.

When making meat or fish pastes, it helps to sprinkle the pulp from time to time with a little wine or water. This softens the fibres and results in a smoother paste. Marinating the wine with ginger or onion for a few hours gives an extra depth of flavour that permeates through the paste, but is not essential.

A meat cleaver is the most efficient utensil for pounding meat, because the weight of its blade and the balance between the blade and the handle minimizes the effort involved. It is also very important to have a large solid chopping board on which to work. This traditional method of making a paste by pounding the meat with a cleaver takes time, but particularly for meat pastes, we have found the results far superior to those from a food processor or liquidizer; however, this is not the case for pastes made from prawns, squid, fish or chicken, where excellent results come from using a food processor.

鮮肉餡

25 g (1 oz) pork back fat
150 g (5 oz) lean boneless pork from the leg or pork chops), cut into small dice
15 ml (1 tablespoon) ginger wine
15 ml (1 tablespoon) cold water

PORK PASTE

Chop the back fat very finely, or put it through the mincer using the fine grille. Mix the fat with the meat and pile onto the centre of the chopping board. Using the blunt edge of a meat cleaver, work from one side to the other across the board, pounding in quick close movements, hardly lifting the blade from the meat. Fold the meat over on top of itself with the flat of the blade and pound across again at right angles to the previous movement. Continue pounding and folding the meat, which will become an homogeneous mass. Lift out the thin threads of tissue as they appear, and from time to time sprinkle the meat pulp with the wine or water; an extra teaspoon of wine or water will result in a smoother, softer paste. Finally the meat pulp will become smooth and almost creamy in consistency, but all this takes time, so allow at least 10 minutes for the job. Pork paste can be made much more quickly in a food processor using the plastic blade attachment, but the results are not as satisfactory. On the whole it is easier to handle small quantities rather than large ones, so if a double quantity of meat paste is required it is better to make it in two separate batches.

Use the pork paste as directed in the following dimsum recipes. This paste can be deep-frozen until it is required, provided that the pork meat is fresh and has not already been frozen. Defrost at room temperature, or in a microwave oven at the defrost setting. Alternatively, you can store the paste wrapped in cling film in a refrigerator for up to 24 hours.

虾肉馅

200 g (7 oz) raw prawns
25 g (1 oz) pork back fat
10 ml (2 teaspoons) egg
   white
15 ml (1 tablespoon) ginger
   wine

PRAWN PASTE

Shell the prawns, de-vein and cut the flesh into small pieces.
Either finely chop or mince the back fat. Place the prawns
and pork fat into a food processor with the plastic blade
attachment. Run for a few seconds and when the prawns and
fat are well mixed, gradually add the egg white and ginger
wine, beating between each addition. Stop working while
the paste is still a little lumpy. Alternatively, use a meat
cleaver and pound the prawns and back fat in the same
manner as in the recipe for pork paste.

This paste cannot be deep-frozen and should be cooked
as soon after making as possible.

鸡肉馅

180 g (6 oz) boneless
   chicken breast
15 ml (1 tablespoon) rice
   wine, preferably
   flavoured with either
   ginger or onion
2.5 ml (½ teaspoon) salt

CHICKEN PASTE

Cut the chicken into small pieces and place it with the other
ingredients into a food processor using the plastic (or pastry)
blade. Run until the chicken is reduced to a smooth paste.
Use as required.

鱼丸

Makes 8

25 g (1 oz) pork back fat
150 g (5 oz) white fish
5 ml (1 teaspoon) rice wine,
   preferably flavoured with
   ginger or onion
5 ml (1 teaspoon) cornflour
20 ml (4 teaspoons) egg
   white

FISH BALLS

*Fish balls are not used as dimsum by themselves, but they
often appear as one ingredient in a mixed meat pot, and so
have been included in this section. They may also be bought
ready made from most Chinese grocers.*

Mince the pork fat using the coarse grille of the mincer.
Remove any skin or bones from the fish and cut it into small
pieces. Place the fish and rice wine into a food processor (or
liquidizer) and run for a few seconds, then add the pork fat
and work until it is a smooth paste. Alternatively, use a
cleaver and pound the fish and fat in the manner described
in the recipe for pork paste. Add the cornflour and egg white
and work until they are well-blended. Bring a large
saucepan of water to almost boiling point. Take a handful of
the fish paste and squeeze it up between the thumb and
forefinger to form a walnut-sized ball. Lift the fish ball with a
spoon and drop it into the water. Repeat the process until all
the fish paste has been used. (If you find it difficult to make
firm balls with your thumb and forefinger, roll the paste into
balls between the palms of your hands.) Simmer the fish
balls until they rise to the surface – about 7 minutes. Then lift
them out and allow to drain. They can be kept in the
refrigerator for 2 or 3 days before use, or they may be
deep-frozen.

牛肉丸

Makes 4 balls

180 g (6 oz) lean beef steak
(rump is best, but topside
can be used)
15 ml (1 tablespoon) ginger
wine
10 ml (2 teaspoons) onion
wine
5 ml (1 teaspoon) light soy
sauce
1.5 ml ($\frac{1}{4}$ teaspoon) sesame
oil
10 ml (2 teaspoons) egg
white
2.5 ml ($\frac{1}{2}$ teaspoon) salt
1.5 ml ($\frac{1}{4}$ teaspoon) freshly
ground pepper

BEEF MEAT BALLS

Trim and cut the beef into small pieces. Then pound it as directed in the recipe for pork paste, sprinkling it from time to time with the ginger and onion wines. When the meat is reduced to a firm smooth pulp, transfer it to a bowl and mix in the rest of the ingredients. Beat the mixture against the sides of the bowl so that any pockets of air are expelled. Divide the mixture into four and, using wet hands, roll the paste between your palms to make 4 balls the size of golf balls. Stand the balls on a plate in a steamer and steam over fast boiling water for 20 minutes. Serve hot with a soy dipping sauce.

Using a food processor to make beef paste gives very disappointing results, and there seems to be no alternative to the traditional method of pounding the meat by hand. These meat balls can be frozen uncooked provided the meat was originally fresh. Steam straight from the freezer for 30 minutes over a high heat.

魷魚丸

Makes 8 balls

250 g (8 oz) prepared squid,
preferably the body sac
only (see diagram on page
23)
7.5 g ($\frac{1}{4}$ oz) pork back fat
2.5 ml ($\frac{1}{2}$ teaspoon) ginger
wine
pinch of sugar
1 garlic clove
2.5 ml ($\frac{1}{2}$ teaspoon) rice wine
pinch of salt and pepper

SQUID BALLS

Cut the squid and the back fat into small pieces and place them with the ginger wine and sugar into a food processor using the sharp blade attachment. Crush the garlic through a garlic press and mix with the rice wine. Add the wine mixture to the squid in the processor and continue working until the mixture is reduced to a smooth paste. Adjust the seasoning and shape the paste into 8 round walnut-sized balls. Stand the squid balls on the oiled base of a steamer and steam over a high heat for 20 minutes. These balls can be deep-fried after they have been steamed.

Squid balls will not deep-freeze well before they are cooked, but they can be made a day in advance, cooked in the steamer, and then reheated by deep-frying when they are required. Store, covered, in the refrigerator.

香菜猪肉丸

Makes 4 balls
180 g (6 oz) pork paste
2.5 ml (½ teaspoon) sugar
1.5 ml (¼ teaspoon) sesame
   oil
10 ml (2 teaspoons) egg
   white
25 ml (1½ tablespoons) finely
   chopped coriander
1.5 ml (¼ teaspoon) salt
1.5 ml (¼ teaspoon) freshly
   ground pepper

PORK AND CORIANDER BALLS

Blend the pork paste with the other ingredients very thoroughly, beating the mixture against the sides of the bowl so that there are no pockets of air trapped in the paste. Divide the mixture into four, wet your hands and roll the paste between your palms into 4 balls the size of golf balls. Have ready a pan of boiling water. Place the meat balls onto a plate in a steamer and steam them over a high heat for 30 minutes. Serve hot with a dipping sauce of soy sauce and chilli oil.

These pork balls can be frozen if the pork meat is fresh; they should be defrosted before being cooked. Alternatively, they can be frozen after being cooked and reheated straight from the freezer in a steamer for 10 minutes, but the flavour is not quite as good as fresh pork and coriander balls.

珍珠丸

Makes 12 balls
60 ml (4 tablespoons)
   glutinous rice
10 ml (2 teaspoons) dried
   shrimps
8 water chestnuts
180 g (6 oz) pork paste
7.5 ml (1½ teaspoons)
   sesame oil
1 spring onion, finely
   chopped
15 ml (1 tablespoon)
   cornflour
pinch of salt and pepper

PEARL BALLS

This dish, in which the meat balls are coated with translucent glutinous rice to look like pearls, is popular at several kinds of Chinese meals. It is often one dish among many at a large dinner, as well as appearing regularly as a dimsum on restaurant menus. Traditionally, pearls bring with them an element of good fortune for the diners, as well as suggesting great wealth and abundance in eating such precious gems.

Wash the rice several times in clean water, until the water runs clear, then cover with fresh water and leave to soak for an hour. Meanwhile, place the dried shrimps in a pan of hot water, bring to the boil and boil them for 2 minutes; this reduces their rather strong flavour. Leave them to soak in the pan for 15 minutes, drain them well and chop with the water chestnuts into rice-sized pieces – or put them both through the mincer. Blend the pork paste with the sesame oil, add the water chestnuts, dried shrimps, spring onion and cornflour and season with salt and pepper. Beat the mixture against the sides of the bowl to expel any pockets of air that may be trapped. Divide the mixture into 12 portions. Wet your hands and roll each portion into a firm ball. Drain and, if necessary, rub the rice in a clean cloth until it is really dry, then roll the pork balls in the rice until they are completely covered. Arrange on a plate in a steamer, allowing about 1 cm (½ inch) space between each and steam for 30 minutes over a high heat.

If you need to make these balls in advance it is better to freeze the meat paste only. Defrost completely, shape into balls and roll in freshly soaked glutinous rice. Cook as above.

鑲 香 菇

Serves 4
8 large-sized Chinese dried
 mushrooms
15 ml (1 tablespoon) egg
 white
5 ml (1 teaspoon) cornflour
75 g (3 oz) prawn paste
pinch of salt and pepper
2.5 ml (½ teaspoon) sesame
 oil
30 ml (2 tablespoons)
 well-seasoned chicken
 stock

腐 皮

STUFFED MUSHROOMS

The dried mushrooms in this recipe give a particularly savoury, slightly smoky flavour to the prawn stuffing. Fresh flat mushrooms can be used instead, but much of the character of the dish is lost. This dish, like many other dimsum, does not have strong seasonings, and should be eaten before any stronger-flavoured small dishes.

Choose even-sized Chinese mushrooms and soak them in warm water for 30 minutes. Cut off and discard the hard stalks (without tearing the caps) and pat the caps dry. Mix the egg white and cornflour into a thin paste and use this to paint the inside of each mushroom. Beat the prawn paste with the salt, pepper and sesame oil. Fill the mushrooms with prawn paste, pressing it down firmly and smoothing over the top with the back of a dampened spoon. Arrange the mushrooms in a shallow dish and pour the stock around it. The stuffing should be well clear of the stock. Steam over a high heat for 30 minutes, then serve at once.

The stuffed mushrooms can be frozen with their cooking liquor after they have been cooked. Defrost and heat in a microwave oven, *or* resteam straight from the freezer for about 10 minutes.

DRIED BEANCURD SKINS

The next three recipes all use dried beancurd skin as a wrapping for various fillings. This is made from the skin that forms on the top of boiling soya bean milk and is lifted off and hung up to dry. When it is dry, beancurd skin is very brittle, breaking and cracking easily, and unfortunately since most beancurd skins come from China, many of the sheets are already badly cracked before we buy them, and these tears cannot be rejoined. This sometimes leads to problems in finding complete lengths without any tears that can be used as wrapping skins: in the recipes we have compensated for this by suggesting rather generous amounts of beancurd skin.

Dried beancurd skin is always soaked in hot water until it becomes soft and pliable so that it can be folded and rolled into various-sized packets, although it still tears easily. If you practise using beancurd skin, you can quickly gain confidence in handling it and achieve very professional results with it.

猪肉鲜丁卷

Makes 10 rolls

FILLING

180 g (6 oz) boneless belly of pork

25 ml (1½ tablespoons) egg white

15 ml (1 tablespoon) finely chopped spring onion

pinch of five spice powder

10 ml (2 teaspoons) grated fresh ginger

1.5 ml (¼ teaspoon) light soy sauce

1.5 ml (¼ teaspoon) salt

2.5 ml (½ teaspoon) cornflour

5 sheets dried beancurd skin

oil for deep-frying (optional)

素鸡

Serves 4

FILLING

15 ml (1 tablespoon) dried shrimps

6 dried mushrooms

15 ml (1 tablespoon) dark soy sauce

7.5 ml (1½ teaspoons) sugar

10 ml (2 teaspoons) oil

2 sheets dried beancurd skin

oil for deep-frying

PORK ROLLS

Mince the pork twice using the coarse grille on the mincer, and mix with all the other ingredients for the filling, beating hard to blend them very thoroughly. Soak the beancurd skins in hot water until they are a light cream colour and very pliable – about 7 minutes, drain, lay them on a flat surface and gently pat dry. Cut them into 10 strips about 10 × 15 cm (4 × 6 inches), trying to avoid any big tears or holes. Paint each skin with a little oil. Pile one-tenth of the meat filling along the bottom edge of a length of beancurd, fold over the sides to close the ends, and roll up the beancurd skin firmly into a tidy, sausage-shaped package. Repeat with the remaining filling and beancurd skins. Arrange the rolls, open flap down on the bottom of an oiled steamer and steam over a moderate heat for 40 minutes.

These beancurd rolls can be steamed in advance and then reheated in a steamer or, after steaming, they can be deep-fried in moderately hot oil for about 30 seconds. They can also be frozen after steaming and then reheated without defrosting either by deep-frying for about 4 minutes or by steaming again for about 10 minutes.

'VEGETARIAN' CHICKEN

Soak the dried shrimps in hot water for an hour. Meanwhile, place the mushrooms in 200 ml (⅓ pint) warm water and leave to soak for 30 minutes. Reserve 150 ml (¼ pint) of soaking water. When the mushrooms are soft, chop the caps finely, discarding the hard stalks. Put the reserved soaking water with the soy sauce and sugar into a small pan and simmer the chopped mushrooms in this stock for 10 minutes. Leave in the stock until required. Drain the shrimps and stir-fry them in 10 ml (2 teaspoons) of oil over a brisk heat until they start to jump – about 2 minutes. Lift them from the pan with a slotted spoon and chop finely. Soak the beancurd skins in hot water for 7 minutes until they are soft. Drain, pat dry and brush a little of the mushroom stock over both sheets. Lay one on top of the other, covering any holes or tears. Sprinkle the whole surface with the chopped shrimps and drained mushrooms. Fold over about 2.5 cm (1 inch) along the length of both sides and as tightly as possible, roll up the beancurd sheets with the shrimps and mushrooms inside the double layer of beancurd skin. Place the roll, loose flap down, on the oiled base of a steamer and steam over a high heat for 40 minutes. Heat the oil for deep-frying moderately hot and deep-fry the roll for 1 minute, turning it once. Drain well and serve either hot or cold, cut into diagonal slices.

蝦肉鮮竹卷

Makes 12 packets

FILLING

100 g (4 oz) raw prawns
20 g (¾ oz) fat pork
10 g (½ oz) lean, unsmoked
　raw bacon
20 g (¾ oz) shelled broad
　beans
2 water chestnuts
5 ml (1 teaspoon) rice wine
pinch of salt and pepper

3 or 4 sheets dried beancurd
　skin
15 ml (1 tablespoon) egg
　white
5 ml (1 teaspoon) cornflour
oil for deep-frying

蛋皮

Makes 12 skins

3 small eggs (size 5)
1.5 ml (¼ teaspoon) salt
25 ml (1½ tablespoons)
　cornflour
45 ml (3 tablespoons) water
2.5 ml (½ teaspoon) rice wine
oil or lard for frying

PRAWN PACKETS

Shell the prawns and de-vein. Put the prawns, pork, bacon, broad beans and water chestnuts through the mincer twice, using a coarse grille both times, then blend the mixture very thoroughly with the rice wine, salt and pepper. Soak the beancurd skins in hot water until they become soft and pliable – about 7 minutes. Drain, pat dry and cut 10 squares each measuring 7 cm (3½ inches) without any tears or holes. Beat the egg white with the cornflour into a thin paste and paint over the beancurd squares. Place about 2.5 ml (½ teaspoon) of the prawn mixture onto the centre of a square and fold it up like an envelope, taking great care that there are no cracks or gaps in the packet. Repeat with the remaining squares. This is a fiddly job and it takes a little practice to avoid any gaps in the packets. When all the packets are completed, arrange them on the oiled bottom of a steamer and steam for 10 minutes. Heat the oil to about 120°C (250°F) and slide the packets in carefully. Deep-fry over a low heat for about 5 minutes. Drain well and serve with a salt and pepper dip.

'EGG-SKINS'

These paper-thin omelettes are used in various dimsum as skins to wrap around different fillings; they are always cooked in a steamer. Stuffed 'egg-skins' can be served in many different ways apart from dimsum, for instance with stir-fried green vegetables or broccoli, as one ingredient in an elaborate pot with many kinds of meat and fish, or smoked and sliced as a cold hors d'oeuvre in a formal meal.

Make a thin batter with the eggs, salt, cornflour, water and wine. Heat a small frying pan – 10 cm (4 inches) in diameter – with 5 ml (1 teaspoon) of oil (or lard) over a high heat. Spoon in 25 ml (1½ tablespoons) of the batter and immediately tilt the pan so the bottom is evenly coated. Cook over a high heat until the egg is just set on top – about 15 seconds, then slide the omelette out onto a flat surface to cool. Continue cooking the rest of the batter in the same way, adding more oil to the pan when necessary.

　　To make larger skins; use a 19 cm (7½-inch) frying pan and the egg mixture to make only 3 omelettes.

Opposite: Steamed Spareribs with Black Bean and Sour Plums (page 39), and Chicken Congee (page 139) served with chopped spring onions and grated ginger

Overleaf: Pearl Balls (page 29) and Prawn Filled Egg Slices (page 33)

鮮肉蛋卷

Makes 12 rolls

150 g (5 oz) boneless pork
(one-third fat)

SEASONING SAUCE

10 ml (2 teaspoons) rice
wine

1.5 ml (¼ teaspoon) salt

10 ml (2 teaspoons) sesame
oil

10 ml (2 teaspoons) very
finely chopped spring
onion

7.5 ml (1½ teaspoons) grated
fresh ginger

7.5 ml (1½ teaspoons)
cornflour

2.5 ml (½ teaspoon) water

12 small 'egg-skins'
oil

DIPPING SAUCE

15 ml (1 tablespoon) chilli
beanpaste

45 ml (3 tablespoons) light
soy sauce

鮮蝦蛋卷

Serves 4

75 g (3 oz) prawn paste

75 g (3 oz) pork paste

SEASONINGS

3.5 ml (¾ teaspoon) salt

10 ml (2 teaspoons) finely
chopped spring onion

5 ml (1 teaspoon) sesame oil

2.5 ml (½ teaspoon) light soy
sauce

pinch of pepper and sugar

3 water chestnuts

15 g (½ oz) bamboo shoots

2 large 'egg-skins'

2 sheets *nori* seaweed

oil

PORK-FILLED EGG ROLLS

Trim any gristle and skin from the pork and put it through the mincer using a coarse grille. Then pound with the blunt edge of a meat cleaver until it becomes a coarse paste, where you can still see small pieces of meat. Mix the paste with the seasoning sauce. Place about 5 ml (1 teaspoon) of the meat filling across the bottom of an 'egg-skin'. Fold the sides over the filling and roll up into a tidy sausage-shaped parcel, about 4 cm (1½ inches) wide. Repeat for the remaining egg-skins. Oil the base of a steamer and arrange the parcels, loose flap down, in the steamer so they do not touch. Steam for 20 minutes and serve very hot with the dipping sauce.

These pork rolls freeze very well cooked or uncooked providing the pork has not previously been frozen. Resteam straight from the freezer for 30 minutes if uncooked and 10 minutes if cooked.

PRAWN FILLED EGG SLICES

The sheets of nori, or laver seaweed, included in this recipe usually come from Japan rather than China. Although laver is familiar in the north-east of China and appears in recipes from that region, the Chinese variety is not usually sold in the West.

Blend the two pastes together with the seasonings. Mince the water chestnuts and bamboo shoots using the coarse grille and add them to the paste. Divide into four and spread one portion over each 'egg-skin'. Lay a sheet of *nori* on top of the paste and spread the remaining paste over the *nori*. Roll up the skins with the filling to make firm sausage-shaped rolls. Oil the base of a steamer and lay the rolls on it so they do not touch. Steam for 20 minutes. Then cut into diagonal slices before serving hot with a soy dipping sauce.

These rolls freeze well *after* cooking. Reheat either by taking the rolls straight from the freezer and steaming for 10 minutes, or defrost and reheat in a microwave oven. Slice just before serving.

紙包蝦

Makes 8 packets
8 raw prawns

MARINADE
15 ml (1 tablespoon) rice
  wine
1.5 ml (¼ teaspoon) salt

oil for deep-frying
1 packet rice paper rounds

五香鴨腳礼

Serves 4
12 ducks' webs
3 spring onions
30 ml (2 tablespoons) oil
2 slices fresh ginger
30 ml (2 tablespoons) rice
  wine
45 ml (3 tablespoons) dark
  soy sauce
600 ml (1 pint) stock
15 ml (1 tablespoon) oyster
  sauce
2.5-cm (1-inch) square of
  dried orange peel (or use
  fresh)
1 petal star anise
pinch of salt and sugar
50 g (2 oz) pork paste
50 g (2 oz) prawn paste
pinch of salt and pepper
2 sheets dried beancurd skin
oil for deep-frying

RICE PAPER PRAWNS

Remove the shells and de-vein the prawns, keeping them whole. Marinate for 20 minutes. Drain and pat dry. Heat the oil. Take a circle of rice paper and place a prawn in the centre. Then quickly (and very gently) loosely gather up the circle to form a bag around the prawn. Lower it into the hot oil. The oil must be hot enough to sizzle when the rice paper touches it, but not so hot that it burns the paper. Deep-fry each prawn packet about 30 seconds, then lift out, and drain. Repeat for all the prawns and serve at once. This dish will not freeze and must be made just before it is served.

DUCKS' WEBS

Ducks' webs (or feet) can be bought ready prepared and deep-frozen from many Chinese grocers. If you wish to prepare your own, see instructions on page 22. Ducks' webs are regarded as a delicacy in China, and are often served as a dish at a large dinner, when they are usually boned before being stuffed.

Wash the ducks' webs. Chop the spring onions into 1-cm (½-inch) lengths. Heat the oil in a frying pan and stir-fry the ginger and onion for 15 seconds. Add the ducks' webs and stir-fry for about 2 minutes, then stir in the rice wine and soy sauce. Continue cooking for another 15 seconds over a reduced heat before pouring in the stock and oyster sauce together with the orange peel, star anise, salt and sugar. Bring to the boil and transfer to a heavy saucepan or casserole. Cover with a lid and simmer over a gentle heat for 75 minutes. While the casserole is cooking, prepare the stuffing by blending the pork and prawn pastes together with the salt and pepper. Soak the dried beancurd skins in hot water for 7 minutes, pat them dry and cut into 12 lengths 5 cm (2 inches) wide. When the ducks' webs are cooked, lift them out of the pan, reserving the cooking liquor, and dry them with kitchen paper. Push a small ball of the stuffing, about the size of a walnut into each 'hand' formed by a duck's web. Wrap a strip of beancurd skin round each web to hold the paste in place. Heat the oil to about 120°C (250°F) and deep-fry the stuffed ducks' webs for 3 minutes, then lift out and drain well. Arrange them in a shallow dish with 75 ml (5 tablespoons) of the reserved cooking liquor and put them into a steamer for 40 minutes over a high heat. Check from time to time that the water does not boil dry.

Ducks' webs can be frozen after they have been deep-fried. To reheat, take them straight from the freezer and steam for 50 minutes.

四宝鸡扎

Makes 8 bundles

250 g (8 oz) boneless
    chicken breast

MARINADE

15 ml (1 tablespoon) ginger
    wine
15 ml (1 tablespoon) onion
    wine
2.5 ml (½ teaspoon) salt
5 ml (1 teaspoon) potato
    flour (or cornflour)

4 dried mushrooms
40 ml (1½ oz) canned
    bamboo shoots
50 g (2 oz) *chahsiu* (see page
    42)
2 sheets dried beancurd skin
10 ml (2 teaspoons) egg
    white
5 ml (1 teaspoon) cornflour
oil for deep-frying

Firewood bundles fastened with
strips of beancurd skin.

FIREWOOD BUNDLES

In traditional versions of this recipe the strips of meat are tied into bundles with strips of winter melon. However these are very apt to break and are harder to handle than beancurd skin, so it has become customary in Chinese restaurants in the West to use beancurd skin for this dish.

Cut the chicken into strips about 1 cm (½ inch) wide and 6 cm (2½ inches) long. Marinate for 30 minutes. Meanwhile, soak the dried mushrooms for 30 minutes in warm water. Discard the hard stalks and cut the caps into slices. Cut the bamboo shoots and *chahsiu* into pieces about the same size and shape as the chicken strips. Soak the dried beancurd skin in hot water for 10 minutes and then cut it into 4-cm (1½-inch) wide strips. Arrange a piece of chicken, *chahsiu*, bamboo shoot and one or two slices of mushroom so that they all lie parallel and fasten them round the middle into a 'bundle' using a strip of beancurd skin. Seal the end with a little egg and cornflour paste. Heat the oil moderately hot — about 150°C (300°F) and deep-fry the bundles for 1 minute. Drain them well and put them onto a plate in a steamer. Steam over a high heat for 30 minutes. Serve hot.

These bundles can be deep-frozen after they have been deep-fried. To finish cooking, take them straight from the freezer together with a little stock and steam for 40 minutes.

五香茶葉蛋

Serves 4

4 hard-boiled eggs
2 teabags (Indian tea)
15 ml (1 tablespoon) soy
    sauce
1 whole star anise
5 ml (1 teaspoon) salt

TEA EGGS

Tap the egg shells gently with a spoon to craze them evenly all over. Place the eggs together with the other ingredients into 600 ml (1 pint) of boiling water. Simmer gently for 30 minutes, then take out the eggs, shell them and cut into quarters. Serve hot.

You will find that the eggs have taken on a lovely pattern, as well as the subtle taste of the cooking liquor.

鑲豆腐

Serves 4

4 squares beancurd, about
350 g (12 oz)

STUFFING

50 g (2 oz) pork paste
50 g (2 oz) boneless and
skinless cod
2.5 ml (½ teaspoon) salt
5 ml (1 teaspoon) light soy
sauce
pinch of pepper

30 ml (2 tablespoons) oil
1 very finely chopped spring
onion
1.5 ml (¼ teaspoon) grated
fresh ginger
15 ml (1 tablespoon) oyster
sauce
15 ml (1 tablespoon) soy
sauce

辣炸豆腐

Serves 4

4 squares beancurd, about
350 g (12 oz)
45 ml (3 tablespoons)
cornflour
oil for deep-frying

DIPPING SAUCE

1.5 ml (¼ teaspoon) chilli oil
1 garlic clove, crushed
10 ml (2 teaspoons) grated
fresh ginger
30 ml (2 tablespoons) soy
sauce
2 spring onions, finely
chopped

STUFFED BEANCURD

Hollow out a small hole about 3 cm (1 inch) across and 1 cm
(½ inch) deep in the top of each beancurd square. Place all
the stuffing ingredients together with the loose bits of
beancurd into a food processor with the plastic blade
attachment and run until the mixture is smooth and
well-blended. Fill the hollows in the beancurd squares with
the processed paste, smoothing over the top with the back of
a wet spoon. Arrange the beancurd squares on a plate that
can stand in the base of your steamer. Heat the oil in a small
pan and fry the onion and ginger for 30 seconds, then add
the oyster sauce and soy sauce together with 15 ml
(1 tablespoon) water. Simmer gently for 3 minutes. Pour the
sauce over the beancurd squares and steam for 20 minutes
over a high heat. Serve hot.
   This dish will not freeze.

CHILLI BEANCURD

Gently dust the beancurd squares with the cornflour. Heat
the oil to a moderate heat – about 150°C (300°F) – and slide
in the beancurd. Deep-fry over a low heat for about
4 minutes until they are golden-brown. Lift them out
carefully, drain and eat hot with the dipping sauce.
Alternatively, the beancurd squares can be gently poached
in 300 ml (½ pint) of good chicken stock, and then eaten with
the same dipping sauce.

Chapter 5 | Pots and small dishes

砂鍋小菜類

There is a wide range of dishes in Chinese cuisine which are often eaten with dimsum meals or for snacks but which in other circumstances may equally well be served as part of an ordinary family meal, although never at a big dinner or banquet. It is this kind of dish, belonging to no particular cooking style, that is the main subject of this chapter.

Fashion dictates the choice of dishes on the menus of restaurants in Hong Kong, Taibei and throughout the Western world (although not necessarily in mainland China, where there are other influential factors) quite as strongly as it influences the clothes people wear. Dishes come and go from the menus, particularly in dimsum menus, where there is relatively much more freedom of choice, and an almost endless range of dishes from which to choose. Almost any dish that does not require skillful or long preparation, is simply cooked, and includes only those ingredients that any Chinese restaurant kitchen would have ready to hand is suitable to be offered as a snack or as a small dish to go with dimsum for a lunch or light meal.

In Hong Kong and Taibei, where many of the regular clientele may eat dimsum at least once a week for lunch, diners are continually searching for something new or interesting on the menu, so even dishes previously reserved exclusively for banquets are now being served as dimsum. Fashion has dictated the introduction of shark's fin soup as a dimsum dish.

Fashion can also dictate the manner in which dishes are served. Many Chinese restaurants in the Western world now serve dishes such as squid with black beans, or stuffed peppers, on *teppans* — flat iron cooking plates that are brought sizzling hot to the table, a practice more usually associated with Indian restaurants in the West. If you can obtain such an iron plate and its wooden base, it is great fun to use. Heat the *teppan* very hot under a grill or in the oven and when the cooking is finished, transfer the food to the *tappan* for serving: we find this is better than trying to do the final cooking of the food in the *teppan* itself.

There is one problem in this group of dishes that is more acute for the domestic cook than for restaurants: that is the problem of quantities. It would not be practical to make many of the dishes described in this chapter in the small quantities usually served at restaurant dimsum meals. We have therefore made the recipes in this chapter small enough to be a dimsum dish shared among four people but large enough to be a one-dish meal for two people. Where it is possible to freeze and store these dishes, we have noted it under the recipes.

鼓汁魷魚

Serves 4

300 g (10 oz) prepared squid
(see page 23)
2 slices fresh ginger
1 spring onion
7.5 ml (1½ teaspoons)
fermented black beans
30 ml (2 tablespoons) oil
10 ml (2 teaspoons) soy
sauce
30 ml (2 tablespoons) water

五香焗肉排

Serves 4

500 g (1 lb) spareribs

MARINADE

25 ml (1½ tablespoons) rice
wine
25 ml (1½ tablespoons) soy
sauce
5 ml (1 teaspoon) salt
30 ml (2 tablespoons) sugar
25 ml (1½ tablespoons)
hoisin sauce
1 square fermented red
beancurd, mashed
(optional)
3 garlic cloves, crushed
pinch of five spice powder

SQUID WITH BLACK BEANS

Score the squid body sac to half its thickness with fine criss-cross cuts and then cut it into 3-cm (1-inch) squares. Cut the tentacles into 4 or 5 pieces. Chop the ginger, spring onion and black beans very finely together. Blanch the squid in boiling water, then immediately dip into cold water and drain. Heat a frying pan or wok with the oil and stir-fry the black beans, ginger and onion for about 30 seconds, then add the soy sauce and 30 ml (2 tablespoons) of water. Crush the beans in the liquid and add the squid. Mix quickly in the sauce to heat through and serve immediately.

SWEET BAKED SPARERIBS

Chop the spareribs into 5-cm (2-inch) lengths, and place them in an ovenproof casserole. Mix the marinade and spoon over the spareribs. Marinate for 1 hour, turning the spareribs in the mixture from time to time so they are all well coated. Preheat the oven to 170°C (350°F, Gas mark 4), cover the casserole and cook for 1¼ hours. Serve hot.

This dish can be cooked in advance and reheated in small helpings in a steamer. If you wish to freeze it, omit the garlic in the first cooking, then reheat in a saucepan with 4 cloves of crushed garlic for 10 minutes before serving.

豉汁蒸肉排

Serves 4
500 g (1 lb) spareribs
3 garlic cloves
25 ml (1½ tablespoons)
    fermented black beans
2 sour plums, stoned
1 fresh chilli, seeded
    (optional)
45 ml (3 tablespoons) light
    soy sauce
10 ml (2 teaspoons) sugar
10 ml (2 teaspoons)
    cornflour
15 ml (1 tablespoon) sesame
    oil

STEAMED SPARERIBS WITH BLACK BEAN AND SOUR PLUMS

Chop the spareribs into 2.5-cm (1-inch) lengths. Crush the garlic, chop the black beans, sour plums and chilli and mix together with the soy sauce, sugar, cornflour and sesame oil. Place the spareribs into a shallow bowl and spoon over the black bean mixture. Take care they are all well-coated and marinate for 1 hour. Steam the spareribs in the marinade over a high heat until they are well cooked – about 40 minutes. Serve hot. These spareribs do not freeze well, but may be kept covered in a refrigerator for 24 hours and reheated in a steamer.

辣 兔 肉

Serves 4
500 g (1 lb) rabbit portions

SIMMERING STOCK

2 spring onions
2 slices fresh ginger
15 ml (1 tablespoon) rice
    wine
15 ml (1 tablespoon) soy
    sauce
600 ml (1 pint) water

30 ml (2 tablespoons) oil
25 ml (1½ tablespoons)
    fermented black beans,
    mashed
25 ml (1½ tablespoons) soy
    sauce
15 ml (1 tablespoon) sugar
2.5 ml (½ teaspoon) salt
2.5 ml (½ teaspoon) Sichuan
    peppercorns, crushed
45 ml (3 tablespoons) chilli
    oil
4 spring onions, finely
    chopped

CHILLI RABBIT

Wash the rabbit portions, put into a pan of boiling water and boil for 5 minutes. Remove the rabbit, rinse and discard the water. Pour the simmering stock into the pan and return the rabbit. Bring to the boil, cover and gently boil until it is just cooked – about 40 minutes. Lift the rabbit out of the stock and when it is cool enough to handle, tear the meat off the bones into shreds. Just before the meal heat a frying pan or wok with 30 ml (2 tablespoons) oil and stir-fry the mashed black beans for about 30 seconds. Then add the soy sauce, sugar, salt, pepper, chilli oil and the rabbit shreds. Mix together very quickly over a high heat and serve at once, sprinkled with the finely chopped spring onions.

塩 椒 蝦

Serves 4

300 g (10 oz) raw prawns

MARINADE

5 ml (1 teaspoon) grated
fresh ginger
15 ml (1 tablespoon) rice
wine

10 ml (2 teaspoons)
cornflour
oil for deep-frying
5 ml (1 teaspoon) salt
2 garlic cloves, crushed

香 酥 魚 塊

Serves 4
FLAVOURED OIL

45 ml (3 tablespoons) oil
3 slices fresh ginger
2 dried chillis
10 ml (2 teaspoons) Sichuan
peppercorns

300 g (10 oz) haddock fillets

MARINADE

2.5 ml ($\frac{1}{2}$ teaspoon) five spice
powder
2.5 ml ($\frac{1}{2}$ teaspoon) salt
5 ml (1 teaspoon) red
vinegar
20 ml (4 teaspoons)
flavoured oil (see below)

BATTER

150 g (5 oz) plain flour
200 ml ($\frac{1}{3}$ pint) cold water

oil for deep-frying

DIPPING SAUCE

20 ml (4 teaspoons) red
vinegar
45 ml (3 tablespoons) light
soy sauce

FRIED WHOLE PRAWNS

De-vein the prawns but do not remove their shells. Rinse well, pat dry and mix with the grated ginger and rice wine. Marinate for 30 minutes, dry again and roll in the cornflour. Deep-fry in very hot oil for one minute, then lift out and drain. Place the prawns with the salt and crushed garlic into a dry frying pan and stir-fry for another minute over a low heat. Serve either hot or cold.

FRIED FISH SLICES

For this recipe you will need a spicy hot oil to enhance the flavour of the marinated fish. Make this oil at least 24 hours before you need it.

Heat the oil in a pan and stir fry the ginger, chillis and peppercorns for about 1 minute over a moderate heat. Remove from the heat and set aside to cool. Strain off the oil and use as required.

Remove the skin from the fillet and cut it lengthways into strips about $1\frac{1}{2} \times 12$ cm ($\frac{1}{2} \times 5$ inches). Mix the marinade and coat the fish strips with it. Leave for an hour. Mix the batter, but do not worry if it is lumpy. Dip the fish strips into the batter before deep-frying them, a few strips at a time, in hot oil. Deep-fry for about 3 minutes, then lift out and cut each strip into 2 or 3 pieces. Serve very hot with the dipping sauce.

蒸鸡脚扎

Serves 4

6 pairs of chicken feet

SEASONING STOCK

45 ml (3 tablespoons) dark
   soy sauce
30 ml (2 tablespoons) rice
   wine
3 slices fresh ginger
3 spring onions
15 ml (1 tablespoon)
   barbecue sauce
7.5 ml (¼ oz) crystal sugar
1 petal star anise
2.5-cm (1-inch) square dried
   orange peel
1.5 ml (¼ teaspoon) freshly
   ground black pepper
600 ml (1 pint) water

叉燒鴨

1 small duck about 1½–2 kg
   (3 4 lb) (If using a goose, It
   may be necessary to
   double the rest of the
   ingredients.)

SEASONINGS

2.5 cm (1 inch) fresh ginger,
   crushed
2 cm (¾-inch) square dried
   orange peel
1 whole star anise
5 ml (1 teaspoon) Sichuan
   peppercorns
10 ml (2 teaspoons) salt

25 ml (1½ tablespoons) water
5 ml (1 teaspoon) maltose,
   or clear honey

PHOENIX CLAWS

If the chicken feet have not already been skinned you will
need to do this by the method described on page 22. Chop
each foot in two across the knuckles. Place the chicken feet
and seasoning stock into a saucepan and bring to the boil.
Cover with a lid and simmer for 1½ hours over a gentle heat.
Serve very hot in small portions with a little of the seasoning
stock poured over. Chicken's feet can be cooked in advance
and reheated by transferring them with a little of the stock to
a bowl and steaming over a high heat for about 20 minutes.
They can also be frozen, then allowed to defrost and
reheated as above.

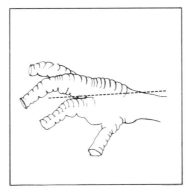

Cut skinned and trimmed chicken's
feet in half along line shown.

CANTONESE ROAST DUCK OR GOOSE

Prepare the duck by cutting off the wing tips and removing
the oil sac from beneath the tail. Place the seasonings inside
the duck and sew up both the neck and back vents very
securely. Pour a kettle of boiling water all over the outside of
the duck and then wipe it dry. Boil the water and maltose in a
small pan to make a syrup and paint the duck with it. Hang
the duck in a current of moving air from 4 to 6 hours. A good
washing day is ideal, for the duck does not need sun, only
wind; or hang it in front of a fan heater running at *cold*.
When the duck is really dry, hang it from the shelf at the top
of a hot 200°C (400°F, gas mark 6) oven with a drip tray
under it. Roast for 15 minutes, then reduce the oven
temperature to 190°C, (375°F, Gas mark 5) and continue
cooking for another 45 minutes to 1 hour depending on the
size of the bird. (Allow about 15 minutes per 500 g (1 lb) and
15 minutes extra.) It may be necessary to turn the duck so it
hangs the other way half-way through the cooking.

When the duck is cool, cut it into quarters, and wrap
and freeze until required. The duck can be served cold, cut
into slices, carved hot in slices, or with hot rice (see page
134). It can be reheated in a microwave oven.

又　燒

Serves 8 as cold dish

500 g (1 lb) boneless,
    skinless belly of pork

MARINADE

45 ml (3 tablespoons) dark
    soy sauce
45 ml (3 tablespoons) rice
    wine
45 ml (3 tablespoons) *hoisin*
    sauce
90 ml (6 tablespoons) sugar
15 ml (1 tablespoon) salt
2 ml (¼ teaspoon) five spice
    powder
3 garlic cloves, crushed

GLAZE

15 ml (1 tablespoon) sesame
    oil
15 ml (1 tablespoon) sugar
15 ml (1 tablespoon) red
    vinegar
pinch of five spice powder

香　豆

Serves 6

125 g (4 oz) dried soya beans
25 g (1 oz) bruised fresh
    ginger
25 ml (1½ tablespoons) salt
1 petal star anise

CHAHSIU

Slices of Cantonese roast pork (chahsiu) are served in many different ways. They can be served as a cold plate with a garnish of boiled soya beans, among other dimsum dishes, but more usually chahsiu is served hot on rice or noodles as a one-dish snack (see Chapters 10 and 11). It is also an ingredient in Firewood bundles (page 35) or chopped as a filling for Chahsiu buns (page 102). Frequently it is used in mixed meat pots and congees. Chahsiu is a specialist dish that is not normally cooked in ordinary restaurants, but in cooked meat shops or noodle and rice houses. When it is available it can usually be seen in the window of the shop. The amount of pork given in the recipe below can be halved without changing the quantity of marinade or glaze.

The belly of pork should be cut into two strips about 5 cm (2 inches) wide and 20 cm (8 inches) long. Mix the marinade in a flat dish and add the pork strips making sure they are completely coated with the marinade. Marinate for 6 hours, turning the pork from time to time so that it is evenly seasoned. Heat the oven to 190°C (375°F, Gas mark 5) and hang the pork strips from the bars of the top shelf of the oven, remembering to put a drip tray under it. Roast for 20 minutes, then paint the pork with the remaining marinade. Continue to cook for another 25 minutes, checking to see that the meat does not burn, and if necessary, repainting with the marinade. While it is cooking, prepare the glaze by heating the sesame oil in a small saucepan and adding the sugar, vinegar and five spice powder. Stir over a moderate heat until all the sugar is dissolved. When the pork is cooked, and while it is still hot, paint all over with the glaze and leave to cool. Before serving, cut into slices.

SPICED BEANS

These beans are served with chahsiu in Cantonese restaurants.

Soak the soya beans in cold water for 12 hours then rinse well and drain. Place the beans in a saucepan with fresh cold water and bring to the boil. Add the ginger, salt and star anise and continue boiling hard for 10 minutes, then reduce the heat and simmer until the beans are soft – about 1½ hours. Drain and serve hot or cold.

紅燒牛肉

Serves 4

350 g (12 oz) thick flank
  steak

MARINADE

15 ml (1 tablespoon) salt
15 ml (1 tablespoon) grated
  fresh ginger
15 ml (1 tablespoon) finely
  chopped onion

SIMMERING STOCK

15 g ($\frac{1}{2}$ oz) boiling spices,
  made up of cloves,
  liquorice powder,
  cinnamon bark, star anise,
  Sichuan peppercorns,
  fennel seeds, dried
  orange peel, all tied into a
  small cloth bag
15 ml (1 tablespoon) rice
  wine
25 g (1 oz) crystal sugar
45 ml (3 tablespoons) dark
  soy sauce
600 ml (1 pint) water

10 ml (2 teaspoons) sesame
  oil

水晶猪蹄

Serves 4

2 pork hocks
2.5 cm (1 inch) fresh ginger,
  crushed
3 spring onions
30 ml (2 tablespoons) rice
  wine
salt and pepper to taste

SPICED BEEF

Rub the beef all over with the salt, grated ginger and onion and leave to marinate for 1 hour. Meanwhile, make the simmering stock by placing the bag of boiling spices together with the rice wine, sugar, soy sauce and water into a thick saucepan and bring it to the boil over a high heat. Reduce the heat, cover the pan and simmer for 30 minutes, then lift out the spice bag and put the stock aside until it is required. Place the beef on an oiled rack over a dry tray in a preheated oven 190°C (375°F, Gas mark 5) for 15 minutes. Then put it into the prepared simmering stock, cover and simmer for 1$\frac{1}{2}$ hours over a low heat. Remove from the heat and leave to cool in the remaining stock. Lift out, drain well and paint with sesame oil before cutting into slices to serve.

CRYSTAL PORK HOCK

Wash the pork hocks and place them into sufficient cold water to cover. Bring to a rolling boil, remove the pork hocks, rinse well and discard the boiling water. Place the hocks into a casserole, again with sufficient water *just* to cover them, and add the crushed ginger, spring onions and rice wine. Cover with a lid and stand the casserole in a pan of boiling water coming about half-way up the side of the casserole. Place the pan and casserole into a preheated oven 150°C (300°F, Gas mark 2), and cook for 4 hours. Strain off the remaining stock and season it to taste with salt and pepper. (Remember the stock will be eaten cold as a jelly and so can stand a little more salt than would be required if it were to be eaten hot.) Take the meat off the bones and cut it into small pieces. Arrange these in the bottom of a glass baking dish. Pour over the stock and leave in a cool place to set. This dish should be mainly jelly with only a little meat in it. Before serving, unmould and cut into thick slices. Serve with a dipping sauce of 45 ml (3 tablespoons) soy sauce and 15 ml (1 tablespoon) red vinegar.

煙燻豬肝

Serves 4

300 g (10 oz) pig's liver in
   one piece

SIMMERING STOCK

2 spring onions
2 slices fresh ginger
15 ml (1 tablespoon) rice
   wine
45 ml (3 tablespoons) dark
   soy sauce
25 g (1 oz) crystal sugar
2.5 ml ($\frac{1}{2}$ teaspoon) salt, or
   more to taste
2 petals star anise
600 ml (1 pint) water

SMOKING MIXTURE

45 ml (3 tablespoons) Indian
   tea
45 ml (3 tablespoons) brown
   sugar
45 ml (3 tablespoons) rice

SMOKED LIVER

Place the simmering stock into a pan and bring to the boil.
Cover and simmer for 30 minutes. Add the liver and
continue simmering with the lid on until the liver is *just*
cooked – about 20 minutes. You can test if the liver is ready
by pricking it with a knife; if no blood runs out, it is cooked.
Leave the liver to soak overnight in the simmering stock. The
next day, line the bottom of a roasting tin with a tight-fitting
lid with kitchen foil and sprinkle on the smoking mixture.
Place the covered roasting tin into a preheated oven 230°C
(450°F, Gas mark 8) and bake for 10 minutes until the
mixture starts to smoke. In the meantime, take the liver out of
the marinade, pat dry and stand it on an oiled rack. When
the mixture is smoking vigorously, stand the rack with the
liver in the tin, cover with the lid and return to the oven. Turn
down the heat to 110°C (225°F, Gas mark $\frac{1}{4}$) and smoke for
5 minutes. Take out and allow to cool before serving cut into
thin slices.

豆花湯

Serves 4

250 g (8 oz) soya beans
5 ml (1 teaspoon) plaster of
   Paris*
8 spring onions
15 ml (1 tablespoon) oil
salt and pepper to taste
20 ml (4 teaspoons) sesame
   oil or chilli oil, depending
   on taste
20 ml (4 teaspoons)
   chopped chives or green
   part of spring onions
1 sheet dried beancurd skin
   (optional)
oil for deep-frying (optional)

Buy fine quality plaster of
Paris from a chemist. Do not
use modelling plaster or any
other substitute plaster.

BEANFLOWER SOUP

*This soup made from curdled soya bean milk is a very
popular breakfast or early morning snack in China, but it can
be eaten at any time of the day. It is traditional to crumble a
deep-fried batter stick (you tiao) into it, but to make these
successfully requires a great deal of skill. We have found that
fresh beanflower soup is very good to eat on its own, or with
a sheet of deep-fried beancurd skin crumbled over as a
substitute for a batter stick. The soya bean milk can be made
in advance and then reheated, but it must be kept cold and
only stays fresh for 24 hours. Commercially produced
brands of soya bean milk cannot be curdled.*

Soak the soya beans in cold water for 24 hours, changing the
water once or twice. Drain the beans and rinse them well in
cold water. Liquidize them into a very smooth purée with
1.65 litres (2$\frac{3}{4}$ pints) of fresh water. We have found that a
liquidizer does this job better than a food processor,
because the latter tends to beat air into the bean purée, and
the bubbles are difficult to remove later. Pour the purée into
a large pan and bring it to the boil. Then, stirring all the time,
boil for 6 minutes. Watch to see it does not burn at the
bottom of the pan. Lift the pan from the heat and allow the
purée to cool. When it can be handled, strain the purée

through a jelly bag or tea towel into a clean pan. Squeeze it very tightly to extract as much liquid as possible. This liquid is now soya bean milk. Return the pan with the soya bean milk to the heat and bring to the boil. Boil for 10 minutes, stirring all the time. Take care it does not boil over at this point. At the same time, heat a small pan with 150 ml ($\frac{1}{4}$ pint) of water to just above blood heat and mix this with the plaster of Paris in a small jug. Remove the soya bean milk from the stove, stir very vigorously and remove the spoon. While the soya bean milk is still moving, pour in the plaster of Paris in a zig-zag movement across the whole surface of the pan. Shake the jug to keep the plaster in suspension while you pour. Stir the milk round *once* more, cover the pan with a lid and leave for 7 minutes for the curd to develop. The soft beancurd can be left at this stage for up to 24 hours in a cold place.

When you are ready to eat the beanflower soup, chop the spring onions finely and stir-fry them in a wok or large saucepan with the oil. Add the soft beancurd and stir over a gentle heat, rather like scrambling eggs, to warm through. Season with salt and pepper to taste and serve in individual warmed soup bowls with a little sesame oil and chopped chives as a garnish. If you wish, deep-fry the sheet of dried beancurd skin in moderately hot oil until it blisters. Drain and crumble the beancurd skin over the beanflower soup.

BIG SOUPS

In recent years a new style of dimsum dish has appeared in some Hong Kong and Taiwanese restaurants. Small individual bowls of particular soups, such as Shark's fin, made from expensive ingredients and normally served only at banquets and big dinners, are now being served as part of a dimsum meal. They can be ordered from the dimsum menu in small quantities to be eaten when and as people please. This freedom gives an almost illicit pleasure to eating a dish traditionally regarded as reserved for only the most formal occasions.

冬菇木耳湯

Serves 4 to 6

6 dried mushrooms
30 ml (2 tablespoons) black
    fungus
3 sheets dried beancurd
oil for deep-frying
2 stalks celery
15 ml (1 tablespoon) sesame
    oil
900 ml (1½ pints) good
    chicken stock
10 ml (2 teaspoons) light soy
    sauce
salt to taste
15 ml (1 tablespoon) potato
    flour mixed with 30 ml
    (2 tablespoons) water

MUSHROOM SOUP

Wash the dried mushrooms very well and soak them in warm water for 30 minutes. Discard their hard stems and cut the caps into thin slices. Soak the black fungus separately in warm water for 30 minutes, then rinse well and cut into thin strips. Deep-fry the sheets of dried beancurd in hot oil for 30 seconds. Drain and crumble them onto a plate. Wash the celery and remove the leaves. Cut the stalks lengthways into thin strips, then slice finely. Heat a saucepan with the sesame oil over a moderate heat and stir-fry the dried mushrooms and black fungus for 30 seconds. Pour in the stock and bring to the boil. Season with soy sauce and salt to taste, lift from the heat and mix in the potato flour mixture very carefully before bringing the soup back to the boil. Stir in the crumbled beancurd sheets and divide among the serving bowls. Garnish with the sliced celery and serve.

酸 辣 湯

Serves 4–6

25 g (1 oz) chicken livers
50 g (2 oz) cooked chicken
1 square beancurd
1 piece wood-ears
15 g (½ oz) pickled bamboo
    shoots, or 25 g (1 oz)
    tinned bamboo shoots
50 g (2 oz) spinach leaves, or
    lettuce
15 ml (1 tablespoon) sesame
    oil
2 spring onions, cut into
    2.5-cm (1-inch) lengths
7.5 ml (1½ teaspoons) freshly
    ground white pepper
800 ml (1⅓ pints) good
    chicken stock
30 ml (2 tablespoons) soy
    sauce
15 ml (1 tablespoon) potato
    flour mixed with 30 ml
    (2 tablespoons) water
40 ml (2½ tablespoons) red
    vinegar
1 egg, beaten
30 ml (2 tablespoons) fresh
    coriander leaves,
    chopped

HOT AND SOUR SOUP

Cut the chicken livers and the chicken meat into matchstick slices. Press the beancurd between two plates for 30 minutes to drain it and then cut into thin slices about 1 cm (½ inch) wide. Soak the wood-ears in warm water for 30 minutes, then wash thoroughly and slice into matchstick shreds. Place the pickled bamboo shoots into a pan of boiling water and return the pan to the boil. Drain and rinse in cold water. Repeat this process two or three times. When they no longer smell sour, cut the bamboo shoots into thin strips. (If using canned bamboo omit the blanching and cut into matchstick strips.) Wash and tear the spinach leaves into strips. Blanch the spinach and wood-ears separately in boiling water for 30 seconds, then refresh in cold water and drain well. All this can be done well in advance.

Just before the soup is needed, heat a large pan with the sesame oil, and stir-fry the onion and white pepper over a low heat for about 15 seconds. Pour in the stock and bring it to the boil before tipping in the chicken livers, chicken meat, wood-ears, bamboo shoots, beancurd and spinach. Stir well to make sure the liver in particular is well separated and bring back to the boil. Add the soy sauce and thicken with the potato flour mixture, lifting the pan from the heat until it is well mixed in. Bring back to the boil again and pour in the vinegar. Check the seasoning, remove from the heat and pour the beaten egg into the pan in a thin stream. Ladle into individual bowls and garnish with coriander before serving as a dimsum dish.

If you wish to serve this soup at an ordinary meal, pour into a soup tureen, garnish with coriander and serve.

SALADS

Salad dishes in dimsum or snack meals can be served in various ways. They can be eaten as a side dish with noodles or rice – for example, a hot salad of choisam is often served with wuntun *noodle soup for an evening snack in Cantonese restaurants. In northern Chinese dimsum meals a small salad may be one of several very small dishes accompanying a bowl of noodles. The quantity in such dishes is often so small that the salad more closely resembles a pickle or relish than a dish. In the following recipes we have suggested serving four people with the quantities given, but these salads can serve six or even eight people.*

涼拌洋荣

Serves 4

100 g (4 oz) cooked chicken
180 g (6 oz) cucumber
50 g (2 oz) cooked ham
15 g ($\frac{1}{2}$ oz) Chinese agar-agar

AGAR-AGAR SALAD

Cut the chicken into shreds and grate the cucumber with the coarsest side of the grater. Cut the ham into thin shreds. Cut the agar-agar into 2.5-cm (1-inch) lengths and soak it in warm water for 4 minutes. Drain and pat dry. Arrange the salad ingredients in a dish, mix the dressing and pour over the salad just before serving.

DRESSING

2.5 ml ($\frac{1}{2}$ teaspoon) prepared English mustard
30 ml (2 tablespoons) light soy sauce
25 ml (1$\frac{1}{2}$ tablespoons) red vinegar
30 ml (2 tablespoons) sesame paste
15 ml (1 tablespoon) sesame oil
pinch of salt

涼拌三絲

Serves 4

100 g (4 oz) dried jelly fish (for preparation see page 22)
180 g (6 oz) cucumber
5 ml (1 teaspoon) salt
50 g (2 oz) dried rice sticks

GREEN AND SILVER SALAD

Have ready the prepared and shredded jelly fish. Roll the cucumber briskly in the salt on a board and leave for 30 minutes to drain. Meanwhile put the rice sticks into boiling water and boil until they are soft – depending on variety between 5 and 7 minutes. Lift out and leave to drain. Rinse the cucumber, dry it and cut into thin shreds the same size as the rice sticks. Mix the jelly fish, cucumber and rice sticks together with the dressing and serve cold.

Make a simple *cucumber salad* by omiting the jelly fish and rice sticks and mixing the cucumber with about half the quantity of dressing given above.

DRESSING

30 ml (2 tablespoons) light soy sauce
15 ml (1 tablespoon) vinegar
15 ml (1 tablespoon) sesame oil
5 ml (1 teaspoon) sugar
2.5 ml ($\frac{1}{2}$ teaspoon) salt

翡翠魷魚

Serves 4

150 g (5 oz) squid sac
150 g (5 oz) broccoli or
  calabrese
10 ml (2 teaspoons) sesame
  oil

DRESSING

10 ml (2 teaspoons) sesame
  paste
15 ml (1 tablespoon) grated
  fresh ginger
15 ml (1 tablespoon) soy
  sauce
15 ml (1 tablespoon) rice
  vinegar
2.5 ml ($\frac{1}{2}$ teaspoon) sugar

涼拌豆芽

Serves 4

250 g (8 oz) bean sprouts

DRESSING

5 ml (1 teaspoon) salt
10 ml (2 teaspoons) sesame
  oil
15 ml (1 tablespoon) rice
  vinegar
15 ml (1 tablespoon) light
  soy sauce
2.5 ml ($\frac{1}{2}$ teaspoon) sugar

油 菜

Serves 4

250 g (8 oz) *choisam* or cos
  lettuce
1 litre (2 pints)
  well-seasoned chicken
  stock
15 ml (1 tablespoon) hot
  peanut oil
45 ml (3 tablespoons) oyster
  sauce

SQUID AND BROCCOLI SALAD

To get a squid sac of about 150 g (5 oz) you need to buy a whole squid of about 300 g (10 oz). Clean and prepare it as directed on page 000. Score the body sac to a depth of about half its thickness with fine criss-cross cuts, then cut the squid into squares about 2.5 cm (1 inch) thick. Wash and cut the broccoli or calabrese into small florets. Put it into boiling water and boil for 4 minutes. Immediately afterwards, refresh under the cold tap and leave to drain. Place the squid into boiling water, bring back to the boil and boil for 30 seconds, then take it out quickly, rinse, drain and toss in sesame oil. It is important not to let squid cook for any longer than necessary or it becomes leathery. Beat the sesame paste with the ginger, soy sauce, vinegar and sugar until it is a smooth cream. Just before serving mix in the cold squid and broccoli.

BEAN SPROUT SALAD

Pick off the roots of the bean sprouts and rinse well. Blanch in a large pan of boiling water for 1 minute and then immediately refresh under the cold tap. Drain well. Mix with the dressing and serve cold.

A HOT GREEN SALAD

Wash and trim the ends of the *choisam* stalks and tie them loosely into two bundles with the stalk ends all together. Bring the chicken stock to the boil. Drop these bundles into the boiling stock and cook until they are just tender – about 2 minutes. Lift out and drain. Lay the bundles on a heated plate and remove the strings. Spoon over the hot oil and oyster sauce and serve immediately.

Opposite: *Chahsiu Pork (page 42) and Green and Silver Salad (page 47)*

Opposite: 'Six Meats' Pot
(page 50)

SMALL POTS

Rows of small clay pots can be seen cooking on gas rings in street restaurants at a Hong Kong night market. The stews in these small pots are made with various inexpensive ingredients already partially cooked so that they need only a final few minutes cooking. Such dishes shared between two people are often eaten as an evening snack, sometimes with a hot salad. Other 'stews' or pots, perhaps requiring longer cooking, are on the menus of dimsum restaurants and can be ordered to follow a few small dimsum dishes, such as jiaozi, fried wuntun and egg rolls to make up a midday lunch. In the West it is often the custom to write such dishes on the menu only in Chinese characters.

西洋菜鸡腿湯

Serves 2 as a complete meal or 4 with other dimsum

250 g (8 oz) whole chicken leg

180 g (6 oz) lean pork shoulder in one piece

2 chicken gizzards, with thick skins removed

6 slices fresh ginger

2 bunches watercress

5 ml (1 teaspoon) salt

CHICKEN AND WATERCRESS POT

Put 1 litre (1¾ pints) of water into a large casserole and bring it to the boil. Add the pork, chicken and gizzards and bring back to the boil. Skim the foam rising to the top, then add the ginger slices, cover the pot and simmer for 30 minutes. Meanwhile, rinse and trim the watercress. After 30 minutes, add the watercress and salt to the casserole and continue to cook for another 3 hours over a low heat. Adjust the seasoning and serve.

This pot can be made in advance and reheated just before it is served.

砂鍋魚湯

Serves 2 as a complete meal or 4 with other dimsum

350 g (12 oz) cod steaks

50 g (2 oz) plain flour

oil for deep-frying

4 dried mushrooms

8 squares fried beancurd, bought ready-fried, or 4 squares fresh beancurd

600 ml (1 pint) good chicken stock

10 ml (2 teaspoons) potato flour mixed with 15 ml (1 tablespoon) water

salt and pepper to taste

5 ml (1 teaspoon) sesame oil

FISH AND BEANCURD POT

Roll the cod steaks in the flour and deep-fry them in moderately hot oil for about 7 minutes. Lift them out, drain well and divide into 4-cm (1½-inch) pieces. Soak the dried mushrooms in warm water for 30 minutes, discard the hard stalks and cut the caps in half. If you have bought ready-fried beancurd, cut each piece into strips about 1 cm (½ inch) wide. (If using fresh beancurd, cut each square in half. Bring a pan of lightly salted water to the boil and blanch each piece for about 20 seconds. Drain well and then deep-fry in moderately hot oil until the beancurd has changed colour to a very light gold. Lift out and drain. Cut into 1-cm (½-inch) slices.) All this can be done well in advance of the meal.

Bring the stock to the boil in the casserole in which you will serve the pot and add the fish, mushrooms and beancurd slices. Bring back to the boil and simmer for about 5 minutes, then lift from the heat and thicken the stock with the potato flour mixture. Return to the boil again, check the seasoning and add the sesame oil before serving.

什錦火鍋

Serves 2 as a complete meal
or 4 with other dimsum

3 pairs duck's webs
(optional)
3 slices fresh ginger
2 spring onions
15 ml (1 tablespoon) rice
wine
4 dried mushrooms
75 g (3 oz) fresh prawns
15 ml (1 tablespoon)
cornflour
1 chicken liver
75 g (3 oz) boneless chicken
75 g (3 oz) prepared squid
sac (see page 23), cut into
bite-sized pieces
15 g (½ oz) smoked bacon
50 g (2 oz) green leaf
vegetable, (choisam,
spinach, lettuce etc.)
600 ml (1 pint) chicken stock
6 fish balls, home-made (see
page 27) or bought
10 ml (2 teaspoons) potato
flour mixed with 15 ml
(1 tablespoon) water
salt and pepper to taste
5 ml (1 teaspoon) sesame oil

滷肉

Serves 2 to 4

2 chicken gizzards
2 chicken thighs
200 g (7 oz) pork shoulder in
one piece

SEASONING SAUCE

100 ml (3½ fl oz) dark soy
sauce
200 ml (⅓ pint) water
15 g (½ oz) crystal sugar
15 ml (1 tablespoon) rice
wine
pinch of five spice powder
2 garlic cloves, crushed

2 squares beancurd
2 hard-boiled eggs, shelled
crystal sugar and salt to taste

'SIX MEATS' POT

Wash the ducks' webs, if necessary skin them according to the instructions given on page 22, and place them in a pan of boiling water with the ginger slices, spring onions and rice wine. Simmer until they are tender, about 1¾ hours. Then lift out, drain, and leave until required. Soak the dried mushrooms in warm water for 30 minutes. When they are soft, discard the hard stalks and cut the caps in halves. Shell the prawns but leave on their tails, and de-vein. Press them flat with the blade of the knife and dust them lightly with cornflour before blanching in boiling water for 30 seconds. Drop them straight from the boiling water into a bowl of cold water to set their shape and then drain and leave until required. Soak the chicken liver in cold water for 20 minutes to remove some of the blood, then cut into thin slices. Cut the chicken meat into thin shreds, and the bacon into matchstick strips. Wash the green leaves and cut or tear them into 5-cm (2-inch) pieces. All this can be done well in advance of the meal.

Just before you wish to eat, bring the stock to the boil in the casserole in which you will serve it and add the chicken shreds. Simmer for 5 minutes, taking care to see they are all well separated. Add the ducks' webs, bacon, prawns and fish balls and finally the squid, liver and green vegetables. Bring back to the boil and boil for 1 minute before lifting the pot from the heat and thickening the stock with the potato flour mixture. Stir well and return to the heat to boil again. Check the seasoning and sprinkle over the sesame oil before serving in the pot in which it was cooked.

MIXED MEATS POT

Wash the gizzards thoroughly, remove the fat and tear off the tough cream-coloured skin. Place the chicken and pork into a pan of boiling water and boil for 3 minutes, then remove from the heat, rinse the meats and discard the water. Put the gizzards, chicken and pork into a clean casserole, pour over the seasoning sauce and bring to the boil. Skim if necessary, cover with a lid and simmer for an hour. Add the beancurd squares and hard-boiled eggs, adjust the seasoning to taste with crystal sugar and salt, and simmer for another 30 minutes. Serve hot in the pot in which it was cooked.

This pot can be made the day before it is needed. It reheats very well.

Chapter 6 | Dumplings

饺子类

There is a whole range of Chinese delicacies that are based on pastry skins, folded and shaped into innumerable intricate forms and filled with an almost endless variety of meat or sweet stuffings. The number of different pastry skins that are used in making such dimsum is almost infinite; many of them made with nothing more than flour and water. A Cantonese master pastry cook a few years ago was said to be able to make over a thousand kinds of pastry — certainly according to a report he produced 112 different types of pastry in one week.

In this chapter we give recipes for about seven different pastries that make various kinds of dimsum. Some are delicate confections that belong almost exclusively to the menus of big dimsum restaurants, particularly in Hong Kong and Taiwan, where dimsum eating is a fashionable pastime for weekends and holidays. Others equally contrived are found on the menus of teahouses in China, where even today it is the habit of many men (but not women) to spend a short time drinking tea, eating a snack and chatting to friends before beginning work. The dimsum served in both these types of restaurant — such as exquisitely shaped *shaomai*, three-coloured balls and transparent *jiaozi*, are never made at home in China. However, less delicate flour and water pastries, which serve as food rather than fun, are made at home. Such dimsum as *jiaozi*, sesame buns, *wuntuns* (though not usually their skins) and rice balls all may be made at home, at festival times if not for every day. In this chapter recipes and methods are given for some of the most practical of both kinds.

Various basic techniques underlie the different recipes, of which the temperature of the water is one of the most important, for it controls the character of the pastry. Cold water and flour make a firm resilient dough, which can be handled and shaped as required. It has a matt white colour and a slippery texture when it is cooked. This type of dough is used for all boiled pasta, such as *wuntun* and *jiaozi*. Dough made with boiling water, on the other hand, always remains soft. It is easier to roll out than cold water doughs and can be made into a very thin skin, but it is less easy to handle and mould and will not hold its shape so well once it is cooked. It has a pearly, translucent look when cooked and is used for all steamed pasta such as simple *shaomai*, steamed *jiaozi* and shallow-fried buns. Finally, a dough made with warm water is the average dough – it can be handled and moulded and will hold its shape well, but it is not as firm as the doughs made with cold water. This kind of dough is used particularly for *shaomai* skins that are to be folded into flower shapes.

The amounts of water to be added to the flour vary between 35% and 55% depending on the softness of the dough required. However, the more water used, the greater is the danger of a leathery pastry – a dry dough produces a brittle pastry. Salt makes the dough more malleable, and is often added in the proportion of 1% to 3% of the quantity of flour used. Just as with Western pastry, all these doughs are quite easy to make after a little practice.

JIAOZI

Jiaozi, sometimes translated as dumplings, are made with a flour and water dough filled with a mixture of minced meat and vegetables. They have been eaten in northern China for well over a thousand years, indeed several have been found in an eighth century tomb on the 'Old Silk Road', which ran from China to Syria. They appear to have been called wuntun *at that time.* Jiaozi *are a robust people's food eaten both for festivals and everyday – as one Chinese friend said 'you can fill yourself with* jiaozi*'. It is the boast of some Chinese that they can eat 60 or 70 – even 80 to 100 – at one sitting.*

Every town in northern China today has its jiaozi *houses. Some are small rooms run by one family, seating at most 10 or 12 people, while others are big state* jiaozi *houses. They are open all day until late in the evening, serving only* jiaozi*, but often with a choice of fillings. We recently ate a memorable lunch in a state* jiaozi *house in a small town in Shaanxi. Four of us ordered 1.5 kilogrammes (3 pounds) of* jiaozi*, which we collected from the serving hatch in a big bowl. Included in the price was a bowl of rather thin cabbage soup, to which we helped ourselves from the communal pot, and a selection of dipping sauces, among them chilli, soy sauce, vinegar and sesame oil. The* jiaozi *skins were soft and smooth without a trace of toughness, and the filling slightly granular in texture, chewy and flavoursome. On another occasion when we were eating* jiaozi *we were given a bowl of garlic cloves and a* *dish of sesame oil to accompany them. This is the Shangdong style.*

Jiaozi may be cooked in three different ways boiling (the most usual), frying or steaming. In this section we first give the recipes for the jiaozi skins for the different methods of cooking and then a selection of fillings that may be used with the skins. Always make the filling before preparing the skins.

DIPPING SAUCES FOR JIAOZI

Soy and vinegar sauce
45 ml (3 tablespoons) soy sauce to 15 ml (1 tablespoon) red vinegar.

Chilli oil and soy sauce
Use either ready-made or home-made chilli oil. Mix 15 ml (1 tablespoon) chilli oil with 45 ml (3 tablespoons) soy sauce.

Crushed garlic sauce
Mix 5 ml (1 teaspoon) crushed garlic with 15 ml (1 tablespoon) red vinegar, 30 ml (2 tablespoons) soy sauce and 15 ml (1 tablespoon) sesame oil.

Garlic and sesame
Break a bulb of garlic into cloves and serve with a small dish of sesame oil. Diners peel their own cloves. Garlic and sesame oil go together particularly well.

水 饺

Makes 40 skins – sufficient for 2 or 3 people

200 g (7 oz) plain flour
100 ml–125 ml (3½–4 fl oz) cold water)
1.5 ml (¼ teaspoon) salt dissolved in the water
flour for rolling

For 80 to 90 skins use:
450 g (1 lb) plain flour
300 ml (½ pint) water

SKINS FOR BOILED JIAOZI

Mix the flour and water together and work into a smooth and elastic dough. Wrap in cling film and leave to rest for 45 minutes. Roll into a long, thin cylinder and cut into 40 equal slices. Roll out each slice on a lightly floured board into a domed disc about 6 cm (2½ inches) in diameter with the edges thinner than the centre.

Fill the *jiaozi* by holding one skin in the palm of your hand and placing a small spoonful of the filling (see following recipes) in the centre. It is better to do this with chopsticks rather than a spoon, since it allows you to position the filling like a little sausage across the skin rather than in a round lump. Bring the two half-moons of the skin up over the filling and pinch in the centre to seal. If necessary, moisten the edge with a drop of water. Pleat the edge closest to you about three times towards the right-hand corner and press these pleats firmly against the edge away from you. Repeat for the other side, pleating three or four times towards the left-hand corner and pinching tightly

Join *Jiaozi* edges in the middle.

Pleat near side to the right.

against the further edge to seal. Make sure the *jiaozi* is completely sealed or the filling will leak out during the cooking. The finished *jiaozi* curls into a crescent shape with the line of the join running across its top — the Chinese call it an 'eye-brow'. Shape all the *jiaozi* skins in the same way; in the beginning this takes a long time, so allow about an hour for the rolling and filling, or enlist some help. With practice, one becomes much quicker. When the *jiaozi* are finished, drop about a third of the *jiaozi* into a large pan of boiling water. Bring back to the boil and pour in a cup of cold water. Bring back to the boil again and add another cup of cold water. Return to the boil once more, then lift out, drain well and keep warm. Repeat this cooking process twice more to cook all the *jiaozi*, then serve them immediately with a selection of the dipping sauces suggested above.

Uncooked *jiaozi* can be deep-frozen, but we have found that it is better not to keep them for more than a week in the freezer. Freeze them on a tray so that their shape is not damaged, then pack in boxes or bags until required. Drop them straight from the freezer into boiling water and cook as fresh *jiaozi*.

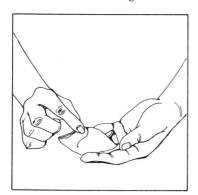

Seal against unpleated side.

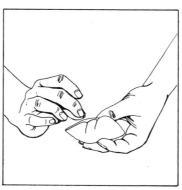

Repeat pleating towards the left.

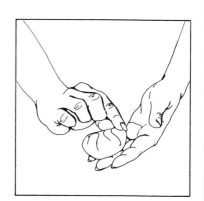

Seal and shape into crescent.

鍋 貼

蒸 餃 皮

Makes 40 skins

12 g (½ oz) lard
100 g (3½ oz) plain flour
100 g (3½ oz) strong flour
100 ml–125 ml (3½–4 fl oz)
     boiling water
1.5 ml (¼ teaspoon) salt
     dissolved in the water

肉 餡

Sufficient for 40 boiled *jiaozi*
or 30 steamed *jiaozi*

180 g (6 oz) Chinese leaves
3.5 ml (¾ teaspoon) salt
275 g (9 oz) pork or lamb
25 ml (1½ tablespoons) water
10 ml (2 teaspoons) soy
     sauce
40 ml (2½ tablespoons)
     sesame oil
3.5 ml (¾ teaspoon) grated
     fresh ginger
1 garlic clove, crushed
2.5 ml (½ teaspoon) finely
     ground black pepper

FRIED JIAOZI OR PAN-STICKERS

Fried *jiaozi* use exactly the same skins and method of shaping as boiled *jiaozi* , but once they are filled, they are cooked in a mixture of oil and steam. Heat a flat-bottomed frying pan and add 45 ml (3 tablespoons) of oil. Put in 10 *jiaozi* and shallow-fry on one side only for 1 minute over a moderate heat. Add 45 ml (3 tablespoons) of water and immediately cover with a lid. Reduce the heat to low and continue cooking for 10 minutes.

SKINS FOR STEAMED JIAOZI

Rub the lard into the flour, then mix in the water. Knead until the dough is smooth and elastic. Cover with a wet cloth and leave to rest for 2 hours. Roll into a cylinder on a floured board and cut into 40 slices. Roll out each slice into a domed disc about 7 cm (2¾ inches) in diameter with the edges thinner than the centre.

Fill the skins with any one of the fillings given in the following section. It is usual to put a little more filling into a *jiaozi* that is to be steamed than into a boiled *jiaozi*. Shape the steamed *jiaozi* in the same way as boiled *jiaozi*, and arrange them on a damp cloth in a steamer so that they do not touch one another. Steam for 20 minutes. Serve immediately after cooking with the dipping sauces suggested at the beginning of this section.

These skins will freeze uncooked if they are filled with fresh ingredients, in which case steam straight from the freezer for 30 minutes. Left-over steamed *jiaozi* can be reheated by deep-frying for about 4 minutes in hot oil.

FILLINGS FOR JIAOZI SKINS

PORK OR LAMB FILLING

Mince or chop the Chinese leaves very finely, but do not put them through a food processor. Sprinkle with salt and set aside for 20 minutes. Then put the leaves into a cloth and squeeze out all the liquid. Cut the meat into small pieces and pound it into a soft pulp using a meat cleaver. From time to time sprinkle with the water during the process. When it is a smooth paste, mix in the rest of the ingredients and blend with the Chinese leaves.

Use this filling with any of the *jiaozi* skins.

素饺

Sufficient for 40 skins
4 dried mushrooms
12 g (½ oz) silk noodles
2 pieces wood-ears
180 g (6 oz) beancurd, about 3 squares, depending on size
150 g (5 oz) Chinese leaves
2.5 ml (½ teaspoon) salt
25 ml (1½ tablespoons) sesame oil
2 finely chopped spring onions

三鲜饺

Sufficient for 40 boiled *jiaozi* or 30 steamed *jiaozi*
100 g (4 oz) raw prawns
25 g (1 oz) dried sea cucumber (for preparation see page 22)
40 g (1½ oz) bamboo shoots
150 g (5 oz) cooked boneless chicken breast
75 g (3 oz) spring onions, finely chopped
5 ml (1 teaspoon) grated fresh ginger
pinch of ground Sichuan peppercorns
2.5 ml (½ teaspoon) salt
40 ml (2½ tablespoons) soy sauce
45 ml (3 tablespoons) sesame oil

VEGETARIAN JIAOZI

Soak the dried mushrooms in water for 30 minutes. When they are soft, discard the hard stalks and cut the caps into tiny morsels. Soak the silk noodles in hot water for 5 minutes to soften, drain well and cut into 1-cm (½-inch) lengths. Soak the wood-ears in warm water for 30 minutes, then rinse well and cut into thin shreds. Wrap the beancurd squares tightly in a tea towel for 20 minutes, to remove some of the excess water. Mince the Chinese leaves, sprinkle them with the salt and leave for 20 minutes before putting them in a cloth and squeezing as dry as possible. Mash the drained beancurd with the sesame oil and finely chopped onions, and blend in the rest of the ingredients.

Use this filling for either fried or boiled *jiaozi*. Serve with a soy sauce dip.

THREE-FLAVOURED JIAOZI

The small pieces of sea cucumber in this filling gives it an attractive chewy texture, but since it needs a lot of preparation, it can be omitted and the amount of chicken increased to 180 g (6 oz).

Shell the prawns and de-vein them. Mince them with the prepared sea cucumber and bamboo shoots twice, using the coarse grille. Put the cooked chicken through the mincer once. Mix all the ingredients together and blend well.

Use this mixture to fill either steamed or boiled *jiaozi*.

小 紅 头

LITTLE RED-HEADS

Colours stand for different moods in different cultures. In China white is the colour of mourning, and red is for celebrations and festivals. Traditional brides in Hong Kong still wear red dresses, good luck banners for the New Year are written on red paper, and these little red-painted cakes are for celebrations and special occasions. Generally speaking, in China sweet pastries are only eaten at such times, but these red-heads taste so good, with or without their red decorations, it seems a shame not to enjoy them more often.

Fills 30 skins

100 g (3½ oz) walnuts

25 g (1 oz) minced pork back fat

25 g (1 oz) fresh white breadcrumbs

50 g (2 oz) granulated sugar

30 steamed *jiaozi* skins (see page 55)

red food colouring (optional)

Toast the walnuts in a dry frying pan over a medium heat until they start to change colour, then chop them very finely, or use a food processor. Mix in the minced pork fat, breadcrumbs and sugar. Blend well.

Take one *jiaozi* skin in your left palm and put a teaspoon of the walnut filling in the centre. Gather up the skin round the filling and lightly pinch in the loose dough over it. Shape the top into 5 flaps taking care to align the two edges of each flap together. Then twist and flatten these flaps into petals all joined together round the top of the filling. Paint the centre of each bun with a little food colouring and stand them on individual squares of non-stick parchment. Steam for 15 minutes.

These little red-heads can be frozen after steaming. Reheat straight from the freezer in a steamer for about 7 minutes.

Put filling in centre of skin.

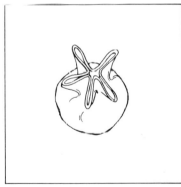
Gather up skin round filling and pinch into 5 flaps.

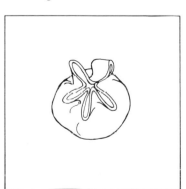
Twist flaps to shape petals.

Finish Little Red-heads.

烧壳

SHAOMAI

Shaomai *are sophisticated tiny mouthfuls of various fillings wrapped in paper-thin dough skins and steamed. They are often folded and shaped into intricate and elaborate forms – and are a complete contrast of style and image to the jiaozi recipes given previously. No one would fill themselves with shaomai – they are essentially fun food.*

We give the recipe for a basic shaomai *dough together with two variations and suggestions for folding the skins into three simple forms. The traditional shape for a rolled out* shaomai *skin is round, but it takes very great skill to roll this dough into circles that are both thin and evenly sized. So we have compromised with a rounded square, which is not so difficult to achieve. All the filling recipes can be interchanged with any of the skins. Always make the filling first, before you make the skins, and always keep the skins under a damp cloth to prevent them drying out. We have given recipes for making 32* shaomai *skins, but fillings for only 30 skins, since we have found that almost inevitably we lose 1 or 2 skins in the rolling out. However, with a little practice one can easily become very skilled at handling this dough and produce very decorative results.*

烧壳皮

Makes 32 skins

45 ml (3 tablespoons)
  boiling water
125 g (4 oz) strong flour
pinch of salt
plain flour for dusting

BASIC SHAOMAI SKINS

Measure the boiling water into the flour and salt and immediately mix until the flour is bound together and the bowl clean. The quantity of water is just sufficient to hold the dough together; it should not be in the least sticky. Wrap the dough ball in cling film, or cover with a damp cloth and leave for 20 minutes for the gluten to develop. Then roll out the dough on an unfloured board to a thickness of about 1 cm ($\frac{1}{2}$ inch) and fold it in half. Continue rolling and folding until the dough is smooth and velvety. Then roll into a straight-sided rectangle about 5 mm ($\frac{1}{4}$ inch) thick and cut into 32 equal-sized squares. It is worth taking care at this stage to make sure the squares are evenly sized since it is hard to correct misshapen skins later, and the look of the finished *shaomai* depends partly on the regularity of the skins. Cover the cut pieces with a damp cloth. Dust the board with flour and roll out one piece of dough until it measures 4 cm ($1\frac{1}{2}$ inches). Roll out another 2 pieces to the same size and shape. Dust them liberally with flour and sandwich them together before rolling out into a 7-cm ($2\frac{3}{4}$-inch) square with rounded sides and corners. The best results come from first rolling each side in turn from the centre of the skin outwards and then rolling the corners diagonally to encourage a round, rather than a square shape. Peel the skins apart and place them in a bowl covered with a damp cloth while you finish rolling out the skins. Use as directed in the following recipes.

If you wish to fold the *shaomai* skins into flower shapes, substitute warm (hand-hot) for boiling water in the above ingredients list. Otherwise the method is the same.

牛肉烧売

Makes 30 *shaomai*

2 dried mushrooms

100 g (3½ oz) lean beef

25 g (1 oz) pork back fat, minced

15 ml (1 tablespoon) ginger wine, or 15 ml (1 tablespoon) *gaoliang* wine plus 2.5 ml (½ teaspoon) grated fresh ginger

50 g (2 oz) Chinese leaves

20 g (¾ oz) bamboo shoots

SEASONINGS

7.5 ml (1½ teaspoons) oyster sauce

7.5 ml (1½ teaspoons) sesame oil

5 ml (1 teaspoon) potato flour or cornflour

2.5 ml (½ teaspoon) salt

5 ml (1 teaspoon) soy sauce

5 ml (1 teaspoon) sugar

pinch of black pepper

30 basic *shaomai* skins

SHAOMAI WITH BEEF AND CHINESE LEAVES

Soak the dried mushrooms in warm water for 30 minutes. Meanwhile, pound the beef and minced pork fat with a meat cleaver (see Chapter 4), sprinkling the meat with the ginger wine from time to time during the chopping. The final result should be like very finely minced meat, slightly coarser than the meat pastes given in Chapter 4. Discard the hard mushroom stalks and chop the caps with the Chinese leaves and bamboo shoots into pieces about the size of half a grain of rice, or use a food processor. Mix the chopped vegetables with the meat very thoroughly, then beat in the seasonings.

Hold one skin in the palm of your left hand and put 5 ml (1 teaspoon) of the filling in the centre. Gather up the sides round the filling and gently make small pleats around the *shaomai* to shape the skin to the filling, leaving the top open and the filling just showing. Finally squeeze the pleated skin against the filling and flatten the bottom of the *shaomai*. Stand on either a damp cloth or on small squares of non-stick parchment in a steamer. Arrange the *shaomai* so they do not touch and steam over boiling water for 20 minutes. Serve immediately with a soy dipping sauce or mix 45 ml (3 tablespoons) soy sauce and 15 ml (1 tablespoon) chilli bean paste.

Always keep the *shaomai* under a damp cloth until they are cooked. Cooked *shaomai* may be frozen, then reheated straight from the freezer by steaming them for 10 minutes.

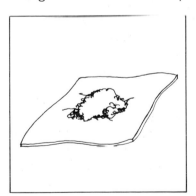

Put filling in centre of skin.

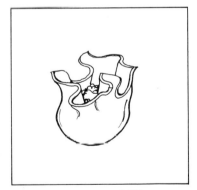

Gather up sides round filling.

蝴蝶烧売

Makes 30 *shaomai*

2 dried mushrooms
100 g (3½ oz) lean pork
15 g (½ oz) pork back fat
75 g (3 oz) bamboo shoots
7.5 ml (1½ teaspoons) egg
  white
1.5 ml (¼ teaspoon) salt
pinch of black pepper
1.5 ml (¼ teaspoon) sesame
  oil
1.5 ml (¼ teaspoon) rice wine
10 ml (2 teaspoons)
  cornflour (optional)
30 basic *shaomai* skins

GARNISHES

12 g (½ oz) finely chopped
  cooked ham
12 g (½ oz) finely chopped
  French beans
1 hard-boiled egg (chop
  white and yolk separately)

BUTTERFLY SHAOMAI

Soak the dried mushrooms in warm water for 30 minutes, then discard the hard stalks and chop the caps finely. Mince the pork, fat and bamboo shoots through the finest grille of the mincer, or use a meat cleaver to chop them finely. Add the chopped mushrooms and beat in the egg white, salt, pepper, sesame oil and rice wine. For a firm textured filling, omit the cornflour, but for a softer filling add the cornflour and blend thoroughly.

Hold a *shaomai* skin in the palm of your left hand and put 5 ml (1 teaspoon) of the filling in the centre. Lift up the two opposite sides and pinch the centres together very firmly. Then draw up the two remaining sides, while keeping the first two still sealed together, and pinch these in the middle to join the original seal. Gently open the tiny 'ears' at the 4 corners with a toothpick and drop fragments of the different coloured garnishes into each. (It in no way detracts from the flavour of the dish if these final garnishes are omitted, but the appearance of the *shaomai* demands them.) Stand on individual squares of non-stick parchment and steam for 20 minutes over boiling water. If they are not to be steamed immediately, cover with a damp cloth. Freeze after steaming and reheat by steaming for 10 minutes straight from the freezer.

Put filling on skin.

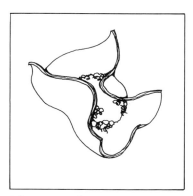
Join centres of opposite sides.

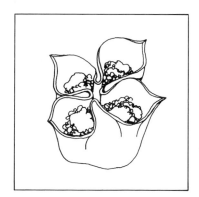
Open out corners for garnish.

Lay skins at right-angles; fill.

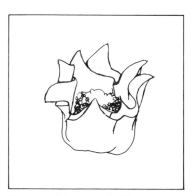
Draw up skins round filling.

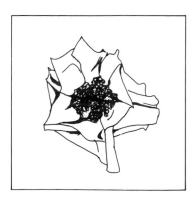
Curl edges out like flower petals.

花烧壳

FLOWER PETAL SHAOMAI

The skins of flower petal shaomai *are more delicate than the other varieties of* shaomai. *Dusting potato flour over the skins allows them to be separated even when they have been rolled out thinner and bigger than skins dusted with ordinary flour.*

Makes 15 *shaomai*

100 g (3½ oz) lean pork from leg or loin

25 g (1 oz) pork back fat, minced

5 ml (1 teaspoon) grated fresh ginger

15 ml (1 tablespoon) rice wine

100 g (3½ oz) spinach

5 ml (1 teaspoon) light soy sauce

5 ml (1 teaspoon) sesame oil

1 spring onion, finely chopped

1.5 ml (¼ teaspoon) salt

SKINS

125 g (4 oz) strong flour

45 ml (3 tablespoons) warm water

potato flour

1 egg white

Pound the pork, minced fat and grated ginger together with a meat cleaver as directed in Chapter 4. From time to time, sprinkle the rice wine over the meat during the pounding. Wash and chop the spinach very finely, removing any tough centre veins, or use a food processor. Mix the meat and spinach together very thoroughly and add the rest of the seasonings. Blend well and leave on one side.

Mix the flour and water together and knead until the bowl is clean and the dough is in a ball. Cover with cling film and leave for 20 minutes. Then roll the dough out on an unfloured board to a thickness of about 1 cm (½ inch). Fold in half and continue rolling and folding until the dough is smooth and velvety. Then roll it into a straight-sided rectangle about 5 mm (¼ inch) thick and cut into 32 equal straight-sided pieces. Dust the board with potato flour and roll out one piece of dough until it measures 4 cm (1½ inches) square, then roll out another two pieces to the same size and shape. As they are rolled out, drop the pieces into a bowl of potato flour. Make sure they are really well-coated in flour before sandwiching them together. With the three pieces on top of each other, roll out first the four corners and then the sides into a 10-cm (4-inch) square, pulling the edges so they blouse and frill. Peel the squares carefully apart and store them in a bowl under a wet cloth until all the skins are rolled out.

Take one skin in the palm of your left hand and paint the centre with lightly beaten egg white. Lay another skin at right angles to the first one so the corners form a star shape. Put 15 ml (1 tablespoon) of the filling in the centre of the skins and then gently draw them up around the filling, leaving the edges to curl away like the petals of a flower, and the top open to show the filling. Press the sides against the filling and flatten the bottoms. Stand each *shaomai* on a square of non-stick parchment and steam for 20 minutes. If they are to wait before being cooked, cover them with a damp cloth and do not allow them to dry out.

These *shaomai* will freeze after being steamed. Take care how they are packed so the skins do not break. Reheat straight from the freezer by steaming for 10 minutes.

鮮蝦燒売

Makes 30 *shaomi*

50 g (2 oz) lean pork, from
  leg or loin
25 g (1 oz) pork back fat,
  minced
15 ml (1 tablespoon) ginger
  wine
100 g (4 oz) raw prawns,
  shelled
50 g (2 oz) bamboo shoots
15 ml (1 tablespoon) finely
  chopped spring onion
15 ml (1 tablespoon) rice
  wine
1.5 ml ($\frac{1}{4}$ teaspoon) salt
pinch of pepper

SKINS
125 g (4 oz) plain flour
45 ml (3 tablespoons)
  boiling water
7 g ($\frac{1}{4}$ oz) lard
pinch of salt
flour

SHAOMAI WITH PORK AND PRAWNS

First make the filling by pounding the pork and minced fat into a smooth paste, sprinkling it from time to time with the ginger wine (see Chapter 4). If you have no ginger wine, add 1 teaspoon of grated root ginger to the meat while you pound it and sprinkle with ordinary rice wine. De-vein the prawns, chop them very finely and mix with the meat. Chop the bamboo shoots to crumbs about the size of half a grain of rice and add them to the mixture with the spring onion and rice wine. Season and blend very thoroughly before putting the filling aside while you make the skins.

Mix the flour, salt and water together, then dot the lard over the dough. Knead very thoroughly, cover with cling film and leave to rest for 20 minutes. The dough should now feel like Western pastry. Roll it out into a rectangle about 5 mm ($\frac{1}{2}$ inch) thick and cut into 32 equal straight-sided pieces. Roll out one piece until it measures 4 cm ($1\frac{1}{2}$ inches) square, then roll out another 2 pieces to the same size. Dust them all liberally with flour and sandwich together before rolling them out to 7 cm ($2\frac{3}{4}$ inches). Peel the skins apart and place them in a bowl covered with a damp cloth while you roll out the remaining dough.

Hold one skin in the palm of your left hand and put 5 ml (1 teaspoon) of the filling into the centre. Gather up the sides and gently pleat the skin so it will fit snugly around the filling, leaving the top open. Finally squeeze the pleated skin against the filling and flatten the bottom of the *shaomai*. Stand them either on individual squares of non-stick parchment or on a damp cloth laid over the bottom of a steamer. Arrange the *shaomai* so they do not touch and steam over boiling water for 20 minutes. Serve immediately with a dipping sauce of 30 ml (2 tablespoons) soy sauce, 30 ml (2 tablespoons) red vinegar and 15 ml (1 tablespoon) sesame oil.

If the *shaomai* are not to be steamed immediately, cover them with a damp cloth. They may be frozen after being cooked. Reheat by steaming, straight from the freezer for 10 minutes.

混沌

WUNTUN

Wuntun *are perhaps the best known of all Chinese pasta in the West. There are two distinct varieties of* wuntun *skins: one is the familiar Cantonese* wuntun *made with an egg noodle dough, while the other is the Shanghai version, which has no egg in it and is basically a* shaomai *dough. Although both varieties are called* wuntun *in Chinese, the Shanghai version when written in Chinese characters has no meaning apart from* wuntun; *the Cantonese written version can also be translated as 'cloud swallow'.*

There are various ways of using wuntun *apart from the* wuntun *noodle soup (page 123) that can be found in Chinese restaurants worldwide: less well known is the Sichuan variety where the* wuntun *are boiled, strained and served in bowls like* jiaozi, *with a very spicy dipping sauce of chilli oil and soy. They may also be deep-fried and served 3 or 4 to a helping as a dimsum dish.*

Cantonese wuntun *skins can be bought from most Chinese grocers, or they can be made at home. They have a limited keeping life in the refrigerator, but* wuntun *made with egg can be deep-frozen after they are filled and before they are cooked. However, great care should be taken in their packing to see that their delicate shapes are not broken.*

Filling wuntun skins:
Place 5 ml (1 teaspoon) of the filling in the centre of a wuntun *skin and fold the skin over the filling to make a triangle, joining the opposite corners. Fold the base of the triangle containing the filling up towards the centre corner, then join the two side corners together with the filling on the inside. Seal these two corners with a drop of water.*

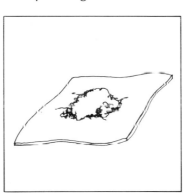

Put filling on *wuntun* skin.

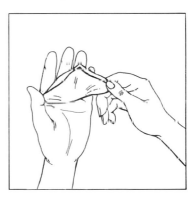

Fold skin over into triangle.

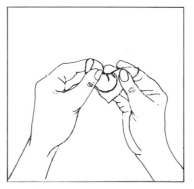

Fold over enclosed filling.

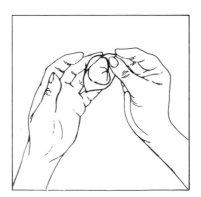

Bring side corners together; seal.

广式云吞

Makes 48 skins

125 g (4 oz) strong flour
15 ml (1 tablespoon) beaten egg
45 ml (3 tablespoons) cold water
cornflour for rolling and dusting

上海式馄饨

Makes 40 skins

125 g (4 oz) strong flour
45 ml (3 tablespoons) cold water
cornflour for dusting

馄饨

Sufficient for 44 skins

75 g (3 oz) chicken breast
75 g (3 oz) lean pork
25 g (1 oz) pork back fat, minced
15 ml (1 tablespoon) rice wine
1.5 ml ($\frac{1}{4}$ teaspoon) ginger juice squeezed from grated fresh ginger
15 ml (1 tablespoon) egg white
pinch of salt and pepper

CANTONESE WUNTUN SKINS

Mix the flour with the egg and water and knead the dough well. Cover with cling film and leave for an hour. When the dough has rested, roll out and fold it several times on an unfloured board until it is quite smooth. Then roll the dough, again on an unfloured board, into a very long narrow strip — about 14 cm (5 inches) wide and thin enough to be able to see the board beneath. If necessary, divide the dough into halves and loop the end across the table, but do not let it stick to itself. (If you have a pasta maker, roll the dough through on its thinnest setting.)

When the dough is as thin as you can make it, dust it very liberally with the cornflour held in a cloth bag and fold into 12 equal-sized layers, piled one on top of the other. Make sure there is plenty of cornflour between the layers or the sheets will not separate when you have finished rolling them out. Roll out the folded layers until they form a rectangle measuring 18 × 16 cm (7 × 6 inches). Trim off about 1 cm ($\frac{1}{2}$ inch) from the uneven edges at the top and bottom and cut the rectangle of pastry into 4 squares of 8 cm (3 inches). Peel apart the 12 sheets of pastry in each square. Dust with additional cornflour and either use immediately or store in a polythene bag in the refrigerator for up to 72 hours. They cannot be frozen.

SHANGHAI WUNTUN SKINS

Use the method described on page 58 for making basic *shaomai* skins; but cut the dough into 40 equal squares and use cornflour for dusting the board and sandwiching the pieces of dough together. Finally roll out the three pieces of dough together into a 8-cm (3-inch) square.

These skins can be kept wrapped in polythene in the refrigerator for 24 hours, but they cannot be frozen.

WUNTUN FOR SOUP

Either Cantonese or Shanghai wuntun *skins can be used for soup* wuntun. *The chicken and pork filling given here can also be used for Sichuan red-oil* wuntun.

Pound the chicken, pork and pork fat into a smooth paste with a meat cleaver (see Chapter 4). During the pounding, sprinkle the meat pulp from time to time with the rice wine. Beat in the rest of the ingredients and use to fill the *wuntun* skins.

Soup *wuntun* made with Cantonese skins can be frozen after they have been filled. Store them carefully so that their rather delicate skins do not break and drop them straight from the freezer into the soup.

云吞湯

Serves 4

75 g (3 oz) green leaves
(spinach, *choisam*,
lettuce, watercress, etc.)
1 litre (2 pints) good chicken
stock
16–24 filled *wuntun*, frozen
or fresh
1.5 ml (¼ teaspoon) sesame
oil

紅油抄手

Sufficient for 44 skins, or for
35 soup *wuntun*
125 g (4 oz) minced pork
2 water chestnuts
5 ml (1 teaspoon) spring
onion, finely chopped
2.5 ml (½ teaspoon) grated
fresh ginger
1 garlic clove, crushed
2.5 ml (½ teaspoon) rice wine
2.5 ml (½ teaspoon)
cornflour
2.5 ml (½ teaspoon) sesame
oil
pinch of salt and pepper

DIPPING SAUCE

45 ml (3 tablespoons) soy
sauce
45 ml (3 tablespoons) chilli
oil
15 ml (1 tablespoon) finely
chopped spring onion
15 ml (1 tablespoon) sesame
oil

炸餛飩

Overleaf: *Cantonese Roast Duck
(page 41) and Hot and Sour Soup
(page 46)*

Opposite: *Boiled Jiaozi (page 53)
and Fried Jiaozi (page 55)*

WUNTUN SOUP

Wash and tear the leaves into 6-cm (2½-inch) pieces. Bring the chicken stock to the boil and drop in the *wuntun* and the green leaves. Boil gently until the *wuntun* rise to the surface, about 3 to 5 minutes. Serve with a little sesame oil sprinkled over the soup.

If using bought *wuntun* skins, cook the filled *wuntun* in a pan of boiling water until they rise to the surface, then transfer them with a slotted spoon to the boiling stock and green leaves. Serve as above.

SICHUAN RED-OIL WUNTUN

This style of wuntun served with a chilli hot sauce is always made with Shanghai wuntun skins. However, this filling can be used for soup wuntun, using either style of skin.

Mix the pork with the finely chopped water chestnuts, spring onion and grated ginger. Blend in the garlic, rice wine, cornflour and sesame oil and season with salt and pepper. Fill the *wuntun* skins as directed on page 63 but put only 2.5 ml (½ teaspoon) of filling in each skin. Have ready a large pan of boiling water and drop the *wuntun* into this pan. When they rise to the surface, skim them off and drain for a few moments. Have 4 small bowls ready with the dipping sauce divided among them and put the *wuntun* into the sauce before serving. Alternatively, serve the *wuntun* in bowls without the dipping sauce and serve the dipping sauce separately in a small bowl at the side.

Another similar recipe for filling *wuntun* uses 25 g (1 oz) raw prawns, shelled and de-veined, 75 g (3 oz) minced pork and some fat, 1 dried mushroom, soaked and chopped and 5 ml (1 teaspoon) sesame seeds. Omit the garlic, but otherwise season as above.

DEEP-FRIED WUNTUN

Use any of the fillings given previously for *wuntun*, but use Shanghai *wuntun* skins only if they are to be cooked immediately after they are made. Filled Cantonese skins can be frozen and dropped into the hot oil straight from the freezer.

Heat the oil for the deep-frying and slide in the *wuntun*. Fry for about 3 minutes, then drain and serve immediately. Deep-fried *wuntun* cannot be frozen.

Chapter 7 | Small pies and rice balls

小餅湯園类

Chinese cooks use a wider range of flours milled from various grains and roots than is customary in Western cooking. In this introduction we explain the differences between some of the most commonly used flours in Chinese cooking and the ways in which these differences are exploited in making doughs and pastry.

Soft wheat flours that have little protein in them – such as Western cake flour – have a gluten content of about 8%–10%. Gluten is the protein constituent in flour that absorbs water and creates the spongy texture of bread when it is baked. Broadly speaking, with a low percentage of gluten in the flour, the cooked dough or pastry will have a finer texture, will be less able to rise and will crumble, while with a higher percentage of gluten, the texture will be more open, the dough will rise and it will flake. The Chinese use both a soft flour very like Western cake flour and a strong flour with a gluten content between 12% and 15% – similar to bread flour in the West. On the whole, a soft flour is better for making doughs that are to be baked or fried and a strong flour is better for steaming, particularly if it has yeast or some other raising agent in it. Strong flours can absorb more water than soft flours. However, all flours attract moisture from the atmosphere; the amount of water a flour can absorb is governed by how dry it is initially. Sometimes, if the flour is very dry, a little extra water has to be added to a dough over and above the amount given in the recipe. The Chinese test flour for dryness by rubbing a little between the thumb and forefinger and listening to the sound it makes – if any. If you can hear a dry, rustling sound like dry sand on a beach, the flour is dry and may require extra water. If it is silent, then the flour has a high moisture content already and probably will not need any extra water.

The Chinese also use a wheat flour from which all the gluten has been removed – wheat starch. This flour has no cohesive quality at all; it cannot rise or hold air, nor can it bind into a dough if it is mixed with cold water, but when it is mixed with boiling water or cooked, it makes a fine smooth jelly without any stickiness. Wheat starch pastes also have the additional quality of being quite transparent when they are cooked. Potato starch is another flour used more often in Chinese cooking than in the West. This very smooth white flour also contains no gluten and its chemical structure is such that when it is mixed with wheat starch and boiling water it makes a dough that is both strong and pliable without being sticky. When cooked it is clear like glass.

There are three basic types of rice in China, long-grain, short-grain and glutinous rice. All these are milled into flour, but only glutinous rice flour is used for cakes and pastries. Making dough or paste from glutinous rice flour can be a little tricky since it easily becomes tough if it is not handled properly. The rice flour dough needs to be steamed and then kneaded very vigorously before it is shaped into individual cakes for steaming. This is because the flour has a high percentage of gluten in it. The gluten must be fully expanded and the chains formed in the structure of the dough when it is cooked broken and regrouped to prevent the dough becoming tough and leathery. However, this technique is not necessary for rice balls that are boiled.

Various kinds of pastry and pie skins have been made in China for at least seven hundred years. A recipe from the eleventh century describes how to make a pie skin and bears a superficial resemblance to several recipes we offer in this book. 'Put oil in a pan and boil it. Then strain it and use it to fry the flour. Remove the flour from the heat and mix it with sugar and wine. Knead the dough until it is smooth. Stuff with bean paste.' Pies made with this recipe and cooked in a dry frying pan covered with a lid have a crumbly biscuit-like outside skin with a soft inner layer much like marzipan. Although the finished pies are unlike anything we have encountered in modern Chinese dimsum, the technique of using cooked flour is still retained in many different styles of cake and pastry cooking in Chinese cuisine. Incidently, we found these pies quite delicious to eat.

餡餅

Makes 8 pies
PASTRY

125 g (4 oz) plain flour
75 ml (5 tablespoons)
   boiling water
flour for rolling

FILLING

450 g (1 lb) fresh spinach*
10 g ($\frac{1}{2}$ oz) lard
2.5 ml ($\frac{1}{2}$ teaspoon) salt
150 g (5 oz) lean boneless
   pork
15 ml (1 tablespoon) oil, or
   lard
5 ml (1 teaspoon) rice wine
10 ml (2 teaspoons) soy
   sauce
10 ml (2 teaspoons) sugar
2.5 ml ($\frac{1}{2}$ teaspoon)
   cornflour made into a
   paste with 5 ml
   (1 teaspoon) water

oil for shallow-frying

DIPPING SAUCE

30 ml (2 tablespoons) soy
   sauce
30 ml (2 tablespoons) red
   vinegar
15 ml (1 tablespoon) sesame
   oil

*If you wish to use frozen
leaf spinach for this recipe,
stir-fry the defrosted
spinach in the lard until it is
soft. Drain well and squeeze
really dry before chopping
finely. Frozen chopped
spinach is not suitable for
this recipe.

SPINACH AND PORK PIES

Mix the flour and boiling water to a dough and knead very thoroughly until it is smooth and elastic. Cover with a damp towel and leave to rest until it is cool, about 30 minutes.

Meanwhile, make the filling. Wash the spinach and remove any tough central veins. Heat a frying pan with 10 g ($\frac{1}{2}$ oz) lard and stir-fry the spinach leaves with the salt until they soften. When the leaves are quite limp, take them out of the pan and allow to cool before squeezing them really dry and chopping into very fine pieces. Mince the pork coarsely and place it into the frying pan with the oil (or lard) and stir-fry the meat for about 1$\frac{1}{2}$ minutes. Add the rice wine, soy sauce and sugar together with 45 ml (3 tablespoons) of water. Reduce the heat and cook for 2 minutes before mixing in the chopped spinach. Finally, stir in the cornflour paste and remove from the heat. Leave on one side until you have finished the pastry.

Divide the dough into 8 equal portions and roll out each portion on a floured board into a thin circle about 13 cm (5 inches) in diameter. Put 15–20 ml (1 heaped tablespoon) of the filling in the centre of each circle. Gather up the edges to close the pie, twist to seal and break off any excess dough from the centre. Make sure the pies are completely sealed and have no holes in them. Pinch and press them into tidy rounds about 6 cm (2$\frac{1}{2}$ inches) in diameter and about 1.5 cm ($\frac{1}{2}$ inch) high.

Shallow-fry the pies in a flat bottomed frying pan containing about 5 mm ($\frac{1}{4}$ inch) oil over a moderately high heat until they are golden and crisp – about 1$\frac{1}{2}$–2 minutes on each side. Serve very hot with a dipping sauce.

These pies can be deep frozen after they have been cooked. Reheat them either in the oven 170°C (350°F, Gas mark 4) for 15 minutes straight from the freezer, or in a frying pan with a little oil for 5 minutes over a high heat. However, we have found that the pastry is never as crisp when it is reheated as it is when it is freshly cooked.

Another version of this recipe uses a small can of red-in-snow instead of spinach. Soak the red-in-snow in clean, cold water for 5 minutes to remove some of the salt before draining it well and chopping into 1-cm ($\frac{1}{2}$-inch) lengths – or use a mincer. Put the red-in-snow into a *dry* frying pan with 10 ml (2 teaspoons) of sugar and stir-fry until the red-in-snow is dry. Remove and put on one side. Cook the pork as directed in the previous recipe using only 5 ml (1 teaspoon) of soy sauce. You can add 2 slices of fresh ginger to the oil if you wish. Add the red-in-snow. Because red-in-snow is so salty, take care not to add salt to any dish in which it is an ingredient. Use red vinegar as a dipping sauce.

夢卜餡饼

Makes 8 pies

250 g (8 oz) white radish
125 g (4 oz) pork
45 ml (3 tablespoons) oil
salt and pepper to taste
pastry (see previous recipe)

蒸炸三鮮盒

Makes 10 patties

50 g (2 oz) lean pork, from
  leg or loin
25 g (1 oz) pork back fat,
  minced
5 ml (1 teaspoon) grated
  fresh ginger
15 ml (1 tablespoon) rice
  wine
25 g (1 oz) cooked chicken
15 g (½ oz) dried sea
  cucumber (for
  preparation see page 22),
  or substitute extra chicken
5 ml (1 teaspoon) sugar
2.5 ml (½ teaspoon) salt
2.5 ml (½ teaspoon) light soy
  sauce

SKINS

125 g (4 oz) plain flour
45 ml (3 tablespoons)
  boiling water
7 g (¼ oz) lard
flour for rolling
oil for deep frying

WHITE RADISH AND PORK PIES

The best known of these pies are those made with white radish and pork. These pies are usually eaten as a snack rather than as one element in a dimsum meal. Allow 3 or 4 pies for each person.

Grate the radish coarsely. Mince the pork and stir-fry it in the oil for 3 minutes. Then add the white radish and continue stir-frying for a few moments. Season with salt and pepper to taste and continue cooking over a moderate heat for 10 minutes until the mixture is soft. Leave to cool until required. Fill the pastry skins as directed in the recipe for spinach and pork pies, but in this case, the finished pie will stand about 2 cm (¾ inch) high. Cook as before and eat with a dipping sauce of 45 ml (3 tablespoons) soy sauce and 15 ml (1 tablespoon) chilli oil.

These pies can be deep-frozen after cooking, and reheated either in the oven 170°C (350°F, Gas mark 4) for 15 minutes or in a frying pan with a little oil for 5 minutes, but the pastry is never as crisp when it has been reheated.

DEEP-FRIED PATTIES

Pound the pork and fat together with the grated ginger as directed in Chapter 4. Sprinkle the rice wine over the meat pulp from time to time to make it softer. Cut the chicken and the prepared sea cucumber into tiny pieces about the size of a grain of rice. Mix them into the meat paste with the seasonings and blend very thoroughly. Set aside while you make the skins.

Mix the flour and water together and then dot the lard over the mixture. Knead the dough very thoroughly before covering with cling film and leaving to rest for about 20 minutes. Roll it out as thinly as possible on a lightly floured board, then roll it up tightly into a cylinder not more than 2 cm (¾ inch) in diameter. Cut the cylinder into 20 slices and roll these slices into rounds about 8 cm (3¼ inches) in diameter.

Hold one circle in the palm of your hand and put 5–7 ml (1 generous teaspoon) of the stuffing in the middle. Moisten the edge and cover with another circle of dough. Pinch the edges tightly together to seal, then twist in the edge to make a coiled rope finish around the patty. Arrange them on individual pieces of non-stick parchment and steam over boiling water for 15 minutes before deep-frying in hot oil until they are golden in colour. Serve at once.

These patties can be frozen after they have been steamed, and then reheated while still frozen in a steamer for 5 minutes before being deep-fried. We have found that deep-frying straight from the freezer does not give really satisfactory results.

柿子餅

PERSIMMON PIES

These pies were a speciality in Xian before the Liberation. In the autumn, when persimmons were in season, they were to be found at almost every food stall in the city, but in particular they were a Muslim delicacy, sold in the Muslim market near the mosque and fried in goat fat. The red dates given in the following recipe are a substitute for the red Chinese hawthorn berries, which are still sold in great quantities during the early autumn in the rural markets around Xian today. They have a flat, slightly bitter taste.

Makes 10 pies
125 g (4 oz) persimmons
50 g (2 oz) lard or solid white
  cooking fat
150 g (5 oz) icing sugar
40 g (1½ oz) plain flour
3 crystallized red dates
50 g (2 oz) preserved winter
  melon
1.5 ml (¼ teaspoon) rose
  water
pastry (see page 68)
oil for shallow-frying

Cut the persimmons open and scrape out the soft flesh, discarding the tough outer skin. Put the flesh through a liquidizer or food processor. Cream the lard or fat and beat in the sugar before adding the persimmon pulp and flour. Put the mixture into a small saucepan and bring to the boil, stirring all the time. Boil gently for about 3 minutes over a low heat. Then lift from the stove and leave to cool while you chop the red dates and winter melon finely. Stir these into the persimmon paste together with the rose water. Leave on one side until required.

Prepare the dough according to the instructions on page 68 and divide it into 10 equal portions. Roll each piece of dough out on a lightly floured board into a circle about 10 cm (4 inches) in diameter and fill with 15 ml (1 tablespoon) of the persimmon cream. Close the buns and shallow-fry in 5 mm (¼ inch) oil as directed over a moderately high heat until they are golden and crisp — about 1½–2 minutes on each side. Serve these pies warm.

These pies can be deep-frozen after they have been cooked and then reheated, but the pastry loses its crispness and is apt to become tough.

六果餅

SIX TREASURES

This sweet filling of various fruits is used to fill these fried pies on special occasions or festivals.

Fills 8 pies
50 g (2 oz) pork back fat
50 g (2 oz) preserved winter
  melon
25 g (1 oz) preserved papaya
25 g (1 oz) preserved
  pineapple
12 g (½ oz) candied orange
  peel or mixed fruit
25 g (1 oz) preserved, stoned
  red dates
12 g (½ oz) pine kernels

Place the pork fat in a dry frying pan and fry it over a low heat so that the fat runs without changing colour. Lift out from the pan with a slotted spoon and chop into small pieces about the size of a currant. Chop all the rest of the ingredients, except the pine kernels to the same size and mix them all together including the nuts.

Use to fill the skin as directed in the recipe for Spinach and pork pies and cook in the same way. These pies can be eaten cold and will keep for about 2 days in a tin. They do not freeze well.

蝦 饺

TRANSPARENT PRAWN JIAOZI

Pastry skins made with wheat starch become almost transparent when they are cooked: this is particularly attractive if they are filled with prawns, which then show through the skins as a delicate pink. These small jiaozi are a most decorative addition to a dimsum repertoire.

Makes 24 *jiaozi*

FILLING
150 g (5 oz) raw prawns

MARINADE
5 ml (1 teaspoon) egg white
5 ml (1 teaspoon) cornflour
a few drops of sesame oil
1.5 ml (¼ teaspoon) salt
pinch of black pepper

10 g (½ oz) back pork fat
25 g (1 oz) lean pork
25 g (1 oz) bamboo shoots

SKINS
100 g (3½ oz) wheat starch
15 g (½ oz) potato flour
200 ml (⅓ pint) boiling water

Shell the prawns and de-vein, then chop finely. Marinate for 20 minutes. Meanwhile, mince the back fat, lean pork, and bamboo shoots, then beat into the prawns. Leave until required.

Sift the flours together into a bowl and pour in the boiling water. Beat hard with a wooden spoon until the paste comes away from the sides of the bowl. Then knead until the dough is smooth and elastic. Roll dough into a sausage and divide into four. Cut each section into 6 equal slices. Put one slice at the edge of the board and press firmly with the blade of the meat cleaver. It will form a thin disc about 8 cm (3 inches) in diameter. Take the disc in the palm of your left hand and put a small spoonful of filling in the centre. Bring the two half-moons of the edges together and pinch in the centre. Then pleat the edge closest to you about three times, travelling towards the right-hand corner and press these pleats firmly against the edge. Repeat on the other side, pleating three or four times towards the left-hand corner (see illustration on page 54). Make sure it is completely sealed and encourage the *jiaozi* to curl into a crescent, with the line of the join running round the top. Stand it carefully on the oiled base of a steamer, covered with a damp cloth. Repeat until all 24 *jiaozi* are prepared. If your dough starts to become dry and crack while you are shaping the *jiaozi*, stand it in a bowl covered with a damp cloth over a pan of very hot water. Take the dough out one piece at a time as you need it. Do not allow the *jiaozi* to touch one another in the steamer. Steam for 15 to 20 minutes. Serve very hot.

These *jiaozi* can be frozen after they have been cooked, then reheated for between 15 and 20 minutes in a steamer.

鸡 饺

TRANSPARENT CHICKEN PASTIES

In this recipe the wheat starch skins used in the previous recipe for transparent jiaozi are prepared and flattened in exactly the same way. However, in this recipe after the skins have been filled, they are folded over into half-moons about 7 cm (2¾ inches) long. The two edges are pinched together and then twisted into a 'rope' finish. Put the pasties onto an oiled steamer and steam for 20 minutes before serving.

As with all pastries made with wheat starch, they must be cooked as soon as they have been made. However, they may be frozen after cooking, then reheated in the steamer for 20 minutes just before they are needed.

Makes 24 pasties

FILLING

50 g (2 oz) raw prawns
125 g (4 oz) boneless
    chicken breast
25 g (1 oz) pork back fat

MARINADE

2.5 ml ($\frac{1}{2}$ teaspoon) sesame
    oil
5 ml (1 teaspoon) soy sauce
2.5 ml ($\frac{1}{2}$ teaspoon)
    cornflour
1.5 ml ($\frac{1}{4}$ teaspoon) salt
pinch of sugar and pepper

2 dried mushrooms
25 g (1 oz) bamboo shoots

transparent *jiaozi* skins

芝麻湯圆

Makes 16 balls

25 g (1 oz) black sesame
    seeds, or white sesame
    seeds or walnuts
25 g (1 oz) pork back fat or
    lard, minced
25 g (1 oz) icing sugar
150 g (5 oz) glutinous rice
    flour
115 ml (7$\frac{1}{2}$ tablespoons) cold
    water

De-vein the prawns and put them with the chicken and fat through the mincer twice, using the coarse grille. Then mix with the marinade and leave for 20 minutes. Soak the dried mushrooms for 30 minutes in warm water, then discard the hard stems and cut the caps into tiny morsels. Either mince or chop the bamboo shoots finely. Mix the mushrooms and bamboo shoots into the minced chicken and prawns and blend thoroughly. Leave on one side until the skins are prepared.

SWEET SESAME BALLS

The traditional way to make these sweet balls was first to shape the sesame filling into marble-sized balls. Then a large tray — up to a metre (3 feet) square — was covered with glutinous rice flour and sprinkled with water from the finger tips. The sesame balls were thrown onto it so that they rolled across the tray as they landed. Then the tray was held at arm's length and shaken. The balls would roll around collecting a coating of the damp rice flour. The tray would be lowered, more water sprinkled over and the balls rolled again until almost all the flour was gone and the balls were thickly coated.

Although originally this sweet was eaten particularly at the New Year festival, it is now made and eaten at all times of the year. It is no longer made only in the traditional manner as this recipe shows.

First make the filling by toasting the sesame seeds (or walnuts) in a dry pan over a moderate heat until they start to colour and dance. Then tip them out onto a board and crush them very finely with a rolling pin. Chop and pound the pork fat until it is smooth, then mix the sesame seeds, sugar and fat together into a firm paste. Roll into 16 marble-sized balls.

Mix the rice flour (which *must* be fresh) and water to a smooth paste and divide into 16 equal balls. Flatten one of these balls into a disc about 5 cm (2 inches) in diameter and put a sesame ball in the centre. Close the rice flour paste around it, and roll into a smooth round white ball. Repeat with the remaining balls.

Have ready a large pan of boiling water and when the balls are all made drop them in and boil gently until they rise to the top – about 5 minutes. Spoon out 4 balls into each bowl with some of the cooking water and serve; it is customary to drink the water while eating the balls. Some people like to sweeten the water with sugar.

Instead of using sesame seeds as a filling, you can substitute about 60 ml (5 tablespoons) of sweet red bean paste (see page 152). Shape into small balls before covering with the rice flour paste.

Savoury rice balls can be made with a filling of finely minced pork, both fat and lean, flavoured with soy sauce, grated root ginger, sesame oil, salt and pepper. Shape and boil as above, but serve these balls in a bowl of fresh seasoned stock.

水晶 三色球

THREE-COLOURED BALLS

These delicate pastries with their brightly coloured fillings appear on some Hong Kong dimsum menus. Although they are sweet, they are served all year round, not just on special occasions. For the recipes for sweet bean pastes, see page 152.

Makes 12 balls
100 g (4 oz) green mung bean paste
100 g (4 oz) red bean paste
100 g (4 oz) white haricot bean paste
 (or use 300 g (12 oz) of one colour paste)
40 g (1½ oz) wheat starch
40 g (1½ oz) potato flour
5 ml (1 teaspoon) sugar
150 ml (5½ fl oz) boiling water

Before making the skins have the bean pastes ready. Sift the wheat starch and potato flour with the sugar and mix with the boiling water. Knead to a smooth dough and then divide into thirds. Roll out one-third into a sausage shape, cut it into quarters, then roll each quarter into a ball between the hands. Roll out one ball with a rolling pin on a pastry board into a circle about 10 cm (4 inches) in diameter. The skin should be thin enough to see the board beneath. If it sticks, put a little oil on the board. Place about 25 g (1 oz) of one colour of beanpaste in the centre of the skin. Gather the edge round the filling to close over the top, pinch to seal and tear away any extra dough. Stand the pastry ball seal-side down on a small square of non-stick parchment and cover with a damp cloth. Roll out the rest of the dough in the same way, changing the colour of the filling as appropriate. Steam over boiling water for 4 to 5 minutes. Remove and serve at once. These transparent balls will not freeze.

If you find shaping these balls difficult, fold each round into a half-moon like the chicken pasties in the previous recipe.

粱毛团

'MILLET-HAIR' BALLS

The 'hair' in the title refers to the coating of glutinous rice in which the balls are rolled before being steamed.

Makes 8 balls
75 g (3 oz) glutinous rice
150 g (5 oz) glutinous rice flour
120 ml (8 tablespoons) cold water
200 g (7 oz) sweet red bean paste (see page 152)

Soak the glutinous rice in cold water for 2 hours, then drain while you make the balls. Mix the flour and water into a smooth thick paste that leaves the bowl clean. Divide into 8 portions and roll each into a ball. Flatten the balls into discs about 9 cm (3½ inches) in diameter. Put a ball of red bean paste in the centre and close the skin around the filling. Shape into a smooth white ball, then roll in the well-drained glutinous rice to coat completely. Stand the balls on an oiled steamer base so that they do not touch, and steam for 30 minutes. Serve hot. These balls will not freeze.

烧饼

SHAOBING

For many centuries China has absorbed food habits from beyond its borders, particularly from Iran and India through Central Asia, and through the great city of Xian. In Xian in the eighth century (then the capital of the Empire and named Changan), there were Zoroastrian temples for Persian merchants, and bakeries sold sesame cakes — 'crisp and fragrant with oil, fresh from the stove' — then called 'foreign cakes'. These were the forerunners of the modern Shaobing.

A good story about shaobing dates from the same early times. One night a traveller in Henan stopped at a small hotel. Around midnight he saw the woman who owned the hotel take a doll from a box, and while he watched, the doll sowed buckwheat seeds in the courtyard. Miraculously, the seeds grew immediately and the doll harvested the grain, ground it into flour and made shaobing from it. These it gave to the hotel owner. The next morning the hotelier served these shaobing to some of the guests, who at once all turned into donkeys. The hotelier took the donkeys and the guests' baggage to market and sold them. However, while she was out, the traveller who had seen what had happened stole some shoabing, and gave them to the woman when she returned. She also turned into a donkey and the man continued his journey riding this new donkey. He rode her for many months until eventually a god felt sorry for her and returned her to her human form.

Makes 5 buns
225 g (8 oz) strong flour
120 ml (4 fl oz) hand-hot water
20 ml (1½ tablespoons) oil and sesame oil (half and half)
40 g (1½ oz) plain flour
sesame oil for rolling
2.5 ml (½ teaspoon) salt
5 ml (1 teaspoon) flour
45 ml (3 tablespoons) sesame seeds

Preheat the oven to 230°C (450°F, Gas mark 8). Mix the strong flour and the water into a dough and knead very thoroughly. Cover with cling film and leave to rest for 30 minutes. Meanwhile, heat the sesame oil mixture in a frying pan over a high heat. Put in the plain flour, reduce the heat and, stirring all the time, cook the flour until it is completely mixed into the oil and golden-brown in colour. Do not let it burn. Remove from the heat and leave on one side. Oil a large flat board with sesame oil and roll out the strong flour dough into a 30-cm (12-inch) square. Sprinkle the fried flour, salt and 5 ml (1 teaspoon) flour over the sheet of dough. Cut about 1 cm (½ inch) off both sides to make a sharp, clean edge and put these scraps of dough in the centre of the square. Tightly roll up the dough from top to bottom into a sausage shape about 4 cm (1½ inches) in diameter. Cut this sausage into 5 lengths, each about 6 cm (2½ inches) wide. Pinch the cut edges on either side to prevent the filling falling out. Roll out one portion into a rectangle about 15 × 8 cm (6 × 3 inches). Fold into thirds and turn the pastry so that the folded top and bottom are now the sides. Roll out again to the same size, fold again into thirds and roll out once more. Sprinkle the top with sesame seeds and press them down gently with a rolling pin. Repeat with the remaining 4 portions. Bake the *shaobing* on a baking sheet in the preheated oven for 10 minutes.

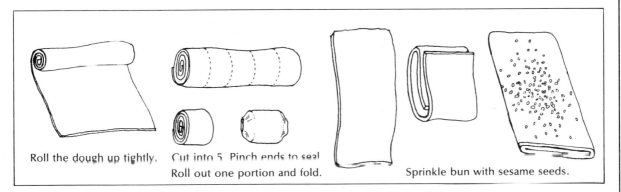

Roll the dough up tightly.

Cut into 5. Pinch ends to seal. Roll out one portion and fold.

Sprinkle bun with sesame seeds.

百果烧饼

Makes 5 buns
FILLING

15 g (½ oz) crystallized winter melon
15 g (½ oz) crystallized papaya
15 g (½ oz) mixed peel or crystallized orange peel
15 g (½ oz) crystallized red dates
15 g (½ oz) walnuts
15 g (½ oz) minced pork back fat

shaobing dough
45 ml (3 tablespoons) sesame seeds
30 ml (2 tablespoons) sugar

FRUIT-FILLED SHAOBING

The next recipe is a variation on the standard shaobing we have given above. They would not be eaten at breakfast, but more likely as a small snack during the afternoon.

Preheat the oven to 230°C (450°F, Gas mark 8).
Chop the fruit and nuts together and beat in the pork fat. Make the *shaobing* dough as directed. When it has been rolled out and folded, roll out once more and put about 30 ml (2 tablespoons) of the filling on the bottom two thirds of one portion of the dough. Fold the top third down and then fold the two thirds together over the bottom third, so all the sweet filling is enclosed. Roll out once again and sprinkle the top with sesame seeds and sugar. Repeat with the remaining 4 portions and bake in the preheated oven for 10 to 15 minutes.

豆沙鍋餅

Makes 4 pancakes
225 g (8 oz) prepared red
   bean paste (see page 152)
125 g (4 oz) plain flour
1 egg, beaten
150 ml (5 fl oz) water
50 g (2 oz) lard or solid
   vegetable fat
caster sugar

SWEET PANCAKES FILLED WITH RED BEAN PASTE

Have ready the prepared red bean paste. Mix the flour, beaten egg and water into a smooth batter. Heat a frying pan with a little of the lard or vegetable fat and make four 20-cm (8-inch) pancakes. When they are cooked on both sides, lift them out onto a flat surface to cool. Spread a quarter of the bean paste onto the centre of each pancake, fold in two sides to cover the paste, then fold over the top and bottom to make square parcels. Heat the remaining fat in a wok or frying pan and carefully slide in the parcels. Fry over a high heat until they are golden-brown on both sides. Turn them out and cut each parcel into quarters. Serve warm, sprinkled with caster sugar.

春卷

Makes 10 rolls
200 g (7 oz) lean pork, cut
   into matchstick shreds

MARINADE
15 ml (1 tablespoon) soy
   sauce
15 ml (1 tablespoon) rice
   wine
5 ml (1 teaspoon) cornflour

50 g (2 oz) bamboo shoots
50 g (2 oz) fragrant leeks*
25 g (1 oz) silk noodles
45 ml (3 tablespoons) oil for
   deep-frying
2.5 ml (½ teaspoon) salt
45 ml (3 tablespoons) beaten
   egg
5 ml (1 teaspoon) cornflour
10 spring roll skins

*or substitute spring onions
and 2 cloves garlic.

SPRING ROLLS

We do not recommend that people try to make their own spring roll skins since this is a very specialized job, demanding a particular kind of griddle. However, they can be bought chilled or frozen at Chinese grocers as well as many delicatessen shops.

Marinate the pork for 10 minutes. Meanwhile cut the bamboo shoots into similar-sized pieces and the fragrant leeks into 2-cm (¾-inch) lengths. Soak the silk noodles in warm water until they are soft – about 10 minutes – then cut them into 2-cm (¾-inch) lengths. Heat a pan with 45 ml (3 tablespoons) oil and stir-fry the pork for about 5 minutes over a moderate heat. Then lift it from the pan with a slotted spoon and leave on one side. When it is cool, mix in the bamboo shoots, fragrant leeks, silk noodles and salt. Divide into 10 portions. Put one portion onto the bottom third of a spring roll skin. Fold the sides over the filling and then roll up the skin into a sausage. Seal the loose end with the egg and cornflour mixture. Heat the oil and fry the spring rolls over a moderate heat until they are golden in colour. Serve at once with a soy sauce and vinegar dip.

春饼

A CHINESE COLD BUFFET FOR THE NEW YEAR

The New Year is a holiday time for everyone in China, including housewives. During the first four days of the holiday they do not cook, but as it is also a time for visiting relatives and close friends, it is customary to prepare great quantities of food in readiness for the holiday. Some families in the north make great trays of jiaozi for their visitors, while others, especially in Hong Kong and Taiwan, go in large family parties to the restaurants. Another custom from eastern China is a form of cold buffet. Numerous cold dishes are prepared as fillings for cold spring rolls. The visitors are invited to help themselves, filling their rolls as they choose, rolling them up and eating them in their fingers — rather like sandwiches.

For this buffet for six people, you should allow about two dozen spring roll skins and prepare at least ten different cold dishes for fillings, as well as a bowl of freshly chopped coriander and another of finely chopped unsalted peanuts (skin before chopping) for additional flavouring. In Taiwan they also use sugar as a flavouring because it is traditional to eat sweet foods at a festival.

Arrange the dishes on a table together with at least six pairs of chopsticks with which people can help themselves to the various dishes. Give everyone a plate and a paper table napkin and encourage them to take a spring roll skin, open it up and select and mix their own fillings for it. Then it is rolled up like a cigar and eaten, held in the fingers. At such a meal you can also serve bowls of raw fruit and Chinese preserved fruits such as winter melon strips, papaya, pumelo, sour plums and crystallized apples, together with sugared nuts and melon seeds.

点菜随心

COLD DISHES FOR THE FILLINGS Serves 6

CHICKEN
Tear 300 g (10 oz) cold roast chicken into thin shreds. Mix 5 ml (1 teaspoon) salt with 2.5 ml ($\frac{1}{2}$ teaspoon) black pepper and 2.5 ml ($\frac{1}{2}$ teaspoon) ground Sichuan pepper, or 5 ml (1 teaspoon) black pepper, in a dry saucepan over a gentle heat for about 2 minutes until it starts to smell good. Sprinkle this mixture over the chicken shreds before serving.

PORK
Put 300 g (10 oz) lean pork cut in one piece into boiling water with a spring onion and a slice of fresh ginger. Skim well, cover the pan, reduce the heat and simmer for 40 minutes. Drain and cut into matchstick strips while the meat is still hot. Mix with 15 ml (1 tablespoon) soy sauce and 5 ml (1 teaspoon) red vinegar. Cool before serving.

PRAWNS

Use 180 g (6 oz) cooked shelled prawns – defrost and drain if necessary. Heat a dry frying pan with 1 clove of crushed garlic and 1.5 ml ($\frac{1}{4}$ teaspoon) salt. When the garlic starts to smell appetizing, add the prawns and stir-fry over a gentle heat until the pan is dry. Turn out and leave to cool.

EGG THREADS

Beat 2 eggs with 5 ml (1 teaspoon) rice wine. Heat a frying pan with a little oil and make 2 plain omelettes. Turn them out and leave to cool before cutting into thin strips. Sprinkle with the same salt and pepper mix used in the chicken filling (see above) before serving.

SQUID

Use 6 very small squid or *calamares*, bought frozen. Clean, remove their heads and scrape off the dark skin, but leave the body sacs whole. Dip them into boiling water for about 1 minute – they will shrink like deflating balloons. Then drain and cut into thin rings. Toss in 10 ml (2 teaspoons) sesame oil, 5 ml (1 teaspoon) vinegar and 1 finely shredded green chilli.

JELLY FISH (prepare 3 days in advance)

Pour boiling water over 100 g (4 oz) jelly fish, which comes preserved in flat sheets. Leave to soak for 3 days in cold water changing the water each day. Cut into very fine threads and dress with 5 ml (1 teaspoon) sesame oil, 5 ml (1 teaspoon) light soy sauce, 2.5 ml ($\frac{1}{2}$ teaspoon) white rice vinegar, 2.5 ml ($\frac{1}{2}$ teaspoon) sugar, and a pinch of MSG (optional).

BEANCURD

Press 100 g (4 oz) of beancurd (about 2 squares) under a plate for 3 hours and drain away the excess water. Cut the firm beancurd into thin slices and mix with 10 ml (2 teaspoons) sesame oil, 1.5 ml ($\frac{1}{4}$ teaspoon) salt and a pinch of MSG.

BEAN SPROUTS

Pick over and rinse 300 g (10 oz) of bean sprouts. Blanch them in boiling water for 1 minute. Immediately afterwards dip in cold water and then drain well. Toss the bean sprouts in 15 ml (1 tablespoon) sesame oil and 1.5 ml ($\frac{1}{4}$ teaspoon) salt.

CELERY

Blanch 6 stalks of celery in boiling water for 1 minute, then dip in cold water and drain well. Cut the celery into thin batons about 4 cm ($1\frac{1}{2}$ inches) long. Toss them in a dressing of 5 ml (1 teaspoon) each sesame oil, white rice vinegar, sugar, grated fresh ginger and a pinch of salt. Marinate for 2 hours before serving.

FRENCH BEANS

Use whole beans, either fresh or frozen. Cook 180 g (6 oz) beans in boiling water until they are just tender, then dip them quickly in cold water and drain well. Cut into 4-cm (1½-inch) lengths, and toss in a dressing made with 5 ml (1 teaspoon) each sesame oil, rice vinegar, sugar, a pinch of salt and 1 crushed garlic clove. Marinate for 2 hours before serving.

AUBERGINE

Cut off 1-cm (½-inch) strips of skin down the length of an 250 g (8 oz) aubergine. Sprinkle with 15 ml (1 tablespoon) of salt and leave to drain for an hour, and then rinse well. Steam the aubergine over boiling water until it is soft – about 30 minutes, and leave to cool. Then tear it into strips and dress with 10 ml (2 teaspoons) soy sauce, 5 ml (1 teaspoon) sesame oil and 2.5 ml (½ teaspoon) red vinegar.

RAW LETTUCE

Wash and cut a lettuce into shreds and serve undressed and raw. The words for lettuce in Chinese also indicate prosperity, so to help provide good luck for the coming year, lettuce is often included in a New Year meal.

鸡肉肠粉

CHICKEN FILLING

Fills 6 rolls

150 g (5 oz) boneless chicken breast

MARINADE

30 ml (2 tablespoons) rice wine

1.5 ml (¼ teaspoons) salt

2.5 ml (½ teaspoon) grated fresh ginger

2 spring onions

SAUCE

60 ml (4 tablespoons) chicken stock

30 ml (2 tablespoons) soy sauce

15 ml (1 tablespoon) melted lard

15 ml (1 tablespoon) sugar

RICE FLOUR SKINS

Rice flour skins are a beautiful pearly white colour and cannot be made at home. They must be bought fresh from the Chinese grocer just before you plan to use them, since they do not keep well and will crack and break when handled if stale. Allow about 15 cm (6 inches) for each roll and 2 rolls for each helping. There are various fillings that can be served in these rolls. We give a selection below.

Cut the chicken meat into pieces about 2.5 cm (1 inch) by 1 cm (½ inch) and marinate with the wine and salt for 30 minutes. Mix in the grated ginger and spring onions cut into 1-cm (½-inch) lengths. Cut the rice skins into 6 lengths about 15 cm (6 inches) long and lay a portion of the filling on the middle third of each. Fold over the top and bottom thirds to cover the filling. Put them onto a plate and steam for 20 minutes. Bring the sauce ingredients to the boil and pour over the rolls before serving.

Other fillings are: 150 g (5 oz) raw prawns, shelled and de-veined, substituted for the chicken; 150 g (5 oz) fillet of beef, cut into thin shreds and marinated in 15 ml (1 tablespoon) soy sauce, 10 ml (2 teaspoons) rice wine and 5 ml (1 teaspoon) sugar and then cooked and served in the same way; about 100 g (4 oz) of *chahsiu* (see page 42) cut into thin slices and cooked and served as the chicken above.

Chapter 8

Pastries and mooncakes

酥饼月饼类

In this chapter we are concerned mainly with one kind of flaky pastry – double-dough – which can be used to make a whole range of pies and cakes. One great quality of double-dough pastry is its versatility: it can be shaped or arranged into many intricate forms, it can be deep-fried or baked in an oven, and has the ultimate merits of being easy to make and good to eat.

Sweet pastries and cakes made with double-dough are sold all over northern China, from a prestigious cake shop in Tiananmen Square in Beijing to country food stores at commune headquarters in Shaanxi and department stores in central Nanjing. We in the West can sometimes buy pastries such as egg custard tarts as takeaways in smart Chinese restaurants. However, double-dough pastry is not limited to sweet cakes. It can also be used for numerous savoury pies and turnovers, which are served at dimsum meals or as a small snack with tea at any time of day.

Some of these pastries, such as chrysanthemum flowers or curry buns, are sold as standard varieties throughout the year, while others, such as various kinds of mooncakes, are made only for a particular season or festival. In recent years, because of their commercial advantages, Cantonese mooncakes (which have a robust crumbly pastry and so are less likely to break in transit and have a much longer keeping life), have been increasingly sold in northern and eastern China alongside the traditional northern varieties made with double-dough pastry. So it is that in September one can now see queues of people waiting outside a Hangzhou cake shop to buy up to eight different varieties of Cantonese mooncake.

We have found that double-dough pastry can be made equally well with either lard or solid vegetable fat. We have also found that these pastries can be deep-frozen very successfully either before or after they are cooked. To use savoury pastries after they have been frozen but not cooked,

Opposite: *Hundred Fruits Suzhou Mooncakes (page 94)*

you can put them straight from the freezer into the oven or deep fat, allowing a little extra time for their cooking. If they have already been baked in the oven, reheat them straight from the freezer in an oven, preheated to 170°C (350°F, Gas mark 4) for 15 minutes. If they have been deep-fried, put them into moderately hot oil for about 4 minutes. Sweet pastries can be frozen before they are cooked and then cooked as directed above; but if they have already been cooked, store for a few days in a cool dry place, but do not freeze. Cantonese mooncakes will keep for several weeks.

The fillings for these pastries are as various as their shapes. Generally speaking, ordinary sweet pastries that have no special festival connotations are filled with either the ubiquitous red bean or red date paste, or less frequently with lotus seed paste, and recipes for these pastes appear in Chapter 11. Of course, you can vary the fillings and experiment with your own combinations, such as chopped preserved fruits in red bean paste, chopped nuts in red date paste, fillings based on pineapple or coconut, or even Western mincemeat — whichever you like best. Each region of China has its own particular recipes. We do not attempt to be comprehensive, but only give a few examples that we have found most satisfactory to both prepare and eat.

The final shape and appearance of the different forms of buns depends entirely on the original arrangement of the double-dough because its texture can be radically changed by varying the alignment of the layers of dough in the pastry. This is done in the initial cutting of the dough before it is rolled out into individual skins. A bun where the skin has the layers of dough exposed when it is rolled out will cook with these layers visible in the final result, while a bun whose outer skin has no striation presents a smooth outer surface, but crumbles and flakes when it is bitten into. The final appearance of a bun can be greatly enhanced by arranging the layers of dough to complement the shape of the bun as in the following recipe for Little Boxes.

Opposite: *Almond Biscuits (page 151), Chrysanthemum Flowers (page 92), and White Rabbits (page 85)*

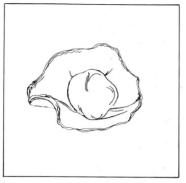

Fold water dough over oil dough.

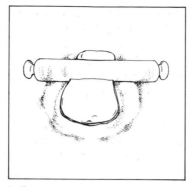

Roll out doughs.

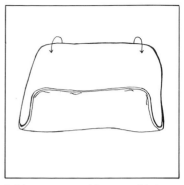

Fold over top and bottom thirds.

Cut rolled up dough into thin round slices.

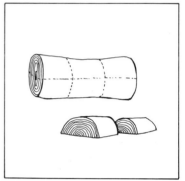

Cut roll of dough into sections; cut sections across into halves.

酥餅

Makes 215 g (7½ oz) dough
OIL DOUGH

25 g (1 oz) lard or solid
   vegetable fat
50 g (2 oz) strong flour

WATER DOUGH

20 g (¾ oz) lard or solid
   vegetable fat
75 g (3 oz) strong flour
45 ml (3 tablespoons) warm
   water

flour for rolling

DOUBLE-DOUGH, BASIC RECIPE

First make the oil dough by rubbing the lard into the flour as one does with Western pastry. When it has the consistency of fine breadcrumbs squeeze the dough together into a ball and leave on one side while you make the water dough. Rub the lard into the flour, then mix in the warm water. It must not be sticky, but should bind together and leave the bowl clean. Knead this dough very thoroughly, for the more it is kneaded, the less likely it is to crack when it is rolled out. Flatten it into a round about 14 cm (5½ inches) in diameter and put the ball of oil dough in the centre. Fold the water dough over to completely enclose the ball of oil dough, and pinch the edges to seal. Roll the ball of doughs between your hands to make sure it is evenly round, then on a lightly floured board, roll it out into a rectangle about 3 mm (⅛ inch) thick. Fold the top and bottom thirds over each other and turn the dough so that the two folds are at the sides of the rectangle. Roll out the dough again into a rectangle about 15 cm × 28 cm (6 × 11 inches) and fold as before. Repeat the rolling and folding once more, then roll the dough out as required in the various recipes. Take great care while handling this dough not to tear or snag the very delicate top layer of skin, and always keep it covered either with a damp cloth or in a polythene bag, since it must not be allowed to dry out during the rolling and shaping.

Deep-frying is the traditional Chinese method of cooking all pastries made with double-dough, and the recipe for dough given above is for this method of cooking. However, in the West it is often easier to bake pastries such as chrysanthemum buns in an oven. Therefore we also give a recipe below for a double-dough that is suitable for baking.

酥餅
OIL DOUGH

25 g (1 oz) lard
50 g (2 oz) plain flour

WATER DOUGH

20 g (¾ oz) lard
50 g (2 oz) plain flour
25 g (1 oz) strong flour
45 ml (3 tablespoons) cold
   water

flour for rolling

OVEN-BAKED DOUBLE-DOUGH

Use the same method given in the double-dough basic recipe and bake at 180°C (350°F, Gas mark 4).

合子酥
LITTLE BOXES

Chestnut paste is not a typical, traditional Chinese filling, but it is increasingly used by overseas Chinese, since it is readily available in the West and the results are good to eat. To make chestnut paste, either shell and boil approximately 1 kg (2 lb) of fresh chestnuts until they are soft and then put them through a mouli (food mill) to remove their skins or buy a can of unsweetened chestnut purée. For 450 g (1 lb) of chestnut purée, melt 50 g (2 oz) lard in a saucepan over a low heat. Mix in 180 g (6 oz) sugar and the chestnut purée, remove from the heat and continue to beat until the paste is smooth. Adjust the sweetness to taste and leave to cool before using. Small crumbs of marrons glacés mixed into the chestnut paste make it particularly delicious, but they can be omitted.

Makes 8 boxes
100 g (4 oz) chestnut paste
215 g (7½ oz) double-dough,
  basic recipe
flour for rolling
clean oil for deep-frying

Have ready the chestnut paste before you make the double-dough. Roll out the dough into a straight-sided rectangle about 2 mm (1/16 inch) thick, then roll it up tightly into a cylinder. Cut the cylinder into 16 equal slices. Put one slice, cut face upwards onto a lightly floured board and gently roll it into a circle about 6 cm (2½ inches) in diameter. Always roll from the centre of the slice to keep the spiral of the layers of dough even. Roll out the remaining 15 slices to the same size. Put about 7 ml (1½ teaspoons) chestnut paste in the centre of one round of dough and cover with another. Pinch round the edges to seal very tightly and then twist the edges into a 'rope' to finish. Repeat for the remaining skins. Heat the oil moderately hot and slide in the pastries. Deep-fry for about 4 minutes until they are a very pale gold. Lift out, drain and allow to cool before eating.

Alternative versions of these buns can be filled with 100 g (4 oz) lotus nut paste, bought ready-made in a can; or made with oven-baked double-dough and baked in a preheated oven 180°C (350°F, Gas mark 4) for 20 minutes on an ungreased baking tray.

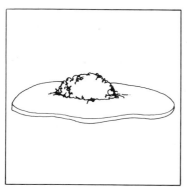
Put filling on centre of one skin.

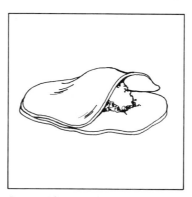
Cover with second skin.

Pinch and twist edges to finish.

芝麻酥餅

Makes 8
25 g (1 oz) walnuts
75 g (3 oz) red bean paste
  (see page 152)
215 g (7½ oz) basic recipe
  double-dough
flour for rolling
1 egg white, lightly beaten
60 ml (4 tablespoons)
  sesame seeds
clean oil for deep-frying

SESAME BUNS

There is a wide range of fillings that can be used for sesame buns. We prefer the one given below, but chopped peanuts can be substituted for the walnuts. Alternatively, toast 45 ml (3 tablespoons) of white sesame seeds in a dry frying pan until they turn pale gold and start to jump, stirring all the time. Remove from the heat and crush them on a board with a rolling pin. Mix the crushed seeds into 50 g (2 oz) of red (or white) sweet bean paste and substitute for the bean paste and walnut filling given below.

Chop the walnuts finely and blend them into the bean paste. Divide the mixture into 8 equal portions, rolling them between your palms to shape into small balls. Make the double-dough as directed, then roll it out into a

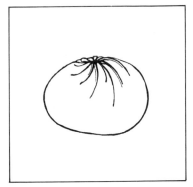

Draw excess dough up in stalk.   Twist off to seal bun completely.

straight-sided rectangle about 2 mm ($\frac{1}{10}$ inch) thick. Roll it up tightly into a cylinder, starting at the narrow side, and cut into 8 equal slices. Lay each slice, cut face upwards, and roll out into a round about 8 cm ($3\frac{1}{4}$ inches) in diameter. Put one ball of filling in the centre of each round of dough, then, holding the bun in your left hand, gently gather the dough up round the filling. Close the top and squeeze the excess dough between the thumb and forefinger of your right hand. Draw the extra dough up into a stalk and then twist and tear it off without breaking a hole in the bottom of the bun. Roll the bun between your hands to form it into a ball and lightly paint it with a little beaten egg white. Sprinkle with sesame seeds. Repeat with the remaining rounds of dough. Heat the oil moderately hot and slide in the buns. Deep-fry until they are a light golden colour, about 3 to 4 minutes. Lift out, drain and allow to cool before eating.

白兔酥

WHITE RABBITS

Festival times in China offer the opportunity for eating sweets and pastries, foods that do not usually appear in day-to-day family meals. In pre-Liberation times great piles of white rabbits made from various flour doughs, sometimes filled with lotus nut paste or sweet red bean paste, appeared on the food stalls in Xian and other cities all over China around the beginning of September. These same rabbits, together with peaches and pears, are nowadays sold for Children's Day on the first of June. Formerly, children in Beijing would be given clay models of rabbits dressed as court officials.

Rabbits and hares are particularly associated with the moon festival, at which time the hare is supposed to be seen in the moon, mixing gold, jade and cinnabar with a pestle and mortar to make the elixir of immortality, as it is still pictured on Cantonese mooncake moulds.

Makes 8 rabbits

100 g (4 oz) red bean paste
(see page 152) or lotus nut
paste (bought canned
ready-made)

215 g (7½ oz) double-dough
for oven baking

4ed food colouring
(optional)

Divide the bean paste into 8 portions and roll into small balls between the palms of your hands. Roll out the double-dough into a straight-sided rectangle about 2 mm (¹⁄₁₀ inch) thick. Roll up tightly into a cylinder starting at the narrower side, then cut it into 4 equal lengths. Cut each length in half to make 8 half-cylinders. Take each half cylinder in turn, with the cut face upwards and pinch each end into a point. Then turn the dough over so that the cut face is downwards, and roll it out into an oval about 8 cm (3 inches) long. Place one ball of the bean paste towards one end of the oval and close up the dough skin, pinching along the line of the join to seal tightly. Then squeeze the bun into a pear shape with your fingers, drawing out the narrow end where there is no filling into the shape of a rabbit's head. Using a pair of very sharp scissors or a razor blade, cut two thin flaps of dough from the front and top of the rabbit's head. Pull them gently upright to make the rabbit's ears. Cut a small scut (tail) at the back in the same way. Take care not to cut through the dough and expose the filling. Paint two red eyes at the sides of the head. Arrange the rabbits on an ungreased oven tray and bake in a moderate oven 180°C (350°F, Gas mark 4) for 20 minutes. If necessary, cover with a sheet of greaseproof paper to prevent them colouring.

Alternatively, use basic double-dough and deep-fry at 150°C (300°F) for 3 minutes. Paint in the eyes after cooking.

Close skin over bean paste.

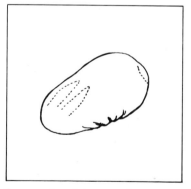

Squeeze bun into pear shape.

Cut dough to make ears and tail.

百合酥

Makes 8

50 g (2 oz) red bean paste
(see page 152)

215 g (7½ oz) basic recipe
double-dough

flour for rolling

clean oil for deep-frying

glacé cherries

LILY PASTRIES

Divide the red bean paste into 8 small balls and have these ready before making the pastry. Make the pastry. Roll the folded dough out to a rectangle approximately 15 × 28 cm (6 × 11 inches), and cut into 8 squares of 7 cm (2¾ inches) each. Take one square in the palm of your left hand and put a ball of red bean paste in the centre. Gently gather up the edges of the skin to cover the filling. When the skin is closed over the filling, hold the gathered dough between the thumb and forefinger of your right hand and, turning the bun round and round in your left hand, squeeze and draw up the excess dough into a long stalk. Finally twist and tear off this stalk of dough, taking care that you do not tear a hole in the bottom of the bun. Roll the bun between your hands to make a round ball, then cut three slashes over the top and down the sides of the bun, all crossing in the centre. (It is best to use a razor blade.) Gently prise the six corners away from the top, leaving only a thin layer of pastry to cover the filling. Have ready a pan of clean oil heated to a temperature of about 120°C (250°F) and slide in the buns with their tops upwards. Deep-fry over a moderate heat for 4 minutes. After about 2 minutes sprinkle a few drops of water with your finger tips over the oil. This causes movement in the oil, which helps shake the thin layers of pastry apart. As they fry, the layers of dough will open out like the petals of a flower. When they are open, lift them out carefully and leave to drain before putting a piece of glacé cherry in the centre of each 'flower'. Allow to get quite cool before eating.

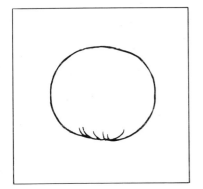

Shape filled bun into a ball.

Cut three slashes across the top.

Deep-fry until petals open

萝卜絲酥餅

Makes 8 buns

50 g (2 oz) lean pork
75 g (3 oz) white radish
25 g (1 oz) pork back fat
salt to taste
215 g (7½ oz) basic recipe
   double-dough
oil for deep-frying

WHITE RADISH BUNS

Cut the pork into very thin shreds. Peel and cut the white radish into similar-sized shreds. Put the pork fat into boiling water for 2 minutes, then drain and cut it into thin shreds. Mix the pork, white radish and pork fat together. Heat a dry frying pan over a moderate heat and stir-fry the mixed shreds until the fat runs and the meat changes colour. Season with salt to taste and leave on one side until required. Roll out the prepared dough into a rectangle about 2 mm ($\frac{1}{10}$ inch) thick and roll up into a cylinder, starting at the narrower side. Cut the dough into 16 equal slices. Roll each slice out, cut face up, into a circle about 8 cm (3¼ inches) in diameter. Always roll from the centre of the circle outwards to keep the spiral of the dough layers even. Pile about 10 ml (2 teaspoons) filling in the centre of one circle of dough and cover with another. Pinch the edges together tightly to seal and twist them into a 'rope' finish. Repeat for the remaining 7 buns. Deep-fry in moderately hot oil, 150°C (300°F), for about 4 minutes. Drain and serve hot with a soy dipping sauce.

芝麻葱饼

Makes 10 biscuits

60 ml (4 tablespoons) sesame seeds

45 g (1¾ oz) lard

125 g (5 oz) strong flour

25 ml (1½ tablespoons) finely chopped green parts of spring onions or chives

pinch of salt

45 ml (3 tablespoons) warm water

flour for rolling

1 egg white, lightly beaten

clean oil for deep-frying

ONION AND SESAME BISCUITS

Toast 30 ml (2 tablespoons) sesame seeds in a dry frying pan over a moderate heat, stirring all the time until they are a light gold colour. Take care they do not burn. Remove from the heat and crush them with a rolling pin on a board. Rub 25 g (1 oz) lard into 50 g (2 oz) strong flour together with the crushed sesame seeds, spring onion and pinch of salt. Squeeze this mixture into a ball and leave while you rub the remaining 20 g (¾ oz) lard into 75 g (3 oz) flour, then mix in the water. Knead this dough until it is smooth and elastic. Flatten it into a round about 14 cm (5½ inches) in diameter and put the ball of onion and sesame dough in the centre. Close up the round of dough over the filling and pinch the edges to seal. Roll out this ball of dough on a lightly floured board to a rectangle about 3 mm (⅛ inch) thick and fold into thirds. Turn so that the folds are at the sides of the dough and roll out and fold again twice again. Finally, roll out into a rectangle about 2 mm (¹⁄₁₀ inch) thick and roll up tightly into a cylinder starting at the narrow side. Cut the dough into 10 equal slices, then with the cut faces up, flatten these slices into discs about 4 cm (1½ inches) in diameter. Paint one side with a little beaten egg white and sprinkle with the remaining 30 ml (2 tablespoons) of untoasted sesame seeds. Deep-fry for about 3 minutes in moderately hot oil before draining and serving hot.

眉毛酥

Makes 10 buns

50 g (2 oz) lean pork

4 dried mushrooms

25 g (1 oz) bamboo shoots

15 ml (1 tablespoon) oil

SEASONING SAUCE

10 ml (2 teaspoons) light soy sauce

10 ml (2 teaspoons) rice wine

2.5 ml (½ teaspoon) cornflour and 5 ml (1 teaspoon) water made into a paste.

215 g (7½ oz) basic recipe double-dough

oil for deep-frying

THREE-THREAD EYEBROW BUNS

Cut the pork into thin matchstick-sized shreds. Soak the dried mushrooms for 30 minutes in warm water, then slice the caps finely, discarding the hard stalks. Cut the bamboo shoots into matchstick-sized strips. Heat 15 ml (1 tablespoon) oil in a frying pan and stir-fry the mushroom shreds for 30 seconds. Add the meat and bamboo shoots and continue stir-frying for another 2 minutes. Pour in the seasoning sauce and mix well. Put on one side until required. Make the double-dough as directed and roll it out into a straight-sided rectangle about 2 mm (¹⁄₁₀ inch) thick. Roll up the dough into a sausage starting from the narrower side and cut it into 10 equal slices. Roll out each of these, cut-side up into rounds about 8 cm (3¼ inches) across. Put about 5 ml (1 teaspoon) filling in the centre of each round. Fold over in half and pinch the edge tightly to seal. Gently pull the left-hand corner of the bun out to lengthen and curve it round into the shape of an eyebrow. Twist the sealed edge into a 'rope' finish. Heat the oil to 150°C (300°F) and fry these buns for about 4 to 5 minutes. Drain well and serve hot, with a dipping sauce of 45 ml (3 tablespoons) soy sauce and 15 ml (1 tablespoon) red vinegar.

Put filling in centre of skin.

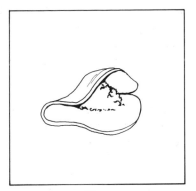

Fold skin over filling.

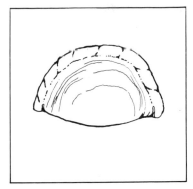

Seal Curry Bun with twisted edge.

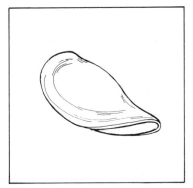

Pull Eyebrow Bun out to lengthen.

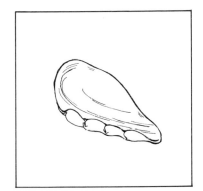

Twist sealed edge to finish.

咖喱肉酥角

Makes 8 buns

75 g (3 oz) lean beef
25 g (1 oz) onion
30 ml (2 tablespoons) oil
5 ml (1 teaspoon) curry
   powder (Chinese if
   possible)
1.5 ml ($\frac{1}{4}$ teaspoon) salt
215 g ($7\frac{1}{2}$ oz) basic recipe
   double-dough
oil for deep-frying

CURRY BUNS

Mince the beef and onion separately, using the coarse grille of the mincer. Heat 30 ml (2 tablespoons) oil in a frying pan and stir-fry the onion for about 30 seconds. Add the curry powder and continue stir-frying for another 30 seconds. Add the minced beef and fry until the meat has all changed colour. Season with salt and put on one side until required. Make the double-dough as directed, then roll it out into a rectangle about 2 mm ($\frac{1}{10}$ inch) thick. Roll it up tightly into a cylinder, starting at the narrow side, and cut into 8 equal portions. Shape each portion into a ball between the hands and roll out into a circle about 8 cm ($3\frac{1}{4}$ inches) in diameter with the centre slightly thicker than the edge. Put about 10 ml (2 teaspoons) curried meat into the centre of each round and fold the dough over into a half-moon covering the filling. Pinch round the edge very tightly to seal, then twist into a 'rope' to finish. Deep-fry in moderately hot oil 150°C (300°F) until golden brown – about 5 minutes. Drain and serve very hot.

蟠桃酥

Makes 10 peaches

25 g (1 oz) walnuts
75 g (3 oz) red bean paste
(see page 152)
215 g (7½ oz) double-dough
for oven baking
beaten egg
red and green food
colouring

PEACHES

Chop the walnuts and mix them with the bean paste. Divide the mixture into 10 portions and roll them into balls between your hands. Roll out the prepared dough into a straight-sided rectangle about 2 mm ($\frac{1}{10}$ inch) thick, and roll the dough up into a cylinder, starting at the narrow side. Cut it into 10 equal slices. Roll out each slice, cut face up into a circle about 8 cm (3 inches) in diameter. Put a ball of the filling in the centre of the dough. Then, holding the circle of dough and the filling in your left hand, gently bring the skin around the filling to enclose it. Pinch the drawn up dough between the thumb and forefinger of your right hand and gently draw the excess up into a stalk (see illustration on page 000). Finally, twist and tear off the extra dough, making sure you do not tear a hole in the bottom of the bun. Roll the bun between your hands into a round ball, then using the edge of a wooden spatula or the back of a knife, shape a division between the two sides as in a peach. Hollow the top – the side away from the join – and fasten on a leaf, made from the extra dough, at the top with a little beaten egg. Paint the leaf green and speckle one side of the bun with red. Do this by running a knife over a brush dipped in red food colouring. Bake in a preheated oven, 180°C (350°F, Gas mark 4) for 20 minutes on an ungreased oven tray. To prevent the 'peaches' browning, it may be necessary to cover them with a sheet of greaseproof paper. Leave to cool before serving.

THE PEAR SELLER

The Chinese have many very good stories that they tell on winter evenings. This tale of the pear-seller is one of our favourites.

One day a farmer was selling some particularly good pears, which he had carried to market in two baskets suspended from his carry pole. A beggar came up and asked to be given a pear. The farmer refused, but after some argument eventually a bystander bought one and gave it to the beggar. A crowd had collected by this time and the beggar told them that he owned an orchard where even better pears were growing, which he would share with them all. When he had finished eating the pear, he made a small hole in the ground and buried the pips, calling for water so that he might water his tree. As the astonished people watched, a tree grew before their eyes, put out branches and burst into flower. They saw the petals fall and the fruit grow and swell until the beggar stretched up, picked the pears and gave them to the crowd.

When the tree was bare, he dug into the ground and pulled out the tree. Then putting it over his shoulder, he walked away. All this time the farmer had watched helpless, since no one wanted to buy his pears, but when the beggar left, he turned back to his baskets only to find them empty and his carry pole gone. He ran after the beggar, but he had disappeared and all the farmer could find was his carry pole round the corner, propped against a wall.

梨子酥

Makes 10 pears

PEARS

Use the same ingredients as for peaches in the previous recipe but cut the rolled up cylinder of dough into 5 equal portions and cut these in half lengthways to make 10 half cylinders. Take one piece of dough and with the cut side up, pinch each end into a point. Turn the dough over and roll it out into an oval about 8 cm (3 inches) long. Then take the oval in your left hand, with the cut side now facing your palm and put one ball of filling in the centre. Close up the dough around the filling and twist off any excess. Mould the bun into a pear shape between your hands. Cut two leaves from the excess dough and stick them to the top of the 'pear' with the beaten egg. Paint the leaves green and either speckle the pear with red food colouring or paint it with the egg to give a yellow colour.

Other fruits, such as oranges, apples or persimmons, can all be made in a similar manner.

蛋撻

Makes 8 tarts
FILLING
100 g (4 oz) sugar
150 ml (5 fl oz) water
2 eggs

215 g (7½ oz) double-dough
for oven baking

EGG CUSTARD TARTS

Prepare the filling first by dissolving the sugar in the water over a low heat, then allow the syrup to cool while you beat the eggs. Pour the cooled syrup into the eggs and mix well.

Make the double-dough as directed. Roll the dough out until it is about 3 mm (⅛ inch) thick, then cut it into 8 rounds about 9 cm (3½ inches) in diameter. (Alternatively, roll up the sheet of dough into a sausage, divide it into four and cut each portion in half lengthways. Roll each piece out into a circle about 9 cm (3½ inches) in diameter.) Press the circles of dough into old-fashioned fluted bun tins and bake them blind for 15 minutes at 180°C (350°F, Gas mark 4). Turn the baked cases out of the tins and stand them on a lightly oiled baking sheet. Divide the egg mixture among them, then return the tarts to the oven to bake until the egg is set – about 25 minutes. Eat warm.

菊花酥餅

CHRYSANTHEMUM FLOWERS

These buns are variously called chrysanthemum flowers or daisy buns, depending apparently on the number of petals cut in the bun. They are usually deep-fried in China, but since it is easy to lose the filling from them during this style of cooking, we have suggested baking them in the oven. However, if you do wish to fry them, substitute the basic dough for the oven-baked double-dough and deep-fry for about 3 minutes at an oil temperature of 150°C (300°F).

Makes 6 flowers

200 g (7 oz) red date paste or red bean paste (see page 152)

215 g (7½ oz) double-dough for oven baking

1 egg, beaten

Have ready the filling before starting to make the pastry. Roll out the dough into a straight-sided rectangle about 2 mm ($\frac{1}{10}$ inch) thick, then roll it up tightly into a cylinder starting at the narrow side. Cut this into 3 equal pieces, then cut each piece lengthways in half, making 6 half cylinders (see illustration on page 82). Take one half cylinder and with the cut face up, pinch each end to seal, before rolling out into a circle about 14 cm (5½ inches) in diameter. Take the circle of dough in your left hand with the cut face downwards against your palm and put about 35 g (1¼ oz) of the filling in the centre. Gently coax and draw the skin over the filling and when it is covered, pinch the gathered dough between your thumb and forefinger of your right hand. Draw up the excess dough into a long stalk, turning the bun round and round in your left hand while working up any thick bumps of dough left by the gathering of the skin around the filling (see illustration on page 85). Finally, twist and tear off the excess dough, making sure you do not leave a hole in the bottom of the bun. Put the bun seal-side down on the board and shape it with your hands into a flat round cake about 7 cm (2¾ inches) in diameter and 1 cm (½ inch) thick. Using a very sharp knife or kitchen scissors, cut a series of slits about 1 cm (½ inch) apart round the entire circumference of the bun, leaving an uncut circle in the centre. Gently twist each segment so that the cut face with the filling is turned upwards, and paint the centre circle with beaten egg. Repeat for the remaining 5 portions of dough, then bake on an ungreased baking tray in a moderate oven 180°C (350°F, Gas mark 4) for 20 minutes.

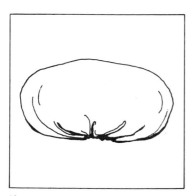

Shape bun into a round flat cake.

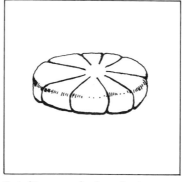

Cut slits around edge of cake.

Twist slits over to make flower.

佛手酥

Makes 6 hands

150 g (6 oz) red bean paste
 or red date paste (see page
 152)
215 g (7½ oz) double-dough
 for oven baking
1 egg, beaten

月饼

BUDDHA'S HANDS

Have the red bean paste ready before making the double-dough. Roll out the dough and shape the buns in the same manner as for chrysanthemum flowers in the previous recipe. Put the closed buns onto a board, sealed side down and shape them into squares about 7 cm (2¾ inches) on each side and approximately 1 cm (⅜ inch) thick. Cut four slits on one side extending 2 cm (¾ inch) into the bun and about 1 cm (½ inch) apart. Twist the five sections into four fingers and a thumb with the beanpaste filling turned upwards. Paint the palm of the 'hand' with beaten egg and bake on an ungreased baking tray in a moderate oven 180°C (350°F, Gas mark 4) for 20 minutes. Leave to cool before eating.

MOONCAKES

Mooncakes are baked specially to celebrate the full moon that comes in the middle of the eighth lunar month, a variable date that falls between mid-September and early October. It is said that under a tyrannical emperor during the sixteenth century, the people organized a revolt through mooncakes. Notes giving the date of a planned uprising were baked in the centre of the cakes, and in this way the news of the impending revolt was carried to every house in the area, and the people were able to prepare for it.

The autumn moon, like the harvest moon in the West, always seems particularly big and close. The traditional belief in China is that the moon goddess was the beautiful Chang-O, the wife of Yi the Archer, one of the gods. She is said to have stolen the elixir of immortality from her husband and sought refuge in the moon, where she can still be seen. In pre-Liberation China, worship of the moon and the moon goddess was strictly a woman's festival, and one in which the men took no part in the lighting of the candles and worshipping at the altar specially put up in the goddess's honour in the courtyard. It was, however, the custom at this time for the men to climb to the tops of hills or gather in the courtyards with their friends to drink wine, eat small snacks and admire the moon. Even today on Hong Kong island both young men and women climb to the top of the Peak, carrying torches and lanterns in the warm darkness, to look at the moon.

Suzhou is famous for its mooncakes and there are many names for different varieties, all using the same pastry and shape but filled with varying ingredients. In the following recipes we give a selection of these fillings.

苏式百果月饼

Makes 5 mooncakes
FILLING

50 g (2 oz) lard
150 g (5 oz) icing sugar
20 ml (4 teaspoons) flour
30 g (1¼ oz) minced pork
    back fat
25 g (1 oz) walnuts
25 g (1 oz) peanuts
25 g (1 oz) almonds
10 g (½ oz) pine kernels
25 g (1 oz) candied orange
    peel, or mixed peel
25 g (1 oz) preserved papaya

215 g (7½ oz) double-dough
    for oven baking
beaten egg white
black sesame seeds or red
    food colouring

芝麻月饼

Makes 5 mooncakes
FILLING

180 g (6 oz) icing sugar
20 ml (4 teaspoons) flour
90 ml (6 tablespoons)
    sesame oil
60 g (2½ oz) sesame seeds
30 g (1¼ oz) walnuts
20 g (¾ oz) pine kernels
15 g (½ oz) almonds
10 g (¼ oz) candied orange
    peel
10 g (¼ oz) preserved
    pineapple
10 g (¼ oz) preserved papaya

HUNDRED FRUITS SUZHOU MOONCAKES

Make the filling first by beating the lard, sugar and flour together with the minced pork fat. Chop the nuts and fruits into small pieces and mix them into the sugar and fat. Leave on one side until required. Roll the dough out into a straight-sided rectangle about 2 mm ($\frac{1}{10}$ inch) thick and roll it up tightly into a cylinder. Cut the dough into 5 equal portions. Take one portion and press it down from the top to flatten it, then roll it out into a circle about 18 cm (7 inches) in diameter. Take it onto the palm of your left hand and put about one-fifth of the filling in the centre. Then gently bring the skin up around the filling until it is completely enclosed. Pinch the gathered dough between the thumb and forefinger of your right hand to seal, and twist and tear away the excess dough, taking care not to tear a hole in the skin (see illustration on page 85). Stand with the seal-side down and shape it into a round, flat- topped bun about 10 cm (4 inches) in diameter 4 cm (1½ inches) thick. Paint the top with beaten egg white and scatter black sesame seeds over one side of it, or paint a red design, such as an H on the top of each bun. Bake on an ungreased baking tray for 20 minutes in a moderate oven 180°C (350°F, Gas mark 4). Leave to cool before eating.

SESAME SEED MOONCAKES

Beat the icing sugar and flour into the sesame oil. Toast the sesame seeds in a dry frying pan over a low heat until they turn golden and start to dance. Then take from the heat and crush them with a rolling pin on a board. Chop the rest of the ingredients and mix with the sesame seeds into the sugar and oil. Follow instructions for rolling, shaping and baking mooncakes as given in Hundred Fruits recipe.

松子棗泥月餅

250 g (8 oz) icing sugar
50 g (2 oz) lard
125 g (4 oz) red date paste
    (see page 154)
25 g (1 oz) pine kernels
12 g (½ oz) almonds
7 g (¼ oz) candied orange
    peel
7 g (¼ oz) preserved
    pineapple or papaya

PINE KERNEL AND RED DATE MOONCAKES

Cream the sugar and lard and mix in the red date paste. Add the rest of the ingredients chopped to about the size of half your small finger nail. This quantity will fill 5 mooncakes.

鷄絲鹹月餅

Makes 5 mooncakes
350 g (12 oz) boneless
    chicken
60 ml (4 tablespoons) white
    sesame seeds
10 ml (2 teaspoons) sesame
    oil
15 ml (1 tablespoon) light
    soy sauce
2.5 ml (½ teaspoon) sugar
1.5 ml (¼ teaspoon) salt

CHICKEN SHREDS MOONCAKES

Not all mooncakes are sweet; this recipe from Shanghai has a savoury filling of chicken and sesame. The pastry dough and the finished shape of the cake are the same as the sweet Suzhou mooncakes given above.

Mince the chicken meat using the fine grille on the mincer and mix with the sesame seeds, sesame oil and soy sauce. Season with sugar and salt. Fill and finish the mooncakes as directed in Hundred Fruits recipe.

台式月餅

Makes 5 mooncakes
350 g (12 oz) white bean
    paste (see page 153)
215 g (7½ oz) double-dough
    for oven baking
red food colouring

TAIWANESE MOONCAKES

Have the white bean paste ready before making the double-dough. Roll out the prepared dough into a straight-sided rectangle about 2 mm ($\frac{1}{10}$ inch) thick, then roll it up tightly into a cylinder. Cut into 5 equal lengths. Press down and flatten one length of the dough while it is still lying on its side, then roll it out into a circle about 18 cm (7 inches) in diameter. Take it in the palm of your left hand and put about 60 g (2½ oz) of bean paste in the centre. Draw up the dough around the filling and pinch the gathered edge to seal over the top. Tear away any excess dough and shape the bun between your hands into a round about 16 cm (6 inches) in diameter and about 2 cm (¾ inch) thick. Paint a red design such as an H in the centre of the cake. Repeat with the remaining lengths of dough, then bake the cakes on an ungreased baking tray in a moderate oven 180°C (350°F, Gas mark 4) for 20 minutes.

蝦仁月餅

Makes 7 mooncakes

100 g (4 oz) pork

12 g (½ oz) raw prawns, shelled

5 ml (1 teaspoon) dark soy sauce

2.5 ml (½ teaspoon) rice wine

pinch of salt and sugar

215 g (7½ oz) double-dough for oven baking

red food colouring

京式月餅

Makes 4 mooncakes

400 g (14 oz) red date paste (see page 154)

215 g (7½ oz) basic recipe double-dough

oil for deep-frying

red food colouring

Opposite: *Lily Pastries (page 86)*

PRAWN MOONCAKES

Prawn-filled mooncakes are not common, but this recipe from Shanghai makes little mooncakes, decorated in the same fashion as the sweet Taiwanese mooncakes in the previous recipe but only about one-third of the size. In the original recipe these mooncakes were baked over the fire in a sort of Dutch oven.

Mince the pork and prawns through the coarse grille of the mincer. Add the soy sauce, rice wine and seasonings and mix very thoroughly. Leave on one side while you prepare the pastry skins. Make the dough and roll it out into a straight-sided rectangle about 2 mm ($\frac{1}{10}$ inch) thick. Roll up tightly into a cylinder and cut it into 7 equal pieces. Turn each piece on its side, cut face upwards, flatten it, then roll out into a circle about 12 cm (4¾ inches) in diameter with the edges thinner than the centre. Put 15 ml (1 tablespoon) filling in the centre of each skin. Hold it in the left hand and draw up the dough round the filling. Close tightly and tear off any excess dough. Put the little cakes onto a board and shape into rounds about 5 cm (2 inches) in diameter. Mark the side opposite the seal with a red design such as an H and bake in a moderate oven 180°C (350°F, Gas mark 4) for 20 minutes, until they are golden. Serve cool.

BEIJING MOONCAKES

Have the red date paste ready before making the double-dough. Roll the dough out into a straight-sided rectangle about 2 mm ($\frac{1}{10}$ inch) thick, then roll it up tightly into a cylinder. Cut into 2 equal lengths, then cut each length in half to make 4 half cylinders (see illustration on page 86). Take one half-cylinder and pinch each end to seal the open edges of the layers, then roll it out into a circle about 18 cm (7 inches) in diameter. Take it onto the palm of your left hand and put a quarter of the date paste in the centre. Draw up the skin around the filling and pinch the gathered edge to seal tightly (see illustration on page 85). Tear off any excess dough, then roll the cake between your hands into a round bun about 8 cm (3½ inches) in diameter and 5 cm (2 inches) thick. Often this shape is described as a 'bald-head' in Chinese recipes. Repeat with the remainder of the dough. Deep-fry these cakes in clean, moderately hot oil 150°C (300°F) for between 2 and 3 minutes. They must not change colour but remain white. Leave to cool before painting a red design such as an H on the top of each. Serve when cool. These mooncakes will keep for several days in a dry place, or they may be deep-frozen uncooked, but allow them to thaw out before frying.

An alternative filling for Beijing mooncakes is red bean paste, flavoured with cassia flowers or ground cinnamon.

広式月餅

CANTONESE MOONCAKES

Cantonese mooncakes look and taste quite different from the other varieties of mooncake made with the double-dough used in the previous recipes. Cantonese pastry is a rich gold colour, sweet and crumbly, more closely resembling the French pâte sablée than flaky pastry. Before being baked, Cantonese mooncakes are pressed into a fluted round mould with an elaborate incised design on the bottom, so that the finished mooncake when it is turned out from the mould has a relief pattern of a good luck symbol embossed on its top. As a substitute for such moulds, you can use a wooden butter mould about 6 cm (2½ inches) in diameter and 2.5 cm (1 inch) deep, or you can shape the cake between your hands into a flattened round of the same dimensions and omit the decoration. It is customary to cut Cantonese mooncakes into segments to serve, since most people find them too filling to eat more than a small quantity at a time.

Makes 5 mooncakes
FILLING

5 small salted eggs (see page 22)
300 g (10 oz) red bean paste (see page 152)
15 ml (1 tablespoon) *Meiguilujiu*, or rose-water to taste

PASTRY

175 g (6½ oz) plain flour
25 ml (2 tablespoons) peanut oil or cooking oil
100 g (4 oz) cane sugar syrup
2.5 ml (½ teaspoon) bicarbonate of soda dissolved in 7.5 ml (2 teaspoons) water
beaten egg for glazing

Prepare the filling first by hard-boiling the salted eggs, then shelling them and discarding the whites. Keep the yolks whole. Flavour the sweet bean paste to taste with either the rose-flavoured Chinese spirit or with rose-water. Then make the pastry by piling the flour onto a flat surface and making a well in the centre. Put the oil, sugar syrup and bicarbonate of soda mixture in the centre and mix together with the fingers. Gently work in the flour, and knead the mixture until your hands are free of dough and it looks shiny and smooth. Leave it to rest for an hour at room temperature. Roll the dough into a sausage and divide into 5 portions. Roll each piece into a ball, then roll out between two pieces of oiled greaseproof paper into circles about 3 mm (⅛ inch) thick and 14 cm (5½ inches) in diameter. Put about 50 g (2 oz) red bean paste very carefully around a hard boiled yolk and place it in the centre of the pastry circle. Close up the pastry around the filling, take great care not to squash the egg, pinch to seal and tear off any excess pastry. Either use a mould (see above) or shape with your hands into a round flat-topped bun about 7 cm (2¾ inches) in diameter 4 cm (1½ inches) high. Repeat with remainder of dough and filling. Paint the top and sides with beaten egg and stand, sealed side down on an oiled baking tray. Bake in a preheated hot oven 230°C (450°F, Gas mark 8) for 8 minutes. Leave to cool before eating.

A simple alternative can be made with canned ready-made lotus nut paste. Allow 400 g (15 oz) for 5 mooncakes.

Opposite: *Transparent Prawn Jiaozi (page 71)*

Here are two more of the most popular recipes for Cantonese mooncakes. Make the the pastry and shape the cakes as in the previous recipe.

火腿月饼
GOLDEN HAM MOONCAKES

Fills 5 mooncakes

100 g (4 oz) icing sugar

10 g ($\frac{1}{2}$ oz) granulated sugar with a few drops of rose water to taste

a very small pinch of five spice powder

40 g (1$\frac{1}{2}$ oz) cooked glutinous rice flour (see page 18)

75 g (3 oz) pork back fat, minced

25 g (1 oz) almonds

25 g (1 oz) crystallized winter melon

25 g (1 oz) walnuts

25 g (1 oz) sesame seeds, toasted

12 g ($\frac{1}{2}$ oz) candied orange peel

15 g ($\frac{3}{4}$ oz) raw unsmoked ham

pinch of salt and pepper

1.5 ml ($\frac{1}{4}$ teaspoon) sesame oil

1.5 ml ($\frac{1}{4}$ teaspoon) rice wine

枣泥月饼
RED DATE MOONCAKES

Fills 5 mooncakes

250 g (9 oz) red date paste (see page 154)

125 g (4$\frac{1}{2}$ oz) icing sugar

45 ml (3 tablespoons) oil

30 g (1$\frac{1}{4}$ oz) preserved winter melon

10 g ($\frac{1}{2}$ oz) candied orange peel

15 g ($\frac{3}{4}$ oz) almonds

25 g (1 oz) cooked glutinous rice flour (see page 18)

5 ml (1 teaspoon) rice wine

Chapter 9 | *Sweet and savoury buns*

包子类

In this chapter we describe a number of different steamed buns, eaten as snacks or light meals everywhere in China and among Chinese communities overseas — they are particularly popular in northern China. They are all made with a leavened dough — usually a yeast dough. We have not, however, included any recipes for ordinary Chinese steamed bread buns (*mantou*) because, according to Chinese eating habits, *mantou* are invariably eaten with a main meal and not as a snack. Unlike the oven-baked breads of the West, Chinese breads and bread buns are cooked in a steamer — although deep-fried bread twists, a speciality of north-western China, are an exception to this rule. Steamed breads have a soft spongy texture and a translucent glow when they first come from the steamer, but they quickly become heavy as they cool, so they should be eaten as soon as possible after they are cooked. However, they do have the advantage of being reheatable, also in a steamer, without spoiling.

The bun recipes we give are made with a bread-dough skin and are filled with a variety of meat and sweet stuffings. Depending on their size, they are called *baozi* or small buns (*xiaolongbao*). *Baozi* are big, about 10 cm (4 inches) in diameter and made with 25 g (1 oz) of bread dough. They are usually stuffed with a variety of cooked meat and sauce fillings, such as chicken or roast Cantonese pork. They are shaped into rounds with a series of pleats around the top gathering up the dough to cover the filling. Generally, they are eaten two or three at a time as a snack on their own rather than as part of a dimsum meal. Small buns are shaped in exactly the same way as the *baozi*, but they are only half the size; 12 g ($\frac{1}{2}$ oz) of dough is sufficient for each bun. Their stuffing is generally made with raw meats or meat pastes, often including expensive ingredients, and they are usually eaten as part of a dimsum meal.

It is perhaps a measure of the tenacity of Chinese

cookery traditions that Chinese chefs as widely separated as street markets in western China, state restaurants in Beijing, demonstrations in a Tokyo department store, and even restaurants in London and San Francisco all hold the *baozi* in the same way as they shape it, bouncing the bun around on their hand as they pleat the dough over the filling. It is also traditional that this form is used only for savoury buns. After they are sealed sweet buns are turned upside down and shaped into 'bald-heads' — a self-explanatory description.

In China leavened bread doughs are usually made with a portion of fermented dough left over from a previous baking. This gives the bread a stronger flavour than doughs made from fresh or dried yeast, but it is also very unstable in its rising potential, and the results from baking with it are usually heavier as well as unpredictable. We have therefore adapted all our recipes for Western-type fresh or dried yeast: we have also found that plain flour with the addition of a little fat gives the best results. The quantity of water used for any bread can vary with the variety of flour used, or even with the weather. *Baozi* dough should be very soft, like 'the lobe of an ear', but it must leave the bowl and hands clean, and not be in the least sticky. We have allowed for a marginal adjustment to the quantity of water in the basic recipe for *baozi* dough that follows.

DOUGH FOR STEAMED BUNS

Makes 12 *baozi or* 20 small buns
10 ml (2 teaspoons) granulated sugar
5 ml (1 teaspoon) dried yeast *or* 7.5 g (¼ oz) fresh yeast
225 g (8 oz) plain flour
15 g (½ oz) lard or solid vegetable fat
flour for rolling

Place the sugar and yeast into 100 ml (3½ fl oz) of warm water and leave until it is foaming — about 10 minutes. Put the flour in a bowl and rub in the lard before mixing in the yeasted water. Add between 40 and 45 ml (2½ and 3 tablespoons) warm water to mix into a very soft, but not sticky dough. Knead the dough on a flat surface until it is smooth and elastic. Cover with cling film or a towel and set aside in a warm place to rise until the dough has doubled in size — up to 3 hours depending on the temperature. While the dough is rising, prepare a filling from one of the following recipes.

FILLING THE BAOZI SKINS
When the dough has risen, divide it into 12 equal portions and roll each into a ball. Have ready 12 small squares of non-stick baking parchment (or oiled greaseproof paper). Using a small rolling pin, roll out one ball of dough on a well-floured board into a circle about 10 cm (4 inches) in diameter. The centre of the circle should be about double the thickness of the edges. Put 15–20 ml (1 generous tablespoon) of filling in the centre of the dough. Then, holding the dough in your left hand and using your thumb to hold in the filling, use the thumb and index finger of your right hand to pleat the edge of the dough, pressing the top

Hold the skin in one hand.

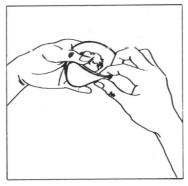

Pleat edge with other hand.

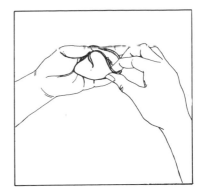

Fold pleats one on another.

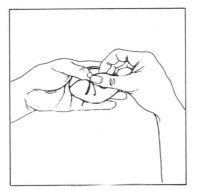

Rotate bun while pleating.

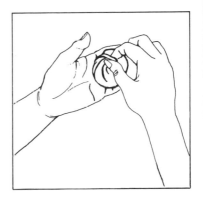

Close bun top by twisting pleats.

edge of each fold very tightly onto the previous pleat. Gently rotate the bun clockwise while pleating the top and take care not to fold in the pleated edge. Finally twist and pinch the pleats to close the bun – it should open again very slightly during the cooking. Shape the bun into a round and stand it on a square of parchment. Repeat with the remaining *baozi* and leave to rise in a warm place for another 30 minutes before steaming for 20 minutes over a high heat. The water must be boiling fast before putting the *baozi* on to steam.

Serve the *baozi* very hot straight from the steamer. These *baozi* will freeze well after cooking. To reheat frozen *baozi*, put them straight from the freezer into a steamer for 10 minutes, over a high heat.

FILLING SMALL BUNS
When the dough has risen, divide it into 20 equal portions and roll each piece into a small ball. Using a small rolling pin and a well-floured board, roll out one ball of dough into a circle about 6 cm (2½ inches) in diameter. Put 15 ml (1 tablespoon) of filling in the centre of the dough. Now, shape and cook as for *baozi* above.

肉巴子

Fills 12 *baozi*

baozi dough

200 g (7 oz) Chinese leaves
or ordinary cabbage (do
not use Dutch white
cabbage)
5 ml (1 teaspoon) salt
300 g (10 oz) lean pork
2 garlic cloves, crushed
50 g (2 oz) spring onions
45 ml (3 tablespoons) oil

SEASONING SAUCE

15 ml (1 tablespoon) rice
wine
30 ml (2 tablespoons) soy
sauce
5 ml (1 teaspoon) sugar
pinch of black pepper
10 ml (2 teaspoons) sesame
oil

又燒巴

Fills 12 *baozi*

baozi dough but add an
extra 5 ml spoon (1
teaspoon) of sugar to the
flour to make a sweeter
dough.
350 g (12 oz) *chahsiu* (see
page 42) or buy ready
made.

SEASONING SAUCE

30 ml (2 tablespoons) soy
sauce
30 ml (2 tablespoons)
barbecue sauce
30 ml (2 tablespoons) sugar
15 ml (1 tablespoon) sesame
oil
15 ml (1 tablespoon)
cornflour
150 ml (¼ pint) water

BAOZI – BIG BUNS

PORK BAOZI

Make the *baozi* dough and leave to rise while you prepare the pork filling. Wash, dry and mince the cabbage leaves coarsely. Sprinkle them with salt and leave to draw out the water. After about 15 minutes squeeze them dry between the hands. Meanwhile, coarsely mince the pork and chop the spring onions finely. Heat a frying pan with the oil and stir-fry the garlic and onion for about 30 seconds. Add the pork and stir-fry over a high heat until the colour of the meat has changed. Reduce the heat and add the seasoning sauce. Stir in the minced Chinese leaves and remove from the heat. Leave to cool before filling the *baozi* skins as directed on page 100. Steam for 20 minutes.

CHAHSIU BAOZI

Make the *baozi* dough and leave to rise while you prepare the filling. Cut the *chahsiu* into small dice about 1 cm (½ inch) square. Mix the seasoning sauce in a saucepan and boil gently until the mixture is thick and syrupy. Stir in the *chahsiu* and leave to cool.

Divide the risen dough into 12 equal portions and roll each into a ball. Roll out each ball on a well-floured board into a circle about 10 cm (4 inches) in diameter. The centre should be about double the thickness of the edge. Hold the circle of dough in your left hand and put 15–20 ml (1 generous tablespoon) of filling in the centre. Gently close up the dough around the filling and pinch tightly to seal. Tear away any excess dough. Stand the *baozi*, sealed side down, on a square of non-stick parchment. Leave the *baozi* to rise in a warm place for 30 minutes. Have ready a steamer with boiling water, but just before putting in the *baozi*, cut an X in the centre of the top of each bun with a knife. Steam for 20 minutes over a high heat and serve very hot. These *baozi* can be frozen after they have been steamed and reheated straight from the freezer in a steamer for 10 minutes.

素包子

Fills 12 *baozi*
baozi dough
1 can (200 g (7 oz))
    red-in-snow
2 squares beancurd
50 g (2 oz) bamboo shoots
50 g (2 oz) fresh mushrooms
15 ml (1 tablespoon) sesame
    oil
5 ml (1 teaspoon) fresh
    ginger, cut into fine
    shreds
7.5 ml (1½ teaspoons) sugar
10 ml (2 teaspoons) soy
    sauce

鸡肉大包子

Fills 12 *baozi*
baozi dough
3 dried mushrooms
300 g (10 oz) boneless
    chicken

MARINADE

2.5 ml (½ teaspoon) salt
10 ml (2 teaspoons) rice
    wine
10 ml (2 teaspoons)
    cornflour

25 g (1 oz) bamboo shoots
45 ml (3 tablespoons) oil
10 ml (2 teaspoons)
    chopped spring onions
5 ml (1 teaspoon) grated
    fresh ginger

SEASONING SAUCE

10 ml (2 teaspoons) rice
    wine
10 ml (2 teaspoons) soy
    sauce
pinch of salt and pepper
5 ml (1 teaspoon) sugar
5 ml (1 teaspoon) sesame oil
5 ml (1 teaspoon) cornflour
100 ml (7 tablespoons) water

VEGETARIAN BAOZI

Make the *baozi* dough and leave to rise while you make the filling. Rinse and drain the red-in-snow very thoroughly before cutting it into 1 cm (½ inch) lengths. Roll the beancurd tightly in a clean towel and press it under a plate for 30 minutes to drain, then cut into thin slices. Chop the bamboo shoots and mushrooms finely, or put them through a mincer using a coarse grille. Heat the sesame oil over a low heat and stir-fry the ginger for 15 seconds, or until it smells good. Then add the red-in-snow and sugar and stir-fry for about 2 minutes. Taste to see if it is too salty, and if necessary, add a little more sugar. Add the bamboo shoots and mushrooms and continue stir-frying for another minute. Finally, add the beancurd slices and soy sauce. Mix well and remove from the heat. Leave to cool before filling the *baozi* skins as directed on page 100. Steam for 20 minutes.

CHICKEN BAOZI

Make the *baozi* dough and leave to rise while you prepare the filling. Soak the dried mushrooms in warm water for 30 minutes, then discard the hard stalks and chop the caps finely. Coarsely mince the chicken meat and marinate for 30 minutes. Chop the bamboo shoots finely — or mince them with the chicken. Heat the oil in a frying pan and stir-fry the onion and ginger for 15 seconds, before adding the minced chicken. Stir-fry over a high heat until all the chicken has changed colour. Add the mushrooms and bamboo shoots and continue stir-frying for another minute. Pour in the seasoning sauce, reduce the heat and scrape the bottom of the pan to free any bits sticking to it. Simmer gently for 5 minutes. Remove from the heat and leave to cool before filling the *baozi* skins (see page 100). Steam for 20 minutes as directed.

猪肉大包子

Fills 12 *baozi*

baozi dough
350 g (12 oz) pork (30% fat, 70% lean)
20 ml (4 teaspoons) chopped onion
20 ml (4 teaspoons) chopped fresh ginger
10 ml (2 teaspoons) yellow beans, mashed
30 ml (2 tablespoons) soy sauce
10 ml (2 teaspoons) sugar
25 ml (1½ tablespoons) rice wine
salt to taste

PORK WITH BEAN SAUCE BAOZI

Make the *baozi* dough and leave to rise while you made the filling. Mince the pork, using the coarse grille of the mincer. Put it into a dry frying pan and stir-fry over a moderate to low heat. If it starts to stick to the bottom, lift the pan from the heat and scrape the meat away from the bottom. Continue in this manner until all the meat has changed colour and the fat is running – about 8 minutes. Lift out the pork with a slotted spoon and stir-fry the onion and ginger in the oil remaining in the pan for about 15 seconds before adding the mashed yellow beans with the soy sauce and sugar. Continue stir-frying for another 30 seconds, then return the meat to the pan. Mix well, season to taste with salt and add the rice wine. Leave on one side to cool before using to fill the *baozi* skins as directed on page 100. Steam for 20 minutes.

肉 笋 馅

Fills 20 small buns

baozi dough
1 dried mushroom
200 g (7 oz) pork
100 g (3½ oz) bamboo shoots
30 ml (2 tablespoons) soy sauce
2.5 ml (½ teaspoon) sugar
10 ml (2 teaspoons) sesame oil
15 ml (1 tablespoon) rice wine
1.5 ml (¼ teaspoon) salt

SMALL BUNS

PORK AND BAMBOO FILLING

Make the *baozi* dough and leave to rise while you prepare the filling. Soak the dried mushroom for 30 minutes in warm water then, discarding the hard stalk, cut the cap into tiny pieces. Put the pork and bamboo shoots through the mincer, using the coarse grille. Mix well with the rest of the ingredients, and put on one side until required. Fill and steam as directed on page 101.

蝦 肉 小 籠包

Fills 20 buns

baozi dough
100 g (3½ oz) raw shelled prawns
200 g (7 oz) pork
25 g (1 oz) spring onions
10 ml (2 teaspoons) sesame seeds
15 ml (1 tablespoon) soy sauce
1.5 ml (¼ teaspoon) salt

PRAWN FILLING FOR SMALL BUNS

Make the *baozi* dough and leave to rise while you prepare the filling. De-vein the prawns, then chop them coarsely. Pound the pork into a paste, as directed on page 26. Chop the spring onions finely and toast the sesame seeds in a dry pan over a moderate heat until they turn golden in colour and start to dance. Stir all the time to prevent them burning and turn out of the pan as soon as they are ready. Mix all the ingredients together and fill the small buns as directed on page 101.

蟹 肉 小 籠 包

Fills 20 buns

baozi dough
180 g (6 oz) pork
25 g (1 oz) pork back fat
90 g (3 oz) crabmeat, fresh or
   tinned
2.5 ml (½ teaspoon) grated
   fresh ginger
2.5 ml (½ teaspoon) salt
10 ml (2 teaspoons) rice
   wine
1.5 ml (¼ teaspoon) ground
   Sichuan pepper

三 鮮 小 籠 包

Fills 20 buns

25 g (1 oz) dried sea
   cucumber (For
   preparation 3 days in
   advance see page 22.)
baozi dough
250 g (8 oz) boneless
   chicken breast
30 ml (2 tablespoons) onion
   wine
30 ml (2 tablespoons) ginger
   wine
50 g (2 oz) raw shelled
   prawns
45 ml (3 tablespoons) light
   soy sauce
2.5 ml (½ teaspoon) salt
45 ml (3 tablespoons)
   sesame oil

CRABMEAT FILLING FOR SMALL BUNS

Make the *baozi* dough and leave to rise while you prepare the filling. Mince the pork and fat together using the coarse grille on the mincer, and mix in the crabmeat. (If using a fresh crab, use both white and brown meat.) Add the remaining ingredients and mix together well. Fill the small buns as directed on page 101.

THREE-FLAVOURED SMALL BUNS

Prepare the sea cucumber as directed. Make the *baozi* dough and leave to rise while you prepare the filling. Pound the chicken breast into a paste sprinkling it from time to time with the onion and ginger wines or use a food processor with the plastic blade attachment. De-vein the prawns and chop them and the prepared sea cucumber into 5-mm (¼-inch) cubes. Blend all the ingredients together and use to fill the small buns as directed on page 101.

MUSLIM RECIPES FOR SMALL BUN FILLINGS

The next two recipes are for Muslim fillings using no pork. Muslim cooking, which is found all over the northern half of China, is popular with many Chinese, not just Muslims. In most towns in northern China there are numerous small one-room restaurants whose doors open straight onto the street and where a choice of dishes is written up on a board hanging clearly visible from the street. Some of these restaurants are run by Muslim families, while others serve standard Chinese dishes. Their menus usually consist of only three or four dishes, such as meat with noodles, meat with noodles and soy sauce, boiling water baozi and French

bean soup; or – typically Muslim – beef or lamb baozi,
vegetarian baozi, stuffed sesame buns and barbecue sauce
for a dip. The baozi in these restaurants are large, so that one
helping of three buns is sufficient for a meal, however the
Muslim recipes that follow are for rather luxurious small
buns served as part of a dimsum meal.

LAMB AND LEEK FILLING FOR SMALL BUNS

Make the baozi dough and leave to rise while you prepare
the filling. Mince the lamb using the coarse grille on the
mincer. Trim, wash and finely chop the leeks. Mix all the
ingredients together and use this mixture to fill the small
buns as directed on page 101.

BEEF AND ONION FILLING FOR SMALL BUNS

Make the baozi dough and leave to rise while you prepare
the filling. Mince the beef coarsely and mix in the rest of the
ingredients. Use this mixture to fill the small buns as directed
on page 101.

香蒜羊肉巳子

Fills 20 buns

baozi dough

250 g (8 oz) lean lamb

100 g (4 oz) leeks

10 ml (2 teaspoons) sesame
oil

2.5 ml ($\frac{1}{2}$ teaspoon) finely
chopped fresh ginger

15 ml (1 tablespoon) soy
sauce

5 ml (1 teaspoon) rice wine

2.5 ml ($\frac{1}{2}$ teaspoon) sugar

1.5 ml ($\frac{1}{4}$ teaspoon) salt

牛肉小籠包

Fills 20 buns

baozi dough

300 g (10 oz) beef, topside
or thick flank

60 g ($2\frac{1}{2}$ oz) finely chopped
spring onions

5 ml (1 teaspoon) finely
chopped fresh ginger

2.5 ml ($\frac{1}{2}$ teaspoon) sugar

15 ml (1 tablespoon) rice
wine

15 ml (1 tablespoon) soy
sauce

10 ml (2 teaspoons) sesame
oil

水煎包子

Fills 14 *baozi*

baozi dough
4 dried mushrooms
25 g (1 oz) dried shrimps
25 g (1 oz) pork back fat
180 g (6 oz) pork
125 g (4 oz) boneless
  chicken
15 ml (1 tablespoon) soy
  sauce
45 ml (3 tablespoons)
  sesame oil
pinch of salt
45 ml (3 tablespoons) finely
  chopped spring onions
7.5 ml (1½ teaspoons) finely
  chopped fresh ginger
40 ml (2½ tablespoons)
  vegetable oil

FRIED MIXED MEATS BAOZI

Make the *baozi* dough and leave to rise while you prepare the filling. Soak the dried mushrooms in warm water for 30 minutes, then discard the hard stalks. Put the dried shrimps into a pan of hot water and bring to the boil. Boil for 2 minutes before leaving them to soak for 15 minutes in the same water. Drain well. Mince the pork back fat then put it into a dry frying pan and cook over a moderate heat until the oil runs out. Leave on one side to cool. Mince the pork, chicken and mushroom caps through the coarse grille of a mincer. Blend in the soy sauce, 15 ml (1 tablespoon) sesame oil, salt, onions and ginger, then add the cooked pork fat, including the rendered oil and the shrimps. Leave on one side until required.

When the *baozi* dough is ready, divide it into 14 pieces. Roll each piece into a ball between the hands and then roll out each ball on a floured board into a circle about 10 cm (4 inches) in diameter, leaving the centres thicker than the edges. Put about 15 ml (1 tablespoon) of the prepared filling in the centre of the dough skin, then pleat up to close as shown in the illustration on page 100. Finally, shape the *baozi* between the fingers so that the bottom of each bun is about 5 cm (2 inches) in diameter and about 6 cm (2½ inches) high. Heat a flat-bottomed frying pan over a low heat with the vegetable oil and remaining 30 ml (2 tablespoons) sesame oil and put in 7 *baozi*. They must not touch. Gently fry for 1 minute over a low heat and then add 30 ml (2 tablespoons) water. Cover the pan with a lid and continue cooking for another 10 minutes over a low heat. From time to time, add another couple of tablespoons of water to prevent the pan becoming dry. Move the buns occasionally in the pan to keep them from sticking. Serve very hot.

An alternative filling for fried *baozi* uses 300 g (10 oz) pork, 50 g (2 oz) water chestnuts, 60 g (2½ oz) finely chopped spring onions, a tablespoon each of sugar and soy sauce together with a pinch of salt. The pork and water chestnuts are put through the coarse grille of the mincer before being blended with the other ingredients.

灌湯包

Makes 24 dumplings
baozi dough
40 g (1½ oz) raw shelled
    prawns
100 g (4 oz) pork
10 ml (2 teaspoons) finely
    chopped spring onions
10 ml (2 teaspoons) sesame
    seeds
10 ml (2 teaspoons) grated
    fresh ginger
5 ml (1 teaspoon) rice wine
flour for rolling out dough
200 ml (⅓ pint)
    well-seasoned jellied
    stock*

*Jellied stock can be made
with pig's trotters or with
veal bones: cook as ordinary
stock but use a little less
water, then strain carefully
into a clean bowl, season
and leave to set.

蓮蓉包

Makes 10 buns
baozi dough
250 g (8 oz) lotus nut paste,
    canned
flour for rolling

'SOUP' DUMPLINGS

These dumplings are said to be the invention of a chef nicknamed Goubuli, who first sold these buns filled with soup stock in Tianjin during the middle of the nineteenth century. Since his time they have become a common feature on many dimsum menus. They are always made small enough to eat in one mouthful so that none of the stock is lost.

Make the baozi dough and leave to rise while you prepare the filling. First de-vein the prawns, then mince together with the pork. Add the spring onions, sesame seeds, ginger and rice wine and blend well. When the dough has doubled in size, divide it into 24 portions and roll out each portion on a floured board into a circle about 6 cm (2½ inches) in diameter. Put a small quantity of the filling in the centre of each round together with 5 ml (1 teaspoon) of the jellied stock. Then fold and pleat the sides round the filling (as directed on page 100) so that the top is almost closed. The finished dumplings should be about the size of a walnut with a tiny hole in the centre of the top. Stand each dumpling on a square of oiled paper or non-stick parchment and leave to rise in a warm place for 30 minutes. Then steam over a high heat for 15 minutes.

LOTUS SEED BUNS

Make the baozi dough and leave to rise. When it has doubled in size, divide it into 10 equal portions and roll out each piece on a floured board into a circle about 10 cm (4 inches) in diameter. The centre should be about three times the thickness of the edge. Put about 25 ml (1½ tablespoons) of the lotus nut paste in the centre of the dough circle. Then, holding the dough skin in your left hand, draw up the edges to cover the lotus nut paste with your right hand. Close the top by squeezing and pinching the dough. If necessary, tear off any excess dough, making sure the buns are completely sealed. Shape into round buns – 'bald heads' as they are called in Chinese – and stand, seal-side downwards, on non-stick parchment to rise for 30 minutes in a warm place. Steam over high heat for 20 minutes.

These buns are best eaten still warm from the steamer, but they will stand reheating. They can be deep-frozen, and then reheated in a steamer for about 10 minutes.

杭州幸運双

HANGZHOU 'FORTUNE' BUNS

These sweet baozi *are a speciality of a big dimsum restaurant in the centre of Hangzhou. It has a rather small front, remarkable only by the official cars that draw up outside from time to time. Inside on the ground floor is a large dining room, where the bare tables are always crowded with people eating many varieties of dumplings such as flower* shaomai, *noodles including cat's ears — another speciality of the house — and* baozi. *Upstairs there is a smaller dining room, where the tables have cloths and people can be entertained to dimsum meals ordered in advance. The 'fortune' buns are sold, sometimes from a stall in the street outside the restaurant, to be eaten at home.*

Fills 8 buns
baozi dough
oil for deep-frying
50 g (2 oz) walnuts
25 g (1 oz) pine kernels
40 g (1½ oz) preserved red
  dates
15 g (½ oz) candied lemon
  peel *and*
15 g (½ oz) candied orange
  peel
  or substitute 25 g (1 oz)
  mixed peel
15 g (½ oz) preserved papaya
25 g (1 oz) raisins
100 g (6 oz) red bean paste
  (see page 152)
pinch of cinnamon

Make the *baozi* dough and leave to rise while you prepare the filling. Deep-fry the walnuts and pine kernels over a moderate heat until the colour just starts to change — about 2 minutes. Then lift out and drain on kitchen paper. Chop the walnuts, red dates, lemon peel, orange peel and papaya finely — 3-mm (⅛-inch) pieces is about right — and mix in the whole raisins and pine kernels. Blend the chopped fruit and nut mixture into the red bean paste and add cinnamon to taste. Divide the filling into 8 portions and shape each into a ball so that it can be handled easily. Divide the risen dough into 8 pieces and roll out each piece into a circle about 10 cm (4 inches) in diameter, making sure that the centres are about 1 cm (½ inch) thick while the edges are only 3 mm (⅛ inch) Put one ball of filling in the centre of a dough circle, then, holding them in your left hand, with your right hand draw up the edges of dough over the filling and pinch tightly to seal. If necessary, tear away any excess dough, and shape the *baozi* with your hands into flat-topped straight-sided buns about 6 × 4.5 cm (2½ × 1¾ inches) and about 2.5 cm (1 inch) high. Stand them, seal-side down, on squares of non-stick parchment and leave to rise for 30 minutes in a warm place before steaming over a high heat for 20 minutes. Eat while they are still warm if possible. These buns reheat very well in a steamer and can be frozen for later use after they have been cooked.

百果包子

Fills 10 *baozi*
75 g (3 oz) pork back fat
75 g (3 oz) walnuts
oil for deep-frying
45 ml (3 tablespoons)
    sesame seeds
50 g (2 oz) crystallized
    winter melon
50 g (2 oz) preserved
    pineapple
50 g (2 oz) preserved
    papaya, or apricot
50 g (2 oz) glaće cherries
75 g (3 oz) preserved red
    dates
15 ml (1 tablespoon) mixed
    peel
5 ml (1 teaspoon) sugar
15 ml (1 tablespoon)
    Meiguilujiu
    (rose-flavoured Chinese
    spirit), optional

Fills 10 *baozi*
300 g (10 oz) unsalted
    peanuts
150 g (5 oz) icing sugar
60 ml (4 tablespoons)
    melted lard
a pinch of cinnamon

CHINESE MINCEMEAT

An alternative filling to lotus nut paste for sweet baozi *is this version of Chinese mincemeat. Use it with the same quantity of* baozi *dough and shape into round buns as directed in the recipe for Lotus Seed Buns.*

Chop the pork back fat into tiny dice and fry in a dry frying pan over a low heat until the fat begins to run and it turns crisp. Do not let it brown. Drain well. Deep-fry the walnuts over a moderate heat for about 3 minutes until they start to change colour, taking care they do not burn. Lift from the fat and drain well on kitchen paper. Toast the sesame seeds in a dry pan over a moderate heat until they start to turn golden and jump in the pan. Stir them continually to prevent them burning and turn out of the pan as soon as their colour has changed. Chop the fruits and walnuts finely and mix in the pork fat, sesame seeds, sugar and *Meiguilujiu*.

NUT BUNS

Remove the peanut skins then toast them in a dry frying pan until they start to change colour. Put them through a food processor (or liquidizer) until they are finely crushed, then mix with the icing sugar and melted lard. Add cinnamon to taste and use this filling in place of the lotus nut paste in the recipe given on page 108.

PEACH BUNS

Large numbers of sweet cakes throughout China are made from baozi *dough filled with sweet red bean paste, shaped and coloured into the forms of different fruits and animals, such as persimmons, hazelnuts, pears, peaches, fish and hedgehogs. All these buns leave a lot of room for the imagination of both cooks and consumers.*

A typical recipe is to make a basic *baozi* dough according to the recipe given on page 100 and after it has risen divide it into 10 portions and roll out each piece into a circle about 10 cm (4 inches) in diameter. Put 30 ml (2 tablespoons) red bean paste onto each circle of dough, and draw up the dough to close around the filling. Seal tightly, tearing off the excess dough, then roll the buns between your hands into rounds with pointed ends. Press the edge of a wooden spatula from the point to the wide end of the bun to mark the divide of a peach and splatter red food colouring from a brush to colour it. Make two leaves from the excess dough, paint them green before sticking onto the wide end of the bun with egg white. Leave to rise on squares of non-stick parchment before steaming for 20 minutes.

千层糕

Makes 8 slices
5 ml (1 teaspoon) dried
    yeast, *or* 10 g (¼ oz) fresh
    yeast
125 ml (4 fl oz) warm water
100 g (4 oz) caster sugar
275 g (10 oz) plain flour
25 g (1 oz) minced pork back
    fat
1.5 ml (¼ teaspoon) ground
    cinnamon
flour for rolling
15 ml (1 tablespoon) sesame
    oil
mixed peel, split almonds

THOUSAND LAYER CAKE

Put the yeast into a small bowl with the warm water and 5 ml (1 teaspoon) sugar and leave for about 10 minutes until it foams. Then tip it into 225 g (8 oz) of the flour and knead into a smooth dough. Cover with a polythene bag and leave to rise for about 3 hours. Meanwhile, put 50 g (2 oz) flour in a small bowl covered with kitchen foil and steam over fast boiling water for 15 minutes. Lift out and allow to cool before mixing in the minced pork fat, 50 g (2 oz) sugar and the cinnamon. Leave on one side until required. When the dough is well-risen, knead in the remaining 50 g (2 oz) of sugar, then roll out on a well-floured board into a 30-cm (12-inch) square. Sprinkle half of the cinnamon flour over two-thirds of the dough. Fold up one third and then fold the doubled dough over the last third. Press each end to prevent the cinnamon flour falling out and roll out the dough again into a 30-cm (12-inch) square. Sprinkle the remaining cinnamon flour over two-thirds of the dough and repeat the folding operation as above. Roll out once again. This time, brush over with sesame oil. Fold again as before and roll out for a fourth time. Brush over with sesame oil and again fold into thirds. Sprinkle the top with mixed peel and chopped split almonds. Lay the dough on a length of non-stick parchment and stand it in a steamer to rise for 30 minutes. Steam over a high heat for 50 minutes and eat hot.

Unfortunately, this cake does not reheat well in the steamer, but when cool, it can be cut into slices and toasted.

刮巴

10 ml (2 teaspoons) dried
   yeast
5 ml (1 teaspoon) sugar
150 ml ($\frac{1}{4}$ pint) warm water
250 g (9 oz) plain flour
7.5 ml (1$\frac{1}{2}$ teaspoons) baking
   powder
12 g ($\frac{1}{2}$ oz) lard
10 ml (2 teaspoons) sesame
   oil

酸 菜 肉 馅

Fills for 12 buns

250 g (8 oz) skinless,
   boneless belly of pork
1 spring onion
75 g (3 oz) canned pickled
   mustard greens
30 ml (2 tablespoons) oil

SEASONING SAUCE

10 ml (2 teaspoons) rice
   wine
45 ml (3 tablespoons) dark
   soy sauce
200 ml ($\frac{1}{3}$ pint) water
7 g ($\frac{1}{4}$ oz) crystal sugar
pinch of five spice powder

60 ml (4 tablespoons)
   coriander
oil for deep-frying
50 g (2 oz) unsalted peanuts

'CUT BUNS

Cut buns are a family recipe, not usually appearing on restaurant menus. They are useful both as a quick snack and also as a dish in a family meal. There are many different fillings that can be used with these buns, and we give two recipes. The name 'cut' comes from the shape of the buns, which look as if they have been cut in half, although in fact they are made by folding the dough.

Mix the yeast, sugar and water and leave to stand for about 10 minutes until it foams. Meanwhile, sift the flour and baking powder together and rub in the lard. Mix in the yeasted water and knead well. Cover with a cloth, or place the bowl into a polythene bag and leave until the dough has doubled in size – between 2 and 4 hours. Divide the risen dough into 12 portions and roll out each into a circle about 8 cm (3$\frac{1}{4}$ inches) in diameter. Paint the top of each circle with sesame oil, then fold over into a half moon. Put each bun onto a square of non-stick parchment. Leave to rise covered with a damp cloth for 30 minutes, then steam for 20 minutes.

    These buns can be deep-frozen after they have been cooked, and will reheat well straight from the freezer in a steamer – allow about 7 minutes re-steaming time.

PORK AND PICKLED MUSTARD GREENS FILLING FOR 'CUT BUNS'

Cut the belly of pork crossways into 12 thin slices. Chop the spring onion finely. Rinse and slice the pickled mustard greens very thinly. Heat 30 ml (2 tablespoons) of oil in a casserole and stir-fry the onion for 15 seconds until it starts to smell good. Add the pork slices and fry until their colour changes. Pour in the seasoning sauce, cover the casserole and simmer for 30 minutes. Add the mustard greens and cook for another 10 minutes.

    Pick over the coriander and chop the leaves finely. Heat the oil in a deep-fat pan and deep-fry the peanuts for 4 minutes over a moderate heat. Drain well and crush or finely chop in a liquidizer.

    Serve the 'cut buns' straight from the steamer, and the pork on a separate dish. Give each person a small bowl of coriander and crushed peanuts. The bun is filled with the meat, seasoned with coriander and peanuts, and eaten held in the fingers.

Opposite: *Cut Buns with Pork and Pickled Mustard Greens filling (page 112) served with coriander and peanuts*

雪 菜 肉 馅

Fills 12 buns

200 g (7 oz) canned
    red-in-snow
150 g (5 oz) lean pork
2.5 ml (½ teaspoon) sugar
30 ml (2 tablespoons) oil
2 slices fresh ginger
5 ml (1 teaspoon) light soy
    sauce
5 ml (1 teaspoon) rice wine
sugar to taste

PORK AND RED-IN-SNOW FILLING FOR 'CUT BUNS'

Wash and soak the red-in-snow for 5 minutes in cold water, drain well and cut into 1-cm (½-inch) lengths. Cut the pork into very thin shreds. Heat a dry frying pan and stir-fry the red-in-snow *without any oil* with the sugar over a high heat until it is dry, about 3 minutes. Turn it out of the pan and leave on one side. Wash the frying pan and reheat it, add the oil and ginger and stir-fry for 15 seconds, then add the meat and continue to cook for another 30 seconds. Stir in the soy sauce and return the red-in-snow to the pan. Mix well over a high heat, then reduce the heat and season with rice wine and sugar to taste. This recipe can be made in advance and reheated when it is required. Serve the 'cut buns' straight from the steamer, with the pork and red-in-snow on a separate plate. Fill a 'cut bun' with the meat and vegetable and eat it held in the fingers.

闹口笑

Makes 16 balls

280 g (10 oz) plain flour
5 ml (1 teaspoon) baking
    powder
25 g (1 oz) lard, or vegetable
    oil
1 egg, beaten
180 g (6 oz) sugar
45 ml (3 tablespoons) water
45 ml (3 tablespoons)
    sesame seeds
oil for deep-frying

LAUGHING MOUTHS

This sweet fried cake is an old-fashioned snack that is still a favourite with children and adults alike.

Sift the flour and baking powder together and rub in the lard. Add the beaten egg, sugar and water. Mix very well into a smooth dough. Shape into a long roll with your hands and divide into 16 equal pieces. Roll each piece into a ball, dip it in water and then roll it in the sesame seeds. Heat the oil until very hot 190°C (375°F) and drop in the balls. After a few moments, reduce the heat and cook until they have puffed up and cracked. Test to see if they are done by pushing a skewer into the centre of one ball. If it comes out clean, they are cooked. Lift out, drain and serve hot or cold.

Opposite: *Little Red-heads (page 57), Flower Petal Shaomai (page 61) on a plate with Butterfly Shaomai (page 60), and Squid with Black Beans (page 38)*

Chapter 10 | Noodles

面类

The rich and the poor in China have eaten noodles for over fifteen hundred years. Made originally with wheat flour, noodles were both a staple for the peasants and a food served at the imperial palace; they were even part of the daily offerings made by the emperor to his ancestors. A long poem written in the fourth century describes the making of pasta and noodles and the foods that should go with them, while an eighteenth-century court gourmet outlined in detail the kind of stock and delicate seasonings that should be poured over noodles. In more recent times their form has attracted a symbolic significance for long life and lasting relationships and noodles have come to be part of New Year menus as tokens of luck, particularly in overseas Chinese communities.

Noodles made with various flours or combinations of flours come in many different forms. The most usual, and probably the most popular, are made with strong wheat flour, sometimes mixed with other flours, and water. Noodles made from this dough and cut into thin strips with a knife are known as knife-cut noodles: at Yangzhou such noodles have been made for a thousand years, and many other places in China claim equal fame for their noodles. Wheat flour noodles made with egg are said to be southern and particularly Cantonese in origin, although, because they are less brittle when dried, they can now be found in northern China as well. Egg noodles are rolled out and cut in the same manner as plain noodles.

Wheat flour dough that is fermented until it can be pulled out into long thin threads is a very old-fashioned style of noodles. Indeed, they are probably the noodles mentioned in the second century as 'swung-noodles'. Nowadays they are usually called 'pulled noodles'. They have an attractive, slightly resilient texture and are pearly-white in colour. White translucent noodles made in quite a different way come from Shaanxi. For these, the wheat starch and rice flour dough is steamed into a firm paste, almost like a blancmange, then sliced into thin ribbons with an implement like a cheese cutter before being dropped into a well-seasoned soup stock. Other noodles popular with country people in northern China, are made from buckwheat flour. These are dark, slightly peppery-tasting noodles, which are never served in Cantonese restaurants in the West. However, these noodles are very popular in Japan, where they are known as *soba*, and they are served in Japanese restaurants in the West.

Rice noodles, which come from the southern part of China, lack the robustness of the northern wheat flour noodles. Unlike the northern wheat noodles they are not a basic staple to be eaten in place of rice, but are eaten in snack dishes or light one-bowl meals. Noodles are also made from mung bean flour, but these dried noodles are considered to be a vegetable, not a grain food, and so are never eaten as a filler with other foods.

In Chinese cuisine noodles can be eaten in many different ways. They may be served in place of rice in northern family meals, although now people must queue to buy ready-made egg noodles in Beijing. They are often eaten as a snack meal in street restaurants or small noodle houses, as well as in state restaurants, where they are considered to be food for the very poor. In an old people's home near Beijing noodles were one of the dishes listed on the weekly menu, while at the other end of the eating spectrum, noodles are often eaten in Hong Kong at the end of a smart dimsum meal as a 'filler'. Soup noodles are a very popular late night snack everywhere.

In the West dried egg noodles – from China or Italy – are easily bought, but since fresh noodles are not difficult to make, particularly with the pasta machines now widely available, and since they taste much better than dried noodles, we have included a few recipes for the kinds of noodles it is possible to make at home. The remaining recipes in this chapter are for dishes using home-made or bought noodles. Generally speaking, any kind of noodle can be used for any kind of noodle dish, but it is usual to use flat noodles for soups and round noodles for frying.

Appetites for noodles vary greatly, as does the difference in weight between fresh and dry noodles. Some people in the West are content with a 75 g (3 oz) helping of dry noodles, while others prefer 125 g (4 oz). Therefore the helpings of noodles in this chapter are given as 500 g (1 lb) dry noodles allowing 125 g (4 oz) per person and 650 g (1 lb 5 oz) fresh noodles allowing nearly 160 g (nearly 6 oz) per person. However, this can be reduced to 350 g (12 oz) of dry noodles or 500 g (1 lb) fresh noodles if desired with no other alteration to the recipes.

愛面

Serves 4–6
450 g (1 lb) strong flour
pinch of salt
2 large eggs (size 2)
100 ml (3½ fl oz) cold water
flour for dusting
10 ml (2 teaspoons) sesame
  oil

FRESH EGG NOODLES

Mix the flour and salt and break the eggs into the flour. Using your hands, gradually work in the egg until the flour resembles the finest oatmeal. Add the cold water and continue kneading and squeezing the dough until it has all stuck together and the bowl is clean. If the flour is very dry and takes up a lot of water, it may be necessary to add another 5–10 ml (1–2 teaspoons) of cold water – but only enough to hold the dough together. Wrap the dough ball in cling film and leave for 30 minutes, before rolling it out into a square about 5 mm (¼ inch) thick on an unfloured board. Fold the square in half and continue rolling and folding until the dough looks velvety with no grain. Finally, roll out the dough to a square about 4 mm (⅙ inch) thick and dust liberally with flour. Fold into thirds and roll out again to 4 mm (⅙ inch) thick. Flour again and fold in half so that the two previous folded edges are together. Using a sharp knife, cut the dough across the folds into strips approximately 3 mm (⅛ inch) wide. Shake the noodles out into lengths, and if necessary, toss in a bowl of flour to keep them separate.

Have ready a large pan of slightly salted boiling water, drop in the noodles and boil until they rise to the surface – about 5 minutes. Lift out, drain and toss in 10 ml (2 teaspoons) of sesame oil. Use as directed.

These noodles can be stored uncooked in the refrigerator for about 24 hours, or they can be deep-frozen. Dry well before freezing by spreading them out, or hanging them up. To cook after freezing, drop them still frozen into boiling water.

A pasta machine makes the whole business of rolling out noodles a great deal easier. Make the dough as directed above and after it has stood for 30 minutes, roll it out until the dough is smooth before putting it through the machine.

Fold rolled dough into thirds.

Cut folded dough in thin shreds.

伊府面

YIFU NOODLES

These noodles are said to have been invented by Yi Bingshou after he retired from palace service to his native Fujian, where he set up a restaurant. These noodles have been taken by Fujian emigrants to many parts of Southeast Asia.

Serves 4–6
500 g (1 lb) dried round egg
   noodles (bought)
salt
clean oil for deep-frying,
   preferably peanut oil

Boil the noodles until soft in lightly salted boiling water, then drain them thoroughly. Divide into 4 equal portions. Heat the oil and deep-fry each portion separately until they are lightly coloured, then drain well before serving either as soup noodles or with a sauce.

拉面

PULLED NOODLES – LAMIAN

In the fifth century noodles were made by mixing flour with meat juices into a dough which was then shaped into thin strips about the size of chopsticks. These were stood in a bain-marie until they had ripened enough to be able to be pulled out into long thin ribbons. Then they were cooked in boiling water. Today professional noodle makers still ferment a dough, now made from flour, egg and water, until it can be pulled out into a skein of noodles like old fashioned knitting wool. They take a lump of dough, the amount for one helping of noodles, and continually banging it into the flour on the table in front of them, pull it out between their hands until it is about a metre (3 feet) long. Then folding it in half, they pull it out again, banging it in the flour as they work. They continue pulling, banging the dough onto the flour and doubling it until the original lump of dough is divided into thin strings. Their skill lies in keeping so many threads of dough separate and unbroken and in the speed with which they work. When the noodles are thin enough, the two ends where they have been held are torn off and the noodles are dropped into boiling water. The noodles are freshly pulled as they are needed, the whole pulling process only taking a few minutes.

We have suggested a less ambitious, if slower, method of pulling noodles in this recipe, but of course there is no reason why you should not try the traditional method. If you do use this method, omit the rolling out of the dough and just divide it into four portions before starting to pull. Also make sure that you have a lot of flour on the table in front of you to keep the threads of dough well-dusted. It is important to have the sauce or soup for the noodles already prepared before you start pulling and cooking the noodles, whichever method you are employing, since once you have started, there is no time to break off and make the sauce.

Serves 4–6
450 g (1 lb) strong flour
1 egg (size 4)
220 ml (7½ fl oz) warm water
7.5 ml (1½ teaspoons) lye
   water
flour for rolling
15 ml (1 tablespoon) sesame
   oil

荞麦面

Mix the flour, egg and water together and knead into a soft smooth dough. Put the dough into a bowl and cover it with a wet cloth. Then put the bowl and wet cloth into a large plastic bag and leave to develop for 24 hours in a warm place – around 27°–30°C (80°–90°F) is ideal. When the dough tears into threads or fine strands, it is ready. Mix in the lye water to remove the strong smell of fermentation and knead the dough on a well-floured board until it is no longer sticky. Then roll it out into a rectangle about 20 cm (8 inches) wide and 5 mm (¼ inch) thick. Cut into 4 long strips each about 5 cm (2 inches) wide. Cut each strip into pieces about 1 cm (½ inch) wide and 5 cm (2 inches) long. Have ready a large pan of boiling water and either a pair of chopsticks or a slotted spoon, together with a large warm bowl containing the sesame oil. Take one strip of the dough and pull it out until it is a ribbon about 1 metre (3 feet) long, then drop it quickly into the boiling water. Continue pulling and dropping in the noodles until the dough is finished (this process may take 30 minutes), but take care in the meantime to lift out the noodles from the water as they rise to the top. They take about 3 minutes to cook. Drain them quickly and put them into the warm bowl with the sesame oil.

BUCKWHEAT NOODLES

Buckwheat noodles are a country people's food in northern China. They are usually eaten in a simple soup with only a little vegetable or onion as additional flavouring. Buck-wheat flour for making fresh noodles can be bought from health food shops as can the ready-made dried buckwheat noodles from Japan.

There is a Chinese tale about buckwheat and a magic fox. A poor student was drinking wine one night when a fox joined him. They drank and made merry, and when the fox came to leave, he thanked his host and said he would be back the following night. So the next day the student bought more wine and the fox came and they drank and had a very good time. Then the fox said 'You've had a lot of expense with me drinking with you, but dig under the floor of your hut and you will find a crock of gold buried there many generations ago.' The student found the gold and he and the fox continued their evenings together. Then one day the fox said that the student should buy up all the buckwheat in the market. The student bought it at a very low price and afterwards there was a drought and he became rich selling the buckwheat. He bought land and became a farmer, but he always consulted the fox before he planted any crop and in the succeeding years he became very wealthy. Finally the farmer died and the fox never visited the family again.

Serves 4
180 g (6 oz) buckwheat flour
180 g (6 oz) strong white
   flour
180 ml (6 fl oz) hot water
flour for rolling

Mix the two flours in a bowl and make a well in the centre. Pour in the hot water and mix to a dough. It should be soft and cohesive, but not in the least bit sticky. If necessary, add another 5 ml (1 teaspoon) water. Knead the dough very vigorously until it is smooth and will bend without cracking or crumbling, then leave it covered for about 30 minutes for the gluten to develop. Divide the dough into two equal portions and, on a well-floured board, roll out one portion into a rectangle about 2 mm ($\frac{1}{10}$ inch) thick. Dust the dough very liberally with the flour and fold into thirds. Dust again and put the two folded edges together so that there are six thicknesses of dough. Using a sharp knife, cut the dough into narrow strips about 3 mm ($\frac{1}{8}$ inch) wide. Shake very gently to unwind the noodles and spread out while making the other half. Bring a large pan of water to the boil and lift from the heat while you slide in the noodles. Return to the heat and as soon as the water boils again, pour in about 150 ml ($\frac{1}{4}$ pint) of cold water. Repeat the boiling and cooling with cold water two or three times until the noodles are cooked – 6 to 7 minutes in all. They should be firm but not hard in the centre: take care not to overcook them. Drain and rinse quickly under cold water before returning to the hot pan. Use as required.

A pasta-maker can be used to cut the well-floured flat sheets of dough into noodles but the initial rolling must be done on a board with a rolling pin.

These noodles cannot be deep-frozen, but they will keep for about 48 hours, uncooked, in the refrigerator.

湯面

SOUP NOODLES

The most usual way to cook noodles in China is in soup. Soup noodles are eaten as light meals or snacks at any time of the day or night. You can use either fresh or dried flat egg noodles, plain noodles (those made without egg) or pulled noodles for soup. Basically, given a good stock, you can use almost any favourite stir-fried dish with noodles in a soup. Stir-fries that are a little sharp or sour in flavour, such as those that include pickled mustard greens or red-in-snow, are particularly good with soup noodles. Soup-noodle dishes in China are generally 'below the level' of written recipes, since most people make the accompaniment for soup noodles from whatever they have to hand at the time, but in the following section we have given a few representative recipes.

120

家常湯面

Serves 4

250 g (8 oz) pork
15 ml (1 tablespoon) rice
  wine
25 g (1 oz) fresh ginger
75 g (3 oz) raw prawns
250 g (8 oz) green
  vegetables: a mixture as
  available of snow peas,
  French beans, *choisam*,
  spinach and watercress
500 g (1 lb) dried flat egg
  noodles, or use fresh
  noodles (see page 116) or
  Lamian (pulled noodles)
  (see page 117)
1½ litres (2½ pints) good stock
salt and pepper to taste

雪里红虾仁面

Serves 4

180 g (6 oz) shelled pink
  prawns

MARINADE

10 ml (2 teaspoons) egg
  white
2.5 ml (½ teaspoon) rice wine
5 ml (1 teaspoon) cornflour
1.5 ml (¼ teaspoon) salt

200 g (7 oz) red-in-snow
15 ml (1 tablespoon) oil
15 ml (1 tablespoon) rice
  wine
1 litre (1¾ pints) lightly
  seasoned chicken stock
500 g (1 lb) egg noodles
15 ml (1 tablespoon) soy
  sauce
15 ml (1 tablespoon) sesame
  oil

FAMILY SOUP NOODLES

Cut the pork into thin slices and marinate it with the rice wine and 5 ml (1 teaspoon) grated ginger for 30 minutes. Shell the prawns and de-vein. Tear the leaf vegetables into 5-cm (2-inch) squares and cut the peas and beans into 2.5-cm (1-inch) lengths. Put the noodles into a large saucepan with lightly salted boiling water and 3 slices of ginger. Boil until cooked – about 4 minutes – then drain and put into fresh hot water to wait until they are required. In a small saucepan, place the pork and prawns with 150 ml (¼ pint) of the stock, and bring to the boil. When it boils, skim off the scum that rises to the top. Meanwhile, in a third pan pour in the remaining stock, add the vegetables and the rest of the ginger cut into thin slices, and bring to the boil. When the scum has stopped rising from the meat and prawns, add the contents of the pan to the stock and vegetables. Simmer for another 2 minutes before checking the seasoning. Drain the noodles and divide them between 4 large bowls. Ladle the soup over the noodles, and serve at once.

If you like a hot seasoning, you can serve a small dish of chilli sauce as a dip to go with soup noodles.

To serve *lamian*, finish making the soup completely and keep it warm while you make the noodles. When all the noodles are cooked, divide them between 4 large warmed bowls and ladle the hot soup over the noodles.

SOUP NOODLES WITH PRAWNS AND RED-IN-SNOW

Marinate the prawns for 20 minutes. Rinse the red-in-snow well, drain and cut into 1-cm (½-inch) lengths. Heat a wok or pan with the oil and stir-fry the red-in-snow over a moderate heat. After a minute add the prawns, rice wine and chicken stock and leave to simmer. Boil a large pan of water and cook the noodles. Meanwhile, mix the soy sauce and sesame oil and divide it among 4 preheated soup bowls. When the noodles are soft, drain them and put them into the soup bowls. Ladle the soup, prawns and red-in-snow over the top and serve.

榨菜 肉絲 湯面

Serves 4
300 g (10 oz) pork
2.5 cm (1 inch) Sichuan
    preserved vegetable
5 spring onions
2 slices fresh ginger
60 ml (4 tablespoons) oil

30 ml (2 tablespoons) soy
    sauce
2.5 ml (½ teaspoon) sugar
black pepper
25 ml (5 teaspoons) sesame
    oil
5 ml (1 teaspoon) potato
    flour
75 ml (5 tablespoons) water
4 small hearts of Chinese
    leaves, *or* 2 leaves of cos
    lettuce
500 g (1 lb) flat noodles

1.2 litres (2 pints) boiling
    unsalted stock

NOODLE SOUP WITH PORK AND SICHUAN VEGETABLE

Cut the pork into matchstick shreds. Slice the Sichuan vegetable finely and cut the slices into thin shreds. Chop the spring onions finely and cut the ginger slices into thin shreds. Heat 45 ml (3 tablespoons) oil in a wok or frying pan and stir-fry the pork for about 2 minutes until it has all changed colour. Lift out the pork with a slotted spoon and put on one side while you reheat the pan and add another tablespoon of oil. Stir-fry half the spring onions and the ginger for 15 seconds, then add the Sichuan vegetable and 10 ml (2 teaspoons) soy sauce together with the sugar, a pinch of black pepper and 5 ml (1 teaspoon) sesame oil. Mix the potato flour with the water and tip it in. Stir well to clean the bottom of the pan, and when it is boiling, return the pork. Leave on a very low heat until required. Blanch the Chinese leaves or cos lettuce in boiling water for 2 minutes, then refresh under cold water. Drain well. Boil a large pan of lightly salted water and cook the noodles until they are just soft – about 4 minutes, depending on variety, then drain. Divide the remaining spring onions, sesame oil and a pinch of black pepper between 4 warm soup bowls. Pour in the boiling stock and add the drained noodles. Put the blanched Chinese leaves on top of the noodles and finally spoon over the pork and its sauce. Serve at once.

过 橋 面

Serves 4
250 g (8 oz) fillet of beef, cut
    into thin matchsticks
250 g (8 oz) calf's liver, cut
    into thin matchsticks
100 g (4 oz) green leaf
    vegetable, such as spinach
1.8 litres (3 pints) fresh rich
    chicken stock,
    well-seasoned and
    unskimmed
500 g (1 lb) flat egg noodles

'CROSSING THE BRIDGE' NOODLES

Fillet of beef and calf's liver are used for this dish because they require a very limited cooking time.

Prepare the meats. Wash and tear the vegetables into 5-cm (2-inch) pieces. Boil the stock. Cook the noodles in boiling water until soft, then drain and keep hot. Have ready a large heated soup bowl. Put the meat and liver shreds in the bottom, pour over the boiling stock, stir for a few seconds and add the vegetables and hot noodles. Stir again and allow each diner to help himself from the big bowl to his individual bowl – so crossing the bridge. The fat in the stock is absorbed by the noodles.

三鮮湯面

Serves 4

350 g (12 oz) fillet of
    haddock or other white
    fish

MARINADE

30 ml (2 tablespoons) egg
    white
15 ml (1 tablespoon)
    cornflour
pinch of salt

oil for deep-frying
4 dried mushrooms
15 ml (1 tablespoon) oil
20 ml (4 teaspoons) chilli
    bean paste (use half the
    quantity for a milder dish)
1.8 litres (3 pints) good stock
15 g (½ oz) fresh ginger,
    crushed
50 g (2 oz) bamboo shoots
50 g (2 oz) raw prawns,
    shelled
15 ml (1 tablespoon) rice
    wine
15 ml (1 tablespoon) soy
    sauce
salt and pepper to taste
15 ml (1 tablespoon)
    cornflour *mixed with*
30 ml (2 tablespoons) water
500 g (1 lb) flat dried
    noodles, or fresh noodles
    (see page 116)
25 ml (1½ tablespoons) finely
    chopped spring onions
50 g (2 oz) spinach or
    choisam, torn into small
    pieces
20 ml (4 teaspoons) red
    vinegar

FISH AND NOODLE SOUP

Skin and cut the fish into small pieces about 2.5 cm (1 inch) square. Marinate the fish for 20 minutes, then deep-fry it in hot oil until it changes colour. Drain well and leave on one side. Soak the dried mushrooms in warm water for 30 minutes. Heat a large saucepan with 15 ml (1 tablespoon) of oil and over a very low heat, gently warm the chilli bean paste. Add the stock and the piece of crushed ginger and simmer gently over a low heat for 30 minutes. Then strain and pour the stock into a clean pan. Drain the mushrooms, discard the hard stalks and cut the caps into quarters. Cut the bamboo shoots into slices. De-vein the prawns and cut them in halves. Put the mushrooms, bamboo shoots and prawns into the prepared stock and simmer for 10 minutes before adding the fish, rice wine and soy sauce. Bring back to the boil, adjust the seasoning with salt and pepper and thicken with the cornflour paste. Boil a large pan of lightly salted water and cook the noodles until they are just soft. Have a large, warmed soup bowl ready with the chopped onion, green vegetable and vinegar in the bottom. Pour in half the boiling soup, then the drained noodles and finally pour over the remaining half of the soup. Serve at once.

羊肉湯面

Serves 4

300 g (10 oz) boneless lamb
15 ml (1 tablespoon) rice
  wine
2 spring onions
3 slices fresh ginger
2 garlic cloves
15 ml (1 tablespoon) soy
  sauce
1 dried chilli
50 g (2 oz) pickled mustard
  greens, canned
15 g (½ oz) fresh chillis
25 g (1 oz) garlic shoots (see
  page 17)
30 ml (2 tablespoons) oil

SEASONING SAUCE

30 ml (2 tablespoons) soy
  sauce
30 ml (2 tablespoons) rice
  wine
10 ml (2 teaspoons) black
  vinegar

500 g (1 lb) flat dried
  noodles, or fresh noodles
  (see page 116)
20 ml (4 teaspoons) finely
  chopped spring onions
1.2 litres (2 pints) lightly
  seasoned boiling stock
30 ml (2 tablespoons)
  chopped coriander

SOUP NOODLES WITH HOT AND SOUR LAMB

Cut the lamb into 2.5-cm (1-inch) pieces and put them with the rice wine, spring onions, ginger, garlic, soy sauce and dried chilli into a saucepan. Cover the meat with water, bring to the boil, then cover the pan and leave over a low heat to simmer for about 1 hour. (Most of the liquid should evaporate.) Meanwhile, rinse the pickled mustard greens and cut them into thin slices, shred the fresh chillis and cut the garlic shoots into short lengths. Heat the oil in a wok or frying pan and stir-fry the mustard greens, chillis and garlic shoots for about 2 minutes until they are soft, then add the seasoning sauce and mix well. When the lamb is cooked, add the stir-fried vegetables and sauce and leave over a very low heat until required. Cook the noodles in lightly salted boiling water until they are just soft, then drain well. Divide the chopped spring onions among 4 heated soup bowls. Pour in the boiling stock, add the noodles, spoon over the lamb with the sauce and vegetables, and garnish with chopped coriander before serving.

云吞面

Serves 4

24 *wuntun* (see page 63)
100 g (4 oz) green vegetable,
  choisam, spinach, or
  lettuce
1.2 litres (2 pints) good
  well-seasoned stock
10 ml (2 teaspoons) rice
  wine
500 g (1 lb) flat noodles

WUNTUN AND NOODLE SOUP

Have the filled *wuntun* ready and the green vegetable washed and trimmed. Prepare the soup by boiling the stock with the rice wine. In a separate pan boil the noodles until they are just cooked and leave in the hot water until required. Add the green vegetable and *wuntun* to the stock and boil gently until the *wuntun* rise to the surface, about 3 minutes. Drain and divide the noodles among 4 soup bowls and ladle over the stock and *wuntun*. Serve at once.

124

四川牛肉面

Serves 4

300 g (10 oz) lean beef shin
30 ml (2 tablespoons) dark
  soy sauce
30 ml (2 tablespoons) rice
  wine
7.5 ml (1½ teaspoons) chilli
  bean paste
2 garlic cloves, sliced
2 spring onions
2 slices fresh ginger
2 petals star anise
1.5 ml (¼ teaspoon) Sichuan
  pepper, ground
50 g (2 oz) green leaf
  vegetable, spinach,
  choisam or lettuce
500 g (1 lb) flat dried
  noodles, or fresh noodles
  (see page 116)
20 ml (4 teaspoons) finely
  chopped spring onions
1.2 litres (2 pints)
  well-seasoned boiling
  stock
pinch of black pepper

猫耳面

Serves 4
NOODLES
180 g (6 oz) strong flour
180 g (6 oz) plain flour
200 ml (7 fl oz) cold water

FOR THE SOUP
300 g (10 oz) boneless
  chicken or pork loin
500 g (1 lb) Chinese leaves
1.8 litres (3 pints)
  well-seasoned stock
15 ml (1 tablespoon) sesame
  oil
15 ml (1 tablespoon) finely
  chopped spring onion

NOODLE SOUP WITH SICHUAN SPICED BEEF

Cut the beef into 2.5-cm (1-inch) cubes and put it into a saucepan with the soy sauce, rice wine, chilli bean paste, garlic, spring onions, ginger and star anise. Add enough water to cover the meat, cover the pan and bring to the boil. Reduce the heat and simmer between 1½ and 2 hours. Towards the end of the cooking time, watch to make sure it does not burn, for there should be very little liquid left. Meanwhile, blanch the green vegetables in boiling water for about 2 minutes, then dip into cold water to refresh. Drain well and keep on one side. Just before the stew is finished cooking, put the noodles into lightly salted boiling water and boil until they are just soft. Drain well. To serve this soup, have ready 4 warmed soup bowls with a teaspoonful of finely chopped spring onions in each. Pour in the boiling stock, then add the drained noodles. Arrange a little green vegetable in each bowl and spoon over the beef and its remaining sauce. Finally dust with a little black pepper and serve at once.

'CATS' EARS' NOODLES

Mix the flours together in a bowl, pour in the water and work into a smooth dough. Leave covered with a damp cloth to rest for an hour. Meanwhile prepare the soup by cutting the meat into very thin slices about 2.5 cm (1 inch) square. Wash and tear the Chinese leaves into 5-cm (2-inch) pieces. Boil the stock in a large pan and check the seasoning; it should be slightly salty because the noodles have no seasoning. Drop in the meat and Chinese leaves, and boil gently for 5 minutes. Put on one side.

Roll out the dough into a long strip and cut into 6 lengths, each about 1 cm (½ inch) wide. Bring a large pan of water to the boil and from one length of dough at a time, tear off tiny pieces – about 1 cm (½ inch) long – and drop them into the boiling water. Continue to tear off the fragments until all the dough is used. At the same time skim off the cooked 'cats' ears' with a slotted spoon as they rise to the surface. Drain the noodles and put into a large, heated serving bowl. Bring the soup to the boil again and pour it over the noodles. Add the sesame oil and spring onion and serve immediately.

家常炒面

Serves 4
100 g (4 oz) boneless
chicken

CHICKEN MARINADE
5 ml (1 teaspoon) rice wine
5 ml (1 teaspoon) cornflour
or potato flour
pinch of salt

4 dried mushrooms
150 g (5 oz) raw prawns

PRAWN MARINADE
5 ml (1 teaspoon) rice wine
5 ml (1 teaspoon) cornflour
or potato flour

50 g (2 oz) green vegetables
(use whatever is available
– choisam, snow peas,
spinach, watercress etc.)
500 g (1 lb) round thin dried
egg noodles
150 ml (5 fl oz) oil
2 slices fresh ginger, finely
chopped
2 spring onions, finely
chopped
45 ml (3 tablespoons) soy
sauce
2.5 ml (½ teaspoon) sugar
5 ml (1 teaspoon) salt
salt and pepper to taste
thickening paste made with
45 ml (3 tablespoons)
potato flour and 45 ml
(3 tablespoons) water

FRIED NOODLES, CHAOMIAN

Fried noodles, made with round egg noodles, are a southern Chinese dish. There are numerous recipes, usually including a selection of pork, chicken, prawns, chahsiu, pig's tripe, squid, dried shrimps and ham together with dried mushrooms, bean sprouts, choisam and other green vegetables. At the most basic level, as in soup noodles, whatever is in the larder can be used to make fried noodles. The noodles themselves are first boiled, then slowly shallow-fried in oil before being served with various stir-fried ingredients mixed into a generous quantity of thickened sauce. We give here one recipe for fried noodles followed by a recipe for 'chop suey', which is not itself a Chinese dish, but a Western adaptation based on Chinese noodle dishes. However, since it is good to eat and so often appears in overseas Chinese menus, we have included a recipe for it.

Cut the chicken into strips about 2.5 × 1 cm (1 × ½ inch), and marinate for 30 minutes. Meanwhile, soak the dried mushrooms in warm water for 30 minutes, then discard the hard stalks and slice the caps. Shell the prawns and de-vein. Marinate them for 20 minutes. Cut the green vegetables into 5-cm (2-inch) lengths. Cook the noodles in boiling water until they have just separated, about 2 to 3 minutes, then drain well. Heat a wok, or large frying pan with 100 ml (3½ fl oz) of the oil and put in the noodles. Keep the pan moving over a moderate heat until the noodles are lightly browned at the bottom, then turn them over and leave them over a low heat to continue cooking. This should take a long time – about 10 minutes – if necessary, add a little more oil to prevent them sticking.

Heat another pan with 45 ml (3 tablespoons) of oil and stir-fry the ginger and spring onions for about 15 seconds. Then add the sliced mushrooms and continue stir-frying over a high heat for another 15 seconds. Add the chicken, and afterwards the prawns and green vegetable and stir-fry for another minute before stirring in the soy sauce, sugar and salt. Pour in 800 ml (1⅓ pints) of water, mix well and bring to the boil. Boil for about 5 minutes, stir in the thickening paste and check the seasoning. Divide the fried noodles among 4 heated plates and spoon the sauce over them. Serve at once.

竹錦炒面

Serves 4

100 g (4 oz) boneless
  chicken

CHICKEN MARINADE

10 ml (2 teaspoons) egg
  white
5 ml (1 teaspoon) cornflour
pinch of salt

75 g (3 oz) lean pork

PORK MARINADE

5 ml (1 teaspoon) light soy
  sauce
2.5 ml ($\frac{1}{2}$ teaspoon) rice wine
2.5 ml ($\frac{1}{2}$ teaspoon)
  cornflour

75 g (3 oz) pink prawns

PRAWN MARINADE

10 ml (2 teaspoons) egg
  white
5 ml (1 teaspoon) cornflour
pinch of salt

25 g (1 oz) raw ham or lean
  bacon
4 dried mushrooms
150 g (5 oz) bean sprouts
2 spring onions
45 ml (3 tablespoons) oil
15 ml (1 tablespoon) rice
  wine
150 ml ($\frac{1}{4}$ pint) good stock
salt and pepper to taste
500 g (1 lb) *yifu* noodles,
  freshly deep-fried (see
  page 117)

'CHOP-SUEY'

Cut the chicken into matchstick strips and marinate for 30 minutes. Cut the pork into matchstick strips and marinate for 30 minutes. Marinate the prawns for 20 minutes. Cut the ham into thin shreds. Soak the dried mushrooms in hot water for 30 minutes, then discard the hard stalks and cut the caps into thin slices. Wash and trim the bean sprouts, blanch in boiling water for 30 seconds, refresh in cold water and drain well. Set aside. Cut the spring onions into 5-mm ($\frac{1}{4}$-inch) lengths. Heat the oil in a wok or very large frying pan and stir-fry the spring onions for 15 seconds, add the mushrooms and fry for another 15 seconds before putting in the meat and prawns. Stir-fry together for about 2 minutes until all the meat has changed colour, then pour in the rice wine and stock. Bring to the boil and add the bean sprouts. Mix well, boil for another minute, and check the seasoning. Arrange a portion of *yifu* noodles on each plate and spoon the meat and vegetables over the noodles. Serve at once.

SAUCES FOR NOODLES

Not all boiled noodles are eaten in soups. They may be mixed with a meat or other highly-flavoured sauce and served either hot or cold. In this section we give a wide variety of different sauces that can be served with either egg noodles or lamian.

Serves 4

40 ml (2½ tablespoons)
vegetable oil and
40 ml (2½ tablespoons)
sesame oil
or 75 ml (5 tablespoons)
peanut oil
15 ml (1 tablespoon) grated
fresh ginger
30 ml (2 tablespoons) finely
chopped spring onion
30 ml (2 tablespoons) light
soy sauce
2.5 ml (½ teaspoon) salt
egg noodles (see page 116)

炸醬面

Serves 4

300 g (10 oz) chicken

MARINADE

15 ml (1 tablespoon) rice
wine
15 ml (1 tablespoon) potato
flour or cornflour
15 ml (1 tablespoon) water
15 ml (1 tablespoon) light
soy sauce
50 g (2 oz) onion
half a cucumber
250 g (8 oz) bean sprouts
30 ml (2 tablespoons) oil

SEASONING SAUCE

4 garlic cloves, crushed
30 ml (2 tablespoons) rice
wine
45 ml (3 tablespoons) soy
sauce
60 ml (4 tablespoons)
barbecue sauce
30 ml (2 tablespoons)
fermented black beans,
crushed
200 ml (⅓ pint) water

egg noodles (see page 116)

FAMILY NOODLES

*This is a very simple domestic recipe, not a dish that would
be served in a restaurant. You can use it in place of rice at an
ordinary family meal, or as a light meal or snack together
with a stir-fried dish or as a 'filler' with a few simple dimsum.*

Heat the oils until very hot and quickly pour them over the
ginger and spring onion so that they sizzle. Mix in the soy
sauce and salt. Boil the noodles as directed on page 116. As
soon as they are drained, toss them in the seasoned oil. Serve
at once.

BARBECUE SAUCE FOR NOODLES

Cut the chicken into small dice and marinate it for 30
minutes. Meanwhile, chop the onion finely, and shred the
cucumber on the coarse side of a grater. Wash and pick over
the bean sprouts, then blanch them in fast boiling water for
30 seconds. Then immediately dip them in cold water to
cool and leave to drain. Heat the oil in a wok or frying pan,
stir-fry the onion for about 30 seconds, add the diced
chicken and continue cooking for another 2 minutes. Pour
in the seasoning sauce and mix well to clean the bottom of
the pan. Bring to the boil and simmer for 15 minutes. Have
the hot boiled noodles ready. Place a portion of noodles into
each plate, divide the cucumber and bean sprouts among
them, pour over the boiling sauce and serve at once.

担担面

Serves 4

SAUCE

30 ml (2 tablespoons) chilli oil

60 ml (4 tablespoons) light soy sauce

40 ml (2½ tablespoons) sesame oil

30 ml (2 tablespoons) finely chopped spring onion

30 ml (2 tablespoons) sesame paste

15 ml (1 tablespoon) black vinegar

egg noodles (see page 116)

DANDANMIAN – CARRY-POLE NOODLES

The name of this recipe comes from the pole carried across the shoulders of the hawkers who sold these noodles in the streets and markets of western China. They carried a pot of sauce, a box of noodles, serving bowls and a small stove, all hanging from the ends of their pole. When they had a customer, they would boil a helping of noodles over the stove and serve them drained and hot with a spoonful or two of the cold sauce.

Mix the sauce ingredients together. Then boil the noodles. As soon as they are drained, mix in the cold sauce and serve at once.

羊肉酱面

Serves 4

2 leg lamb chops, weighing about 450 g (1 lb)

40 g (1½ oz) fresh ginger in one piece, crushed

25 g (1 oz) dried red dates

2.5-cm (1-inch) cinnamon stick

1.5 ml (¼ teaspoon) fennel seeds

25 g (1 oz) crystal sugar

45 ml (3 tablespoons) dark soy sauce

15 ml (1 tablespoon) rice wine

500 g (1 lb) dried round egg noodles or *lamian* (see page 117)

15 ml (1 tablespoon) sesame oil

15 ml (1 tablespoon) finely chopped spring onions

SOYA LAMB SAUCE FOR NOODLES

This recipe is said to come from Hangjia Lake in Zhejiang, where the fattened lambs or goats that are used for this dish are sold in the markets only at the time of the autumn festival.

Cut the lamb into 4 equal portions, removing the bones. Put them into a saucepan with the ginger, red dates, cinnamon stick and 900 ml (1½ pints) of water and bring to the boil. Skim off the scum that rises and add the fennel, sugar, soy sauce and rice wine. Cover tightly with a lid and simmer over a low heat for about 1 hour, after which the liquid should be reduced to about one quarter. Cook the noodles in boiling water until they are soft, then drain them and toss in the sesame oil and chopped spring onion. Divide among 4 heated plates. Arrange a slice of lamb over each plate of noodles, strain the sauce, pour over and serve.

Opposite: *Steamed Pork Baozi (page 102) and fried White Radish and Pork Pies (page 69)*

棒棒煨汁伴面

Serves 4

egg noodles (see page 116)
30 ml (2 tablespoons) oil
350 g (12 oz) cooked
  chicken
200 g (7 oz) bean sprouts
150 g (5 oz) snow peas, or
  French beans
3 garlic cloves

SEASONING SAUCE

90 ml (6 tablespoons)
  sesame paste
90 ml (6 tablespoons) light
  soy sauce
40 ml (1½ tablespoons) sugar
10 ml (2 teaspoons) sesame
  oil
40 ml (1½ tablespoons) red
  vinegar
75 ml (5 tablespoons) chilli
  oil
30 ml (2 tablespoons) finely
  chopped spring onions
30 ml (2 tablespoons) grated
  fresh ginger

椒麻汁伴面

Serves 4

7.5 ml (1½ teaspoons)
  sesame seeds
70 ml (4½ tablespoons) chilli
  oil
60 ml (4 tablespoons)
  sesame paste
90 ml (6 tablespoons) dark
  soy sauce
10 ml (2 teaspoons) sesame
  oil
2.5 ml (½ teaspoon) sugar
90 ml (6 tablespoons) red
  vinegar
7.5 ml (1½ teaspoons)
  crushed garlic
15 ml (1 tablespoon) finely
  chopped spring onion
pinch of cayenne pepper

egg noodles (see page 116)
30 ml (2 tablespoons) oil

COLD NOODLES WITH A CHICKEN AND SESAME SAUCE

Boil the noodles as directed on page 116 until they are soft. Drain well. While they are still hot, toss them in the oil and leave to cool. Tear the cooked chicken into thin shreds. Wash and pick over the bean sprouts before blanching them in boiling water for 2 minutes. Drain well. Trim the snow peas and cook in boiling, lightly salted water for 4 minutes. Drain them well. Crush the garlic and mix the seasoning sauce. Toss the chicken with the vegetables and garlic. Divide the cold noodles among 4 plates and put a portion of the chicken and vegetables on top of each. Pour over the seasoning sauce and serve.

A CHILLI SAUCE FOR COLD NOODLES

Serve cold noodles and chilli sauce with other small dishes, such as beef cooked in soy sauce, served either hot or cold, a vinegar-dressed cucumber salad and a soup to make a light lunch.

Toast the sesame seeds in a dry pan over a moderate heat until they start to turn golden brown and dance. Stir all the time to prevent them burning and immediately tip them out onto a board and crush them with a rolling pin. Mix the crushed sesame seeds with the rest of the sauce ingredients into a smooth paste. Boil the noodles as directed on page 116. When they are cooked, drain well and toss in the oil before putting on one side to cool. When the noodles are cold, mix with the chilli sauce and serve.

Opposite: *Singapore Noodles (page 130)*

米粉

星加坡炒米粉

Serves 4

250 g (8 oz) lean boneless
   pork*, cut into matchstick
   shreds

PORK MARINADE

10 ml (2 teaspoons) soy
   sauce
10 ml (2 teaspoons) rice
   wine
2.5 ml ($\frac{1}{2}$ teaspoon) sugar
10 ml (2 teaspoons) potato
   flour or cornflour

150 g (5 oz) pink prawns

PRAWN MARINADE

half an egg white
2.5 ml ($\frac{1}{2}$ teaspoon) rice wine
5 ml (1 teaspoon) cornflour
1.5 ml ($\frac{1}{4}$ teaspoon) salt

350 g (12 oz) dried rice
   noodles
1 egg + remaining yolk and
   half white
4 fresh chillis
1 green pepper
50 g (2 oz) bamboo shoots
4 spring onions
60 ml (4 tablespoons) oil
4 slices fresh ginger
salt and pepper to taste
5 ml (1 teaspoon) curry
   powder
10 ml (2 teaspoons)
   shachajiang, or barbecue
   sauce

*Or use *Chahsiu* pork and
omit the marinade.

RICE NOODLES

There are several varieties of rice noodles. Fresh soft noodles called he, or hefen, are flat, about 1 cm ($\frac{1}{2}$ inch) wide and can be bought ready-made from many Chinese grocers. Dried rice noodles are thin, round noodles. They can be deep-fried and used in place of yifu noodles in the recipe for 'chop suey' given on page 126.

SINGAPORE NOODLES

There is a large Fujian Chinese community in Singapore, whence this recipe originated. It is very similar in style to many Fujian noodle dishes with the addition of curry powder and chillis.

Marinate the pork for 30 minutes. Marinate the prawns for 20 minutes. Soak the noodles in cold water for 5 minutes, then drain well. Beat the eggs and cook them as an omelette in a frying pan with a little oil. When it is set, turn it out and cut into thin shreds. De-seed the chillis and pepper and cut them into shreds. Cut the bamboo shoots into matchstick pieces. Cut the spring onions into 1-cm ($\frac{1}{2}$-inch) lengths. Heat 60 ml (4 tablespoons) oil in a wok or large frying pan and stir-fry the ginger and onion for 15 seconds. Add the pork and continue to stir-fry for another 30 seconds. Tip in the prawns, bamboo shoots, chillis and green pepper and stir-fry for another 2 minutes. Season with salt and pepper and stir in the curry powder and *shachajiang*. Add the egg shreds and rice noodles with 600 ml (1 pint) water and simmer for about 5 minutes. Finally stir-fry until all the water evaporates. Check the seasoning and serve on 4 separate heated plates.

If you want a hotter dish, add 1.5 ml ($\frac{1}{4}$ teaspoon) chilli oil with the curry powder.

牛肉炒合粉

Serves 4
350 g (12 oz) lean beef

MARINADE

5 ml (1 teaspoon) soy sauce
5 ml (1 teaspoon) rice wine
5 ml (1 teaspoon) oil
5 ml (1 teaspoon) cornflour

20 ml (1 rounded
   tablespoon) fermented
   black beans
4 slices fresh ginger
2 spring onions
250 g (8 oz) bean sprouts

SEASONING SAUCE

200 ml ($\frac{1}{3}$ pint) water
15 ml (1 tablespoon) oyster
   sauce
15 ml (1 tablespoon) dark
   soy sauce
10 ml (2 teaspoons) potato
   flour or cornflour

45 ml (3 tablespoons) oil
5 ml (1 teaspoon) sesame oil
450 g (1 lb) fresh rice
   noodles

HEFEN AND BEEF WITH A BLACK BEAN SAUCE

Cut the beef into thin slices and marinate for 30 minutes. Chop the black beans and ginger and cut the spring onions into 2.5-cm (1-inch) lengths. Pick over the bean sprouts and rinse well. Mix the seasoning sauce and then heat a wok or frying pan with the oil, and stir-fry the spring onions, ginger and black beans together for 15 seconds. Add the meat and stir-fry for another 1 to 2 minutes. Then mix in the bean sprouts and continue stir-frying for 15 seconds before pouring in the seasoning sauce. Bring to the boil and sprinkle over the sesame oil. Keep the beef warm while you heat the rice noodles by sliding them into a large pan of boiling water. Quickly bring the water back to the boil and lift out the noodles. Drain them for a few seconds, then divide them among 4 heated plates. Spoon over the beef and sauce and serve at once.

福建炒米粉

Serves 4
4 dried mushrooms
15 ml (1 tablespoon) dried
   shrimps
45 ml (3 tablespoons) oil
300 g (10 oz) lean pork, cut
   into matchstick shreds
45 ml (3 tablespoons) soy
   sauce
15 ml (1 tablespoon) rice
   wine
200 g (7 oz) Chinese leaves
   finely sliced
100 g (4 oz) carrot, shredded
1 stalk celery, shredded
450 g (1 lb) dried rice
   noodles
salt and pepper to taste

FUJIAN RICE NOODLES

Soak the dried mushrooms in warm water for 30 minutes, discard the hard stalks and cut the caps into thin slices. Put the shrimps into a small pan of hot water and bring to the boil. Boil for 2 minutes, then leave to soak in the hot water for 15 minutes. Heat a wok or frying pan with the oil and stir-fry the shrimps and mushrooms for about 15 seconds. Add the pork. When the meat has changed colour, add the soy sauce and rice wine and continue stir-frying until the pan is almost dry. Add the vegetables and mix well over a high heat. Pour in 400 ml ($\frac{2}{3}$ pint) of water and bring to the boil. Rinse the rice noodles and add them to the pan. Cover and simmer over a low heat for 2 minutes, then stir-fry until the pan is dry. When the cooking is finished, season with salt and pepper to taste and serve at once.

Chapter 11 | Rice

飯類

Rice is a special and most favoured grain in Chinese terms. Every grain is precious. There are numerous folk sayings against its waste. In the south of China, rice has been a basic staple in the diet for more than three thousand years and remains so today. However, in the north where rice cannot generally be grown, during the seventh century BC it was used as a food offering to see the dead on their way in the afterlife, and a thousand years ago, even at the Imperial court, rice was a luxury. In the 1930s before the Liberation rich people in the north ate rice only for special occasions, and today it is still not regarded as a basic staple in the north, but as a luxury food. With such a long history of use and cultivation, it is hardly surprising that there are literally thousands of varieties of rice. Both the taste and particularly the aroma of different rices can vary enormously. Chinese connoisseurs and gourmets before the Liberation had very strong preferences for a particular variety or even one grown in a particular district — as they do in Hong Kong and Taiwan today. Yangzhou rice was said to be outstandingly good.

Nowadays in the West we have a more limited choice of rice. We can buy long-grain rice, which is the standard Cantonese rice, as well as an American variety of short-grain rice similar to one grown in Taiwan and some eastern areas of China, which is stickier than ordinary long-grain rice. There is also an expensive variety of rice — xiangmi — which has a penetrating fragrance when cooked and may be an acquired taste for some people. Glutinous rice, as its name suggests, is very sticky when it is cooked and is also a luxury rice. It is used primarily to make wine, but it also forms the basis of almost all Chinese sweet rice dishes. (Pudding rice is not suitable for any form of Chinese rice cooking.)

In Chinese meals the balance between grain food in the form of rice, noodles or mantou (steamed bread) and other dishes is always strictly maintained. Fundamentally, food is grain and the other dishes are there to make it more interesting. It may be an example of the almost subconscious freedom associated with dimsum or 'not-real-meal-eating' that in such a style of eating, the balance between grain and the other dishes is relaxed and it is acceptable to eat only the luxurious without its customary fillers, although in many dimsum dishes the balance is retained in the dish itself between the grain or skin and the filling.

The basic method of cooking rice by boiling has remained virtually unchanged in the last three thousand years. Perhaps it says something about the quality of rice that, uniquely among grain foods, it can still be cooked by an original primitive method and yet be appreciated by sophisticated, modern palates. To achieve good boiled rice depends on two elements: the quantity of water and the speed at which it is cooked. A measure of slightly more water than rice by volume, 6 parts water to 5 parts rice, gives the best result. A useful rule of thumb is to cover 300 g (10 oz) or more of rice with water to the depth of the first joint on one's thumb. Always cook rice in a pan with a tight-fitting lid. Boil it over a moderate heat until all the water evaporates, then cook it very slowly in its own steam before allowing the rice to dry in the heat of the pan for a while before serving.

白飯

Serves 4

600 g (1 lb 4 oz) long-grain
  rice
1 litre (1¾ pints) water

BOILED RICE

Wash the rice very thoroughly in several lots of cold water. Drain well and put it into a pan with the measured water. Cover the pan and bring quickly to the boil. Reduce the heat and boil gently until all the water has evaporated, about 20 minutes. Then turn the heat down to the lowest possible setting and leave the rice to steam for 10 minutes *with the lid on*. Turn off the heat and leave for an additional 15 minutes, still with the lid on, for the rice to dry.

Electric rice cookers are now widely available in the West. They automatically boil and then dry the rice.

Always keep left-over cooked rice covered in the refrigerator. It can be reheated by adding approximately 15 ml (1 tablespoon) of water to 250 g (8 oz) cooked rice. Cover closely and put into a preheated oven 190°C (375°F, Gas mark 5) for 30 minutes.

In the following recipes we give a selection of one-dish snack meals that have boiled rice as their basic ingredient. They are not usually eaten as part of dimsum meals, but as simple lunches or evening snacks. Such dishes are more common in southern China than in the north.

咸飯

Serves 4

15 ml (1 tablespoon) black
   fungus or *muer*
4 dried mushrooms
125 g (4 oz) bamboo shoots
45 ml (3 tablespoons) oil
50 g (2 oz) boneless chicken,
   shredded
50 g (2 oz) pink prawns,
   peeled
15 ml (1 tablespoon) soy
   sauce
salt and pepper to taste
450 g (1 lb) long-grain rice
900 ml (1½ pints) good stock
50 g (2 oz) fresh coriander,
   finely chopped
10 ml (2 teaspoons) hot
   chicken fat

CORIANDER RICE

Soak the black fungus in hot water for 20 minutes, then rinse well and cut into thin slices. Soak the dried mushrooms in hot water for 30 minutes, discard the hard stalks and slice the caps finely. Finely chop the bamboo shoots. Heat 45 ml (3 tablespoons) oil in a wok or large frying pan and stir-fry the vegetables with the chicken shreds and prawns for 3 minutes. Add the soy sauce and adjust the seasoning with salt and pepper. Remove from the heat. Wash the rice in several lots of water and drain well. Cook it with the stock in a covered saucepan until all the stock has evaporated, about 20 minutes. Then tip the stir-fried vegetables and chicken and prawns on top of the rice, cover tightly again and cook for an additional 15 minutes over a very low heat before adding the chopped coriander. Mix all the meat and vegetables into the rice and serve immediately, sprinkled with the melted chicken fat.

叉燒飯

Serves 4

425 g (15 oz) rice
720 ml (1¼ pints) water
450 g (1 lb) *chahsiu*,
   home-made (see page 42)
   or bought
2 bundles *choisam*, about
   450 g (1 lb)
30 ml (2 tablespoons) oil
200 ml (⅓ pint) chicken stock
15 ml (1 tablespoon) soy
   sauce
pinch of salt and pepper to
   taste
10 ml (2 teaspoons) potato
   flour made into a paste
   with 20 ml (4 teaspoons)
   water

CANTONESE ROAST PORK WITH RICE

This dish may equally well be served with noodles instead of rice.

Wash the rice thoroughly in several lots of clean water, drain well and put it with the measured water into a pan. Bring quickly to the boil, reduce the heat and cover the pan. Simmer for 20 minutes, then turn the heat to the lowest possible setting and leave the rice to steam with *the lid still on*. Turn off the heat, and with the pan still covered leave the rice for an additional 15 minutes to dry. Meanwhile, prepare the *chahsiu* and sauce. Cut the *chahsiu* into slices about 5-mm (½-inch) thick. Wash and cut the *choisam* into 5-cm (2-inch) lengths. Heat a wok or large frying pan with the oil and stir-fry the *choisam* for about 3 minutes until it starts to soften. Add the *chahsiu* slices and continue to stir-fry for another minute before pouring in the chicken stock and soy sauce. Bring to the boil, adjust the seasoning with salt and pepper, then reduce the heat and stir in the thickening paste. Bring to the boil again, stirring all the time, then remove from the heat and put on one side until required. When the rice is ready, divide it among 4 preheated plates and spoon over the *chahsiu* and sauce. Serve at once.

牛楠烩饭

RED-COOKED BEEF AND RICE

This red-cooked beef stew is also frequently served with noodles in northern Chinese restaurants as a snack. In northern restaurants, the stew may also be served in individual small portions as part of a dimsum meal. These small portions are reheated in small bowls in a steamer when they are required.

Serves 4

500 g (1 lb) shin of beef
15 g (½ oz) fresh ginger, sliced
3 spring onions
3 garlic cloves
30 ml (2 tablespoons) rice wine
45 ml (3 tablespoons) dark soy sauce
1 litre (1¾ pints) water
25 g (1 oz) crystal sugar
1.5 ml (¼ teaspoon) salt
1 petal star anise
5-cm (2-inch) cinnamon stick
425 g (15 oz) long-grain rice
720 ml (1¼ pints) water
4 cos lettuce leaves

Cut the beef into 5-cm (2-inch) cubes and drop them into boiling water to seal the meat juices. Bring the water back to the boil and boil for 30 seconds, then lift out the meat and discard the water. Rinse the meat cubes in clean water and return them to a clean pan with the ginger, spring onions cut into 5-cm (2-inch) lengths, garlic cloves, rice wine, soy sauce, water, sugar, salt, star anise and cinnamon. Bring to the boil and skim off any foam that rises. Reduce the heat. Cover the pan with a tight-fitting lid and leave to simmer for 3 hours. About 45 minutes before the meat is finished, wash the rice very thoroughly and put into a pan with the measured water. Bring quickly to the boil, reduce the heat and cover with a close-fitting lid. Simmer until all the water has evaporated, about 20 minutes, turn the heat to its lowest setting and leave the rice, still covered, to dry for 10 minutes. Finally, turn off the heat and leave for another 15 minutes, still with the lid on. Wash and blanch the lettuce leaves in boiling water for 30 seconds, then refresh them in cold water. Drain well and tear into 5-cm (2-inch) pieces. When everything is ready, divide the rice among 4 bowls, arrange a few pieces of lettuce over the rice and spoon the beef and sauce on top.

If you can get *choisam* in place of cos lettuce it is even better and more authentic. Boil the *choisam* in water for about 2 minutes, then drain and cut into 8-cm (3½-inch) lengths.

滷肉饭

Serves 4

180 g (6 oz) onion
45 ml (3 tablespoons) oil
180 g (6 oz) coarsely minced pork
15 ml (1 tablespoon) rice wine
60 ml (4 tablespoons) dark soy sauce
150 ml (¼ pint) water
2.5 ml (½ teaspoon) sugar
pinch of five spice powder

SPICED PORK ON RICE

Chop the onion very finely and stir-fry it in the oil in a wok or large frying pan until it is lightly browned. Add the minced pork and continue to stir-fry for about 3 minutes, until all the meat has changed colour. Now add in the rice wine, soy sauce and water together with the sugar and five spice powder. Simmer the meat and onion in the sauce for 20 minutes over a low heat, then serve on plain boiled rice as directed in the previous recipe.

蒸鸡饭

Serves 4
425 g (15 oz) long-grain rice
775 ml (1⅓ pints) water

1 kg (2 lb) chicken portions

MARINADE

15 ml (1 tablespoon) rice
wine
15 ml (1 tablespoon) light
soy sauce
1.5 ml (¼ teaspoon) salt
10 ml (2 teaspoons) potato
flour

8 dried mushrooms
5 slices fresh ginger

OPTIONAL SAUCE

15 ml (1 tablespoon) melted
lard
15 ml (1 tablespoon) dark
soy sauce

15 ml (1 tablespoon) finely
chopped spring onions

STEAMED CHICKEN AND RICE

Bowls of steamed rice cooked with either chicken or Chinese sausage on top are very popular simple lunch dishes in Hong Kong. The flavour of the chicken or sausage permeates through the rice giving it a wonderful, delicate aroma. Traditionally this dish is cooked in individual bowls in a steamer, but we have adapted the recipes below for a Western oven. If you wish to cook in the traditional manner with a steamer, put the soaked rice and measured water into 4 small bowls. Arrange either the chicken, mushrooms and ginger or the sliced sausage on top of the rice. Cover each bowl with kitchen foil and steam for 1½ hours, or until the rice is soft. Take care the steamer does not boil dry.

Wash the rice and soak it in the measured water for an hour. Meanwhile, chop the chicken (including the bones) into bite-sized pieces and marinate for 30 minutes. Soak the mushrooms in warm water for 30 minutes, discard the hard stalks and leave the caps whole. Bring the rice and measured water to the boil over a high heat and boil for 1 minute only. Tip the rice and water into an ovenproof casserole and lay the chicken, mushrooms and ginger on top. Cover with a close-fitting lid and cook in a preheated oven 170°C (350°F, Gas mark 4) for 40 minutes. Before serving you can mix the sauce ingredients and pour them over the rice and chicken. Finally, sprinkle over the spring onions and serve.

As an alternative to the chicken in the steamed rice you can slice 4 Chinese sausages and put them on top of the rice before cooking it. You can use either pork or liver sausages. Both varieties are available at Chinese grocers. It also improves the appearance of the dish if you stir-fry a bundle of *choisam*, or a few cos lettuce leaves in 45 ml (3 tablespoons) of oil for about 3 minutes. Cut them into 8-cm (3¼-inch) lengths and add them to the rice and sausage casserole just before serving. Some people also like to add a tablespoon of melted lard mixed with soy sauce to the rice when it has finished cooking.

NEW YEAR CAKE

The first day of the New Year is by custom a day on which the Chinese housewives do not cook, but they will serve food prepared in advance of the festival. The Chinese New Year is calculated according to the old lunar calendar and the actual date of the New Year changes like the date of Easter.

This traditional New Year cake of white radish and rice comes from the south-eastern part of China. Visiting is a major activity in the traditional New Year festivities in China and these cakes are taken as gifts to friends and relatives. Many families, including May Huang's in Taiwan, order a number of these cakes to be specially made before the festival.

When this cake is fresh, it can be eaten cold just as it is, but after a few days, it is customary to cut it into slices and shallow-fry it before serving with garlic, soy sauce or chilli sauce.

250 g (8 oz) long-grain rice
300 ml (½ pint) water
450 g (1 lb) white radish
5 ml (1 teaspoon) salt
2.5 ml (½ teaspoon) black
  pepper

Wash the rice well and leave it to soak in the measured water for 12 hours. Then tip the rice and water into a liquidizer, or food processor, and run until the rice is a very fine paste – at least 10 minutes. Peel and grate the white radish, using the coarsest side of the grater. Put it into a large, thick-bottomed pan and gently stir-fry it without any oil, until the radish is soft – about 4 minutes. Add the rice paste and turn the heat very low. Bring the mixture to the boil, stirring all the time to prevent it from sticking to the bottom of the pan, then remove from the heat and season with salt and pepper. Line a small bamboo steamer, or an ordinary Western steamer with a wet cloth and pour the rice and radish mixture into it. Steam over fast boiling water for 1 hour. When it is cooked, a skewer inserted into the centre will come out clean. Turn out onto a plate, peel off the cloth and cut into slices with a wet knife.

BEEF AND SPRING ONION FRIED RICE

Serves 4

25 g (1 oz) lard
450 g (1 lb) lean beef, cut
  into very small dice
400 g (14 oz) cold cooked
  rice
salt and pepper to taste
75 g (3 oz) spring onions,
  very finely chopped

Melt the lard in a large frying pan or wok and stir-fry the beef until it has all changed colour. Mix in the rice and continue stir-frying very quickly over a high heat until the rice is hot. Season and serve decorated with the finely chopped spring onions. The hotter and quicker this dish is cooked, without burning, the better the results.

揚州炒饭

Serves 4
2 dried mushrooms
50 g (2 oz) pink prawns,
   peeled
25 g (1 oz) cooked chicken
50 g (2 oz) cold roast pork or
   cooked ham
3 spring onions
3 eggs
60 ml (4 tablespoons) oil
30 ml (2 tablespoons) green
   peas (use frozen)
400 g (14 oz) cold cooked
   rice, well-separated
10 ml (2 teaspoons) salt
pinch of pepper to taste

YANGZHOU FRIED RICE

In the beginning of the seventh century the Emperor of China was said to be inordinately fond of 'golden rice' – stir-fried egg and rice. When he visited Yangzhou, the people who knew of his tastes gave him their version of this dish, and the Emperor was delighted to find such excellent fried rice in which every grain was coated individually in the egg. Five hundred years later, Yangzhou was still famous for 'silver coated in gold', but in the intervening years other ingredients had been added. It is this dish, which after another eight hundred years, we know as Yangzhou fried rice.

Rice for frying is better if it is cooked the day before and allowed to dry out in the refrigerator overnight before being fried. Check before adding it to the egg that any lumps of rice are broken up and that all the grains are separated.

Soak the mushrooms in warm water for 30 minutes, discard the hard stalks and cut the caps into thin slices. If the prawns are large, cut them in half. Dice the meats and chop the spring onions finely. Beat the eggs. Heat a large frying pan or wok with the oil and stir-fry half the chopped spring onion for 30 seconds. Add the meat and prawns. Stir-fry for 2 minutes. Add the mushrooms, peas and beaten egg. Continue stir-frying, adding more oil if necessary, until the egg just begins to set, about 2 minutes, then mix in the rice and continue to stir-fry for another 3 minutes. Adjust the seasoning and decorate with the remaining spring onion.

RICE CONGEE

Rice congee is like a thin rice porridge, flavoured with various additional foods such as fish, chicken, duck, etc. It is not considered to be made properly if you can see the rice without the water or the water without the rice. Any rice porridge which is made with left-over rice is a poverty dish with a different name. Rice congee is mainly a southern dish, but other congees made with grains such as millet or wheat are eaten in most areas of China. Simple congees are eaten by traditional families for breakfast and are also considered suitable food for the old or very young. More elaborate versions of rice congee with more ingredients are often eaten as a late-night snack. Still other congees are made especially for festivals or special occasions, such as an eight-jewelled congee, cooked to bring prosperity in the New Year. As well as rice, it has broad beans, soya beans, red beans, cow peas, dried mushrooms, water chestnuts, plus yams, which are boiled separately and added at the last moment. It can be seasoned with either salt or sugar.

In the following congee recipes you can use either short-grain or long-grain rice. A measure of 10 parts of water to 1 part of rice gives an ideal congee consistency.

鸡 肉 粥

Serves 4

150 g (5 oz) rice

2 litres (3⅓ pints) good
  skimmed chicken stock or
  water

4 dried mushrooms
  (optional)

100 g (4 oz) boneless
  chicken breast

5 ml (1 teaspoon) grated
  fresh ginger

10 ml (2 teaspoons) finely
  chopped spring onions

5 ml (1 teaspoon) sesame oil

艇 仔 粥

Serves 4

150 g (5 oz) rice

2 fresh scallops, or 12 g (½ oz)
  dried scallops

50 g (2 oz) fresh squid

50 g (2 oz) pig's liver

75 g (3 oz) cooked duck (see
  page 41) or raw chicken

50 g (2 oz) raw prawns,
  shelled

25 g (1 oz) unsalted peanuts

oil for deep-frying

25 g (1 oz) dried rice sticks

salt and pepper to taste

4 spring onions, finely
  chopped

soy sauce

sesame oil

CHICKEN CONGEE

Wash the rice and bring it to the boil in the chicken stock. If you are using dried mushrooms, soak them in hot water for 30 minutes, discard the hard stalks and cut the caps into thin slices. Cut the chicken into thin shreds and after 20 minutes add them to the rice in the stock. Continue boiling gently for another 20 minutes, adding the mushrooms when they have finished soaking. Serve in individual bowls into which you have already divided the grated ginger, spring onions and sesame oil. Serve at once.

SAMPAN CONGEE

Until recently in the Hong Kong typhoon shelters there were numerous sampans or small one-oared, flat-bottomed boats covered half over with a barrel roof, often made from bamboo matting, available for hire. Before the tunnel was built, they would take late night revellers across the harbour after the ferries had stopped for the night, while others offered more esoteric entertainment. This congee, or late-night snack, particularly in some versions of the recipe that include a lot of shellfish and seafood, traditionally good for sexual performance according to Chinese thinking, might alternatively be called 'brothel-broth'.

Rinse the rice and put it into 2 litres (3 pints) of clean water. Wash the scallops and cut into pieces before putting them into the water with the rice. Bring the rice and scallops to the boil and boil gently for 30 minutes. Meanwhile, cut the squid into thin shreds, slice the liver very thinly and tear the cooked meat into thin strips. De-vein the prawns and cut in halves. Skin the peanuts by dipping them in boiling water, then deep-fry for about 3 minutes before draining and crushing them. Deep-fry the rice sticks until they puff up, then crumble them coarsely and put on one side. When the rice is nearly cooked, add the squid shreds, the strips of duck and prawns and continue cooking for another 7 minutes before dropping in the slices of liver. Cook for 2 more minutes and season to taste with salt and pepper. Serve at once in a big bowl, with small bowls of finely chopped spring onions, the crushed peanuts, crumbled rice noodles, and soy sauce and sesame oil as additional seasonings for the diners to use as they please.

A far less elaborate fish congee can be made with a fillet of cod and a little ginger and spring onions. Cook 150 g (5 oz) rice in 2 litres (3 pints) of water as before for 20 minutes. Then add 150 g (5 oz) of cod cut into bite-sized pieces and season with salt and pepper. Continue boiling for another 20 minutes while you cut 3 slices of ginger into hair-like threads and finely chop 4 spring onions. Serve the congee in a big bowl and have small dishes of ginger, spring onion and sesame oil on the table so that the diners may flavour their congee as they please.

糯米

GLUTINOUS RICE

The grains of glutinous rice are whiter, harder and rounder than those of ordinary rice, and when they are cooked are much stickier. Glutinous rice is used for making rice wine as well as special festival or celebration dishes and stuffings where its stickiness will bind the other ingredients together. It is never eaten as plain boiled rice with other dishes.

粽子

BAMBOO LEAF PACKETS

This recipe and the one following for lotus leaf packets are both said to commemorate the same historical event. Around 300 BC, the poet Qu Yuan, a native of Hubei and a Privy Councillor to the Prince of Chu, was sent into exile south of the Yangzi. He was so distressed with his disgrace that he committed suicide by drowning himself. It is said that the people of the district, with whom he was popular, threw rice into the river to feed his ghost, but the fish always ate the rice before it could reach the bottom of the river where he was. So they took to wrapping the rice in bamboo leaves and making it into packets that the fish could not eat.

These packets of rice were formally a festival food prepared especially for the double fifth, a time when Hong Kong still celebrates Qu Yuan with its dragon boat races. According to the legend, at the time when Qu Yuan jumped into the water, the fastest boats on the river set out to save him, and it is their fruitless dash that is still recreated in modern times in Hong Kong harbour. However, nowadays big bowls of bamboo leaf packets can be seen throughout the year in backstreets in China, swathed in quilts to keep them warm, and Cantonese restaurants in the West serve lotus leaf packets as a standard dimsum dish.

Makes 10 packets

600 g (1 lb 4 oz) glutinous
    rice

20 bamboo leaves

350 g (12 oz) red-cooked
    pork or mixed meats (see
    page 50)

3 small eggs (size 5 or 6),
    hard-boiled

5 dried mushrooms

15 ml (1 tablespoon) dried
    shrimps

1½ litres (2½ pints) stock or
    water

Rinse the rice thoroughly in several lots of water, then soak it in clean water for an hour. Wash the bamboo leaves and blanch them in boiling water for 5 minutes. It is probably easiest to do this in a large frying pan. Keep them wet until required. Cut the pork or other red-cooked meat into 2.5-cm (1-inch) cubes, and cut the hard-boiled eggs into quarters. Soak the dried mushrooms in warm water for 30 minutes, discard the hard stalks and cut the caps into halves. Soak the dried shrimps in hot water for 20 minutes, then drain well. When the rice has soaked sufficiently, drain it well and mix it with the dried shrimps. Divide the rice into 20 equal portions. Take two bamboo leaves and lay them on top of one another. Fold them over to form a cone, making one end of the leaves longer than the other. As you fold them over, make a double fold at the bottom to seal the end. Put in one portion of rice and shrimps and then add one or two cubes of meat, about 5 ml (1 teaspoon) of the sauce in which the meat was cooked, a quarter of an egg and half a mushroom. Then cover with another portion of rice. Fold over the short end of the bamboo leaves to enclose the filling and fold the long end over the top and around the side to make a pyramid. Tie firmly into shape with string.

Boil the packets for an hour in the stock or water, then serve hot or deep-freeze and reheat when required, either in a steamer or in a microwave oven. Chopped peanuts can be mixed into the rice in place of the shrimps.

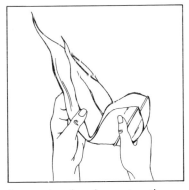
Put two bamboo leaves together.

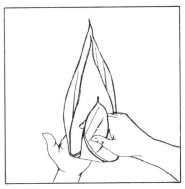
Make double fold at base of cone.

Fill cone with rice, meat, etc.

Cover with short end of leaf.

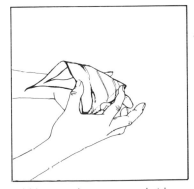
Fold long end over top and sides.

八宝黏米鸡

Makes 1 packet, serving
2 to 4

250 g (8 oz) glutinous rice
pinch of salt
5 ml (1 teaspoon) melted
lard
75 g (3 oz) boneless chicken
breast

75 g (3 oz) lean boneless
pork
25 g (1 oz) *chahsiu* (see page
42) or use more pork
3 dried mushrooms
15 ml (1 tablespoon) melted
lard

thickening paste made with
5 ml (1 teaspoon)
cornflour mixed with
10 ml (2 teaspoons) water
3 lotus leaves
a little vegetable oil

MARINADE

5 ml (1 teaspoon) light soy
sauce
5 ml (1 teaspoon) grated
fresh ginger
2.5 ml ($\frac{1}{2}$ teaspoon)
cornflour
pinch of salt

SEASONING SAUCE

10 ml (2 teaspoons) rice
wine
10 ml (2 teaspoons) light soy
sauce
5 ml (1 teaspoon) sugar
1.5 ml ($\frac{1}{4}$ teaspoon) black
pepper
1.5 ml ($\frac{1}{4}$ teaspoon) salt
75 ml (5 tablespoons) water

LOTUS WRAPPED CHICKEN AND GLUTINOUS RICE

Wash the glutinous rice and then soak it in clean cold water overnight. The next day, drain the rice well. Cover the bottom of a steamer with a clean cloth and spread the rice over it. Steam for 40 minutes. Then tip into a bowl and mix with the salt and melted lard. Cut the chicken into bite-sized pieces and marinate for 30 minutes. Cut the pork and *chahsiu* into thin slices. Soak the dried mushrooms in warm water for 30 minutes, discard the hard stalks and cut the caps into quarters. Heat a frying pan or wok with 15 ml (1 tablespoon) lard and stir-fry the pork, *chahsiu* and chicken for 1 minute. Tip in the seasoning sauce and boil for another 2 or 3 minutes. Thicken with the cornflour paste and put on one side until required.

Select lotus leaves that are least damaged and boil 3 of them in a large pan for about 3 minutes to soften. Spread them out flat, pat dry very gently and paint with a little vegetable oil. Cut away the hard centre veins where the stalk joins the leaf. (Lotus is a variety of water lily with a round leaf.) Lay one on top of the other to cover the holes and tears, so you have one complete round.

Pile one-half of the rice in the centre of the lotus leaf about 1 cm ($\frac{1}{2}$ inch) high and 10 × 8 cm (4 × 3$\frac{1}{4}$ inches). Then put the cooked meat and its sauce in the centre of the pile of rice and cover with the remaining rice. Fold over the lotus leaves, not too tightly, to make a tidy oblong parcel. Put it onto a plate in a steamer with the ends tucked underneath and steam for 40 minutes. Serve hot. Open up the packet and eat the filling, not the lotus leaves.

If you wish to cook the rice in a pan, rather than in a steamer use equal quantities of water and rice, volume measure, soak for one hour, then drain and put into a pan with the measured water. Bring to the boil and boil for about 20 minutes, or until soft. Mix in the salt and lard.

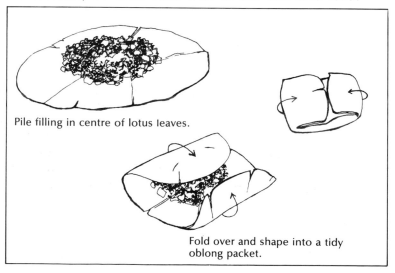

Pile filling in centre of lotus leaves.

Fold over and shape into a tidy oblong packet.

添饭

CELEBRATION RICE

This recipe comes from Taiwan, where when a baby boy is a month old celebration rice is cooked and given to all the friends and relatives of the family. This recipe is the simple unadorned peasant dish, but 'rich people' add chestnuts, pine kernels and bamboo shoots as well as a kind of onion reminiscent of a French shallot.

Serves 4 or more
600 g (20 oz) glutinous rice
700 ml (1¼ pints) water
150 g (5 oz) lean boneless
   pork

MARINADE

15 ml (1 tablespoon) soy
   sauce
15 ml (1 tablespoon) rice
   wine
4 dried mushrooms
10 ml (2 teaspoons) dried
   shrimps
45 ml (3 tablespoons) oil
30 ml (2 tablespoons) soy
   sauce
30 ml (2 tablespoons) rice
   wine
60 ml (4 tablespoons) water

Wash the rice and soak it in the measured water for an hour. Then bring it to the boil over a high heat, cover, reduce the heat to low and simmer for about 20 minutes until all the water has evaporated. Turn down the heat to its lowest setting and allow the rice to dry for about 10 minutes with the lid still on. Meanwhile, cut the pork into matchstick shreds and marinate it for 20 minutes. Soak the dried mushrooms in warm water for 30 minutes, cut the caps into thin slices and discard the hard stalks. Put the dried shrimps into a pan of hot water and bring them to the boil. Boil for 2 minutes, then leave in the pan of hot water for an additional 15 minutes. Drain well and chop coarsely.

   Heat a frying pan or wok and add the oil. Stir-fry the shrimps and mushrooms for about 30 seconds before adding the pork. Finally, pour in the soy sauce, rice wine and water and bring to the boil. Reduce the heat and simmer for 5 minutes. When the rice is cooked, mix in the stir-fried pork and serve.

SWEET GLUTINOUS RICE DISHES

Sugar was expensive and precious in pre-Liberation China, and to offer a sweet dish either at a meal or at the temple showed honour.

凤梨甜饭

Serves 4 to 6
45 ml (3 tablespoons) oil
250 g (8 oz) cooked
   glutinous or plain rice
150 g (5 oz) sugar
75 g (3 oz) fresh pear
75 g (3 oz) banana
75 g (3 oz) fresh pineapple
3 preserved red dates,
   chopped
15 ml (1 tablespoon)
   seedless raisins

PINEAPPLE RICE

Heat the oil in a frying pan and stir-fry the rice for 30 seconds, breaking up any lumps. Add the sugar, the pear, cored and cut into 1-cm (½ inch) wedges, the banana and pineapple, cut into similar pieces. Stir-fry for about 4 minutes over a low heat until the sugar has melted, mix in the preserved red dates and raisins and serve. You can also leave until cold and then serve, but do not leave more than 3 hours before serving, or the fruit will begin to discolour.

Chapter 12 | Sweets and cakes

甜菜美

In China sweet dishes are luxury foods; many are served only on occasions such as weddings and festivals when sweets and pastries are prepared specially. The Chinese, whose day-to-day diet contains very little sugar, relish sweets as extraordinary treats. It may be for this reason that Chinese sweet dishes often seem overly sweet to Western tastes, but it should be remembered that they are not usually eaten at the end of a full meal, but as snacks and refreshments between meals.

Sometimes in the course of large dinners or banquets, expensive ingredients such as 'silver-ears' are served as a sweet soup to mark the change of mood in the procession of dishes, but most sweet soups, made from less luxurious ingredients like mung beans and red dates, are eaten as ordinary afternoon or evening snacks. The sweet fritters, fruits and jellies that feature in Chinese cuisine are sometimes included in a dimsum meal if one of the diners feels like something sweet, but more usually they are eaten as afternoon or evening snacks with tea, just as we might eat cake with afternoon tea. Cakes and biscuits are not eaten with dimsum meals, but along with tea at virtually any time of the day or night.

Sweets, toffee and candied fruits are considered nibbles, not necessarily to be served with tea, but picked up and eaten as you please throughout the day at least among the well-to-do. When there are visitors to the house, housewives often provide small bowls of sweets, candied fruits and nuts or melon seeds for the guests' refreshment.

None of the recipes we give in this chapter is difficult, or demands a great deal of skill, unlike some Chinese sweetmeats. However, in handling the melted sugar for the various toffees, we think a sugar thermometer is almost essential, unless you are very skilled at judging sugar temperatures. We also found it was very helpful to have a marble slab on which to work the melted sugar, although a

Opposite: *Braised Sweet Potatoes (page 149) shown with plates of Three-Coloured Balls (page 73)*

good smooth large metal sheet can be substituted.

The Chinese use maltose, a sweet syrup extract from wheat, rather than sugar in many of their sweet recipes. It is not as sweet as sucrose and hardens at a lower temperature than sugar syrups.

芝 蔴 糖

100 g (4 oz) white sesame
  seeds
100 g (4 oz) granulated sugar
50 g (2 oz) maltose
50 ml (2 fl oz) water
sugar thermometer

SESAME BRITTLE

Put the sesame seeds in a clean dry pan and cook them over a moderate heat until they start to change colour and dance, stirring all the time. Spread them out on a cold flat board – ideally it should be marble, but it is possible to use either wood or metal. Leave to cool. Have a rolling pin ready. Put the sugar, maltose and water into a pan and stir over a moderate heat until the sugar has dissolved. Reduce the heat, stop stirring and allow the syrup to boil gently until its temperature reaches 140°C (280°F) or 'small crack'. Immediately pour the syrup over the sesame seeds on the board. Push up the seeds from the sides to cover the syrup. Working quickly, roll out the toffee until it is about 3 mm ($\frac{1}{8}$ inch) thick. All the sesame seeds should be included in the toffee. Cut into 4-cm (1$\frac{1}{2}$-inch) squares and leave to cool before eating.

Another version of this brittle can be made with 100 g (4 oz) peanuts. Remove their skins and then deep-fry in hot oil for about 3 minutes before draining well and spreading them out on the flat board.

糖 核 桃

150 g (5 oz) shelled walnut
  halves or cashew nuts
75 ml (5 tablespoons) sugar
75 ml (5 tablespoons) water
oil for deep-frying

SWEET WALNUTS

Put the nuts, sugar and water into a small pan and bring to the boil. Reduce the heat and simmer for 5 minutes, then remove from the heat and leave the nuts to soak in the syrup for 4 hours, turning them from time to time to make certain they are all well-coated in the syrup. Heat the oil very hot, put in the nuts and deep-fry them over *a low heat* until they are golden brown – about 4 minutes. Lift the nuts from the oil with a slotted spoon and spread them on a plate to cool. Serve cold. These nuts can be stored for a few days in an airtight container.

Opposite: *Lotus Wrapped Chicken and Glutinous Rice* (page 142)

花生酥

50 g (2 oz) plain flour
75 g (3 oz) peanuts
125 g (4½ oz) sifted icing
   sugar
125 g (4½ oz) maltose
sugar thermometer

PEANUT TOFFEE ROLL

Put the flour into a clean, dry cake tin and bake it in a low oven for 30 minutes, stirring it from time to time. Meanwhile, skin the peanuts by dipping them in boiling water, then toast them in a dry pan over a moderate heat until they darken slightly, stirring all the time to prevent them burning. Tip them into a food processor or liquidizer and grind into a coarse powder. Mix the cooked flour, ground peanuts and icing sugar on a large flat board (preferably made of marble), and have ready a rolling pin. Heat the maltose over a low heat until it reaches 102°C (215°F) stirring all the time to make sure it does not burn at the bottom of the pan. The temperature of the maltose is quite critical to the success of the toffee: if it is too high, the toffee becomes brittle, but if it is too low, the toffee will not set. As soon as it has reached the correct heat, tip the maltose onto the pile of flour mixture on the board. Quickly sprinkle some of the flour mixture on top of the maltose and roll it out into a thin rectangle. Sprinkle with the flour mixture again, fold into three and roll out again into a thin rectangle. Time is of the essence during this operation. Ideally it should be coated with the flour mixture, folded and rolled out seven times, but often it becomes too hard to roll after the fifth or sixth time. Finally, roll the toffee up into a tight sausage shape and with a very sharp knife cut it into round slices, like pin-wheels. Wrap each slice in a small square of non-stick parchment, or better still, cellophane sweet papers, and store in a closed container.

Another version of the soft toffee rolls in the previous recipe can be made with sesame seeds. Use 75 g (3 oz) of either white or black sesame seeds. If you use black seeds, also include a pinch of salt and an extra 12 g (½ oz) of icing sugar in the recipe. The sesame seeds should be toasted over a moderate heat in a dry pan until they start to dance. Then mix them with the 50 g (2 oz) of baked flour and grind them to a fine powder in a food processor. Mix this powder with the icing sugar and pile them all in the centre of a large flat board, preferably marble. Melt the maltose and bring it up gently to 102°C (215°F), before tipping onto the board and rolling and folding in the same way as in the previous recipe.

杏仁脯

1 kg (2 lb) fresh apricots
300 g (10 oz) sugar

PRESERVED APRICOTS

A favourite Chinese sweetmeat is preserved apricots. They can also be included in fillings for various sweet pastries and buns. This recipe originally came from an eighteenth-century Chinese farmer's almanac. We have adapted it for a modern Western kitchen. Preserved apricots are said to keep well, but we have been unable to test their keeping qualities!

Cut the apricots in half and remove the stones. Fill each hole with 5 ml (1 teaspoon) of sugar and arrange the apricots in a bowl. Scatter the remaining sugar over the fruit and put the bowl in a steamer. Steam over fast boiling water until the juice runs from the apricots. Then lift them from the bowl with a slotted spoon onto a baking tray lined with greaseproof paper, reserving the sugar and fruit juice in the bowl. Put the apricots into a very low oven for 12 hours, then return them to the bowl of fruit syrup. Leave to soak for 12 hours before repeating the drying in the oven. Continue the cycle of soaking and drying until all the fruit syrup has been absorbed – about 5 to 7 days. (Between soakings store the fruit syrup in the refrigerator.)

紅枣綠豆湯

75 g (3 oz) mung beans
50 g (2 oz) pearl barley
14 dried red dates
25 g (1 oz) glutinous rice
sugar to taste

FOUR FRUITS SOUP

Soak the mung beans overnight in cold water, then rinse well. Soak the barley, red dates and rice separately for 3 hours in cold water, rinse well and drain. Remove the stones from the dates, and chop into small pieces. Put all the soaked ingredients into a pan with 1.8 litres (3 pints) water and boil gently for 1½ hours. Add sugar to taste and serve either hot or cold.

Another variation of this recipe can be made by omitting the barley but adding small rice balls at the very last minute. Mix 75 g (3 oz) glutinous rice flour with 55 ml (3½ tablespoons) cold water and knead into a smooth paste. Shape into 20 small round balls about the size of a thumb nail and drop these into the soup about 1 minute before you serve it. When they rise to the surface they are ready. Serve at once.

紅棗核桃湯

Serves 6

40 g (1½ oz) dried red dates
40 g (1½ oz) glutinous rice
75 g (3 oz) walnuts
75 g (3 oz) sugar, or to taste

芝蔴糊

Serves 4

30 ml (2 tablespoons)
    glutinous rice
50 g (2 oz) black sesame
    seeds
20 unsalted peanuts
800 ml (1⅓ pints) water
90 ml (6 tablespoons) sugar,
    or more to taste

WALNUT AND RED DATE SOUP

Wash the red dates thoroughly and soak them in cold water for 3 hours. Put them into a pan and simmer until they are soft, about 20 minutes. Wash the glutinous rice well and soak it in cold water for an hour, then drain well. Remove the date stones and chop the dates and walnuts into small pieces about the size of a grain of rice. Put dates, walnuts, drained rice and 800 ml (1⅓ pints) of water in a pan and bring to the boil, stirring from time to time. Simmer until the rice is soft, about 20 minutes. Remove from the heat and add sugar to taste. Return to the heat to dissolve the sugar, then pour into a serving bowl. You can serve this soup tepid, or if you prefer it, cold.

SESAME SEED SOUP

About two thousand years ago a peasant called Liu went into the mountains to gather medicinal herbs. While he was wandering in a lonely valley he met two goddesses picnicking on the grass. He joined them, and as it grew late, they invited him to go back with them to their cottage further up the valley. There it was always springtime, the grass and trees were green and the birds sang. The air was full of the scent of flowers, but Liu was homesick, and after about six months he left the valley and went down the mountain to his village. As he approached, it looked strange and unfamiliar. He saw no one he knew. He spoke to the people he met, and eventually, an old man remembered hearing of someone from the village who long ago had never returned from the mountains. But, he explained, seven generations had passed since that time. Liu told his story and the people asked him what he had eaten while he lived with the goddesses that he should look so young after so long a time and he told them — rice and sesame.

Rinse and soak the rice in cold water for an hour. Toast the sesame seeds in a dry pan over a moderate heat until they start to dance, stirring all the time to prevent them burning — about 4 minutes. Skin the peanuts by dropping them in boiling water, then rubbing off the skins. Put the peanuts and sesame seeds into a food processor or liquidizer and run until reduced to a fine powder. Drain the rice and add it with 400 ml (⅔ pint) clean water to the mixture in the food processor. Blend until the mixture is very smooth; some recipes recommend passing the mixture through a fine cloth to make sure the soup is smooth. Pour the mixture into a pan and add another 400 ml (⅔ pint) water and bring gently to the boil. Cook over a low heat for about 15 minutes until the mixture has thickened. Towards the end of the cooking stir in the sugar to taste. Serve warm.

雪白銀耳

Serves 4 to 6

12 g (½ oz) silver wood-ears
1.2 litres (2 pints) water
300 g (10 oz) crystal sugar
2 kiwi fruit

SILVER WOOD-EARS SOUP

Soak the silver wood-ears in hot water for 30 minutes, then rinse well and trim off any yellow or coarse bits. Put the trimmed wood-ears in a bowl with the water and crystal sugar. Steam for an hour, then add the flesh of the kiwi fruits, peeled and cut into slices, and continue steaming for another 5 minutes before serving. If you wish, you can serve this soup chilled, in which case omit steaming the kiwi fruit.

Fruit drained from a small can of mandarin oranges or red cherries can be substituted for the fresh kiwi fruit.

馬蹄酪糕

Serves 6

300 ml (½ pint) water
100 g (4 oz) sugar
50 g (2 oz) potato flour
100 g (4 oz) canned water
  chestnuts, drained
25 g (1 oz) lard

WATER CHESTNUT JELLY

Mix the water gradually with the sugar and potato flour, adding a little at a time and mixing well between each addition to prevent the flour forming lumps. Liquidize or coarsely grate the water chestnuts and stir them into the potato flour mixture. Leave to sit for 30 minutes. Meanwhile, lightly grease a shallow baking dish which will fit in your steamer with a little lard. Melt the remaining lard in a saucepan and, stirring all the time, gently cook the water chestnut mixture over a low heat until it thickens and just comes to the boil. Pour it into the greased dish and steam over boiling water for 25 minutes. Leave to cool a little before unmoulding and cutting into squares to serve. This jelly tastes much better if it is served warm rather than cold. It can be kept for a day or so in the refrigerator. Return it to the steamer and steam for about 5 minutes to warm through before serving.

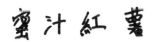

Serves 4 to 6

500 g (1 lb) sweet potatoes
  (the purple skinned
  yellow-fleshed variety is
  best)
150 g (5 oz) crystal sugar
200 ml (⅓ pint) water
25 ml (1½ tablespoons) good
  honey (acacia, orange
  blossom or cassia flower)

BRAISED SWEET POTATOES

This is a delicious dish, not nearly as sweet as one might imagine from the ingredients, but with an unusual flavour rather similar to such tropical fruits as pawpaws or mangoes. The Chinese usually boil or steam sweet potatoes in their skins to prevent them losing their flavour.

Peel and cut the potatoes into big wedge-shaped pieces. Dissolve the sugar in the water in a large thick-bottomed pan, then add the potatoes and honey. Bring just to the boil and simmer very gently for 30 minutes with the pan covered. Afterwards, remove the lid and continue simmering until the potatoes are completely soft – about 30 to 40 minutes. Take care towards the end of the cooking time, if the syrup is much reduced, that they do not burn. Lift the potatoes carefully onto a serving dish and pour the remaining syrup over them. Chill before serving.

酥酪集珍

SWEET POTATO BALLS

Many Buddhist temples in China in the past had a high reputation for their cooking, and people would go especially to eat a meal cooked in the temple style. This recipe comes from the Kaiwuan Temple in Fujian.

Makes 16 balls

500 g (1 lb) sweet potatoes (white-fleshed variety)

60 ml (4 tablespoons) plain flour

75 g (3 oz) sugar

30 ml (2 tablespoons) beaten egg

flour for rolling

50 g (2 oz) sesame seeds

oil for deep-frying

FILLING

20 g (¾ oz) crystallized winter melon

10 g (½ oz) candied orange peel or mixed peel

20 g (¾ oz) unsalted peanuts

Peel the sweet potatoes and cut them into pieces. Put them into a steamer and steam until very soft, about 20 minutes. Meanwhile, prepare the filling. Chop the winter melon and orange peel finely together. Skin the peanuts by dropping them in boiling water, then deep-fry them in clean hot oil for about 1 minute before draining and chopping them finely. Mix the peanuts with the winter melon and orange peel. When the potatoes are soft, transfer them to a bowl and mash into a smooth dough with the flour and sugar, then beat in the egg. Put the potato dough onto a lightly floured board and knead well. If the dough is too soft to hold its shape, add a little more flour. Divide into 16 portions, and using floured hands, flatten each portion into a round about 7 cm (2¾ inches) in diameter. Put 2.5 ml (½ teaspoon) filling in the centre of each round and fold up the potato skins to cover the filling. Roll into smooth balls about the size of a walnut. Roll the balls in the sesame seeds before deep-frying them at a low heat 170°C (350°F) until the skins are golden brown. Serve at once.

蒸蛋糕

STEAMED EGG CAKE

This recipe was given in a Chinese farmer's almanac published in northern China in the eighteenth century. It was called Foreigner's cake *and is familiar to us all in the West as a fatless sponge: take 500 g (1 lb) white flour, 16 eggs, 500 g (1 lb) sugar and a little yellow wine. Mix extremely evenly and put in the oven. In the following recipe, we give a modern Chinese version of this cake from a book published in Hong Kong in 1976, which makes no mention of its foreign origins.*

6 eggs

250 g (8 oz) sugar

180 g (6 oz) flour

Line the sides of a loose-bottomed 20-cm (8-inch) cake tin with greaseproof paper. Put the eggs in a bowl with the sugar and beat very well. (We find we get better results by standing the bowl over hot water during the beating.) Beat until the eggs leave trails on top of the surface. Sift the flour and fold it in, moving always in one direction. Put the mixture into the cake tin and steam over a high heat for 50–60 minutes. Take care that the steamer lid is close-fitting and keep the steamer topped up with boiling water.

高朋香蕉

Serves 4

4 or 5 bananas
2 egg whites
45 ml (3 tablespoons)
   cornflour
45 ml (3 tablespoons) plain
   flour
60 ml (4 tablespoons) water
clean oil for deep-frying
icing sugar

BANANA FRITTERS

Peel the bananas and cut them into bite-sized pieces. Whisk the egg-whites until they form peaks. Mix the water and two flours into a very stiff batter. Heat the oil very hot then fold the egg whites into the batter. Dip the banana pieces into this mixture and drop them, a few at a time, into the oil. Fry until they are golden brown, about 1 minute, then lift them out and drain for a few seconds before sprinkling with icing sugar. Serve immediately.

These fritters can also be made with apples. Use 4 or 5 crisp well-flavoured apples such as Coxes or Granny Smiths. Peel, core and cut into quarters or sixths and dip them in the batter. Deep-fry as above.

芝麻糕

25 g (1 oz) glutinous rice
   flour
25 g (1 oz) black sesame
   seeds
12 g (½ oz) sugar
2.5 ml (½ teaspoon) sesame
   oil
approximately 25 g (1 oz)
   lard
icing sugar

SESAME BISCUITS

Put the rice flour in a dry, clean cake tin and bake it in a preheated oven at the lowest setting for 30 minutes, stirring it round from time to time. Toast the sesame seeds until they start to dance in a clean, dry pan over a moderate heat. Place the toasted sesame seeds on a flat board and crush them with a rolling pin. Mix the crushed seeds with the cooked flour, sugar and sesame oil. Knead the mixture adding sufficient lard to make a firm cohesive ball. Dust a set of madeleine moulds with icing sugar. Divide and shape the sesame paste into small balls and press one small ball into each shape. Then tip out and place on a serving plate. These sweet biscuits will keep for about a week in a cold place.

杏仁糕

Makes 10 biscuits

60 g (2½ oz) lard or soft white
   cooking fat
75 g (3 oz) caster sugar
1 egg (size 4)
2.5 ml (½ teaspoon) almond
   essence
200 g (7½ oz) plain flour
5 ml (1 teaspoon) baking
   powder
1.5 ml (¼ teaspoon) salt
beaten egg for glazing
10 split almonds

ALMOND BISCUITS

Cream the lard and sugar, then beat in the egg and flavouring — or use an electric mixer and beat them all together for 2 minutes. Sift in one-third of the flour together with the baking powder and salt and beat well. Pile the remaining flour onto a pastry board and put the rather sticky dough in the centre. Knead gently until all the flour has been taken up. Roll the dough into a long sausage and divide it into 10 equal portions. Roll the portions between your hands into balls, then flatten them gently into discs about 1 cm (½ inch) high and 10 cm (4 inches) in diameter. Arrange them on a lightly greased tray, and with the tip of your finger make a deep indentation in the centre of each biscuit. Paint with the beaten egg and place a split almond on top of each biscuit. Bake for 15 minutes at 200°C (400°F, Gas mark 6).

沙其馬

sesame oil
200 g (7 oz) self-raising flour
2.5 ml (½ teaspoon) baking
  powder
2 eggs, beaten
clean oil for deep-frying
30 ml (2 tablespoons) white
  sesame seeds

SYRUP

175 g (6 oz) sugar
60 ml (4 tablespoons) honey
60 ml (4 tablespoons) water
7.5 ml (1½ teaspoons)
  sesame oil
5 ml (1 teaspoon) white rice
  vinegar

SHAJIMA

This biscuit is eaten everywhere in China, but it is particularly popular in the south. It was originally a Manchu recipe and it is interesting that the name Shajima makes no sense in Chinese.

Oil an oblong baking tin 20 × 30 cm (8 × 12 inch) with sesame oil. Mix the flour, baking powder and beaten eggs together and knead into a smooth, slightly shiny dough, or use a food processor. Roll out the dough on an unfloured board into a rectangle about 5 mm (¼ inch) thick, and cut into long strips about 5 cm (2 inches) wide. Cut each strip into very thin shreds about 3 mm (⅛ inch) thick. Separate the shreds and drop them, a few at a time, into very hot oil. Fry for about 1 minute until they are light gold in colour, then lift them out and leave to drain. When all the strips are fried, put the syrup ingredients into a large saucepan and melt the sugar over a low heat. When it has melted, turn up the heat and bring to the boil, stirring all the time. After it has boiled for 4 minutes, remove from the heat and carefully mix in all the fried shreds, taking care not to crush them. When they are completely coated in the syrup, spoon them out onto the oiled baking tin and press down flat. Sprinkle with sesame seeds and leave to cool. Cut into oblongs or squares before serving.

VARIOUS SWEET PASTES

The different pastes made according to the following recipes would not be eaten on their own, but are used to make the numerous sweet fillings that are described in other recipes throughout this book. All these pastes freeze well and should be allowed to completely defrost before using them as directed.

紅豆沙

Makes approximately 400 g
  (14 oz) bean paste
180 g (6 oz) red adzuki beans
caster sugar
50 g (2 oz) lard

RED BEAN PASTE

Rinse the beans and soak them overnight in clean water. The next day rinse again and put them into a saucepan with 800 ml (1⅓ pints) water. Bring to the boil, add another 150 ml (¼ pint) cold water, and bring back to the boil. Turn down the heat and simmer the beans until they are really soft – about 1½ hours. If necessary, add more water. When the beans are ready, strain off the remaining water and put the beans into a *mouli-legumes* (food mill) using the finest grille, or use a wire sieve. Stand the *mouli* in a bowl of clean water. Work the beans through the *mouli* or sieve, using the water to wash out the soft flesh so that only the hard shells are left in the *mouli*, and the pulp is in suspension in the water. Discard the hard shells. Leave the water and bean pulp to

Hold *mouli* in water to wash bean flesh from hard shells.

settle for at least 30 minutes, then carefully pour away the clear water from the top before straining the remaining water and bean pulp through a fine cotton cloth, or better still a jelly bag. Squeeze tightly to get rid of as much water as possible.

Now weigh the squeezed bean pulp and allow an equal quantity of caster sugar to bean pulp. Melt the lard in a large saucepan, add the sugar and one-third of the bean pulp. Cook the mixture over a low heat, stirring all the time until the sugar has dissolved. Then add the rest of the bean pulp and boil over a low heat, beating all the time until the paste comes clean away from the bottom of the pan – about 15 minutes. The longer it takes, within reason, the better. Remove and allow to cool before using.

If you wish to use this red bean paste as a stuffing for mooncakes or other *baked* (rather than steamed) pies, add 90 ml (6 tablespoons) of plain flour just before removing the bean paste from the heat. Beat the flour in well and remove from the heat.

白豆沙

WHITE BEAN PASTE
Use 180 g (6 oz) white haricot beans in place of the red adzuki beans in the previous recipe. Soak them overnight and then, depending on their age, boil them for up to 2 hours before sieving them. Otherwise the method is the same as for red bean paste.

綠豆沙

GREEN BEAN PASTE
Substitute 180 g (6 oz) mung beans for the red adzuki beans. Soak them overnight and then boil for between 1 and 1½ hours. Sieve and treat as the red beans above.

栗泥

Makes approximately 700 g
  (1½ lb) chestnut paste
25 g (1 oz) lard
approximately 200 g (7 oz)
  icing sugar depending on
  taste
1 × 439 g (15½ oz) can
  chestnut purée

CHESTNUT PASTE
Melt the lard in a large saucepan and add the sugar and chestnut purée. Bring to the boil, beating hard all the time. Test to see if it is sweet enough for your taste. If not, add more sugar. Boil, gently beating all the time for about 3 minutes over a low heat, before tipping into a bowl to cool. Use as required.

枣泥

Makes approximately 350 g
(12 oz) red date paste
250 g (8 oz) dried red dates
180 g (6 oz) caster sugar
25 g (1 oz) lard
60 ml (4 tablespoons) plain
flour

茶

RED DATE PASTE

Wash the dates thoroughly and soak them in cold water for 4 hours. Then rinse again and put them into a pan with 600 ml (1 pint) of water. Simmer until they are really soft, about 1 hour. If necessary, add a little more water. Strain off the remaining water and reserve. Allow the dates to cool slightly, then rub them through a strong sieve to remove their skins and stones. This takes time and is quite hard work: use a little of the reserved water to help the date pulp through the sieve. Weigh the resulting date pulp – 250 g (8 oz) of dates will usually result in about 180 g (6 oz) pulp – and allow an equal quantity of caster sugar.

Melt the lard in a saucepan and add the sugar and date pulp. Beat over a low heat until the sugar has melted, then continue beating while the mixture boils gently for about 3 minutes. Add the flour, spoonful by spoonful and beat between each addition. Turn out of the pan and leave to cool.

CHINESE TEA

Tea is an integral part of a dimsum meal, and tea drinking accompanies a large number of the small snacks and refreshments that are eaten throughout the day in the Chinese world. The history of tea-drinking goes back nearly two thousand years in China. Originally, tea was considered to be a medicinal drink. For the last one thousand years tea has been a most highly prized commodity, both by the Chinese community itself and by the merchants from Asia and later from the West who sought to buy it. Even today the wealthy in Taiwan will pay enormous sums for the very best teas picked at exactly the right moment, and it is said even now little or none of the best tea ever leaves China, but is drunk by a privileged few.

There are hundreds of different teas grown in most parts of southern China. They have names whose significance is similar to that of regional or local wines in France. For instance, the name Longjing belongs to a speciality green tea, greatly prized, from a group of communes in Zhejiang, just as a wine like Monbazillac marks the produce of a group of villages in Guyenne. A wine name of this kind indicates the locality of origin, the type and within limits, the quality of the wine; the same is true of the names of teas in China. The time when the leaves are picked – for instance early in the season – gives extra and even more specialized quality to the tea. There are three different methods of preparing Chinese tea and teas are classified accordingly. Usually a district will specialize in one particular kind of preparation, with local variations, but the same tea leaves can be prepared by any of the methods.

The most highly esteemed teas are the green or

unfermented teas, for which the leaves are lightly rolled and immediately steamed to prevent any fermentation, after which they are baked dry. By this process the leaves remain green and the flavour of the tea is light and astringent. Green teas should never be made with boiling water or they will taste bitter. The best flavour comes when the water is 60°C (170°F) but green tea can stand a temperature of 70°C (190°F) — the boiling point of water is 100°C (214°F). Longjing from Zhejiang is one of the most admired green teas, which has small flat leaves that look like dried rosemary. Longjing from Jiangsu is sold in the West.

Almost as greatly prized as green tea is oolong, or half-fermented, tea. Oolong is made from leaves that are allowed to ferment for a short period, then steamed to prevent any further fermentation. It has a dark colour, but is more astringent than fully fermented teas. An apocryphal story says that oolong tea was discovered when workers, frightened by a snake, left the green tea to ferment for a period by mistake before starting to steam it. It was first mentioned in the eighth century, but it was not until about eight hundred years later that it became really well known. The most famous varieties come from Fujian, including one called 'Iron Goddess'. It is said that one day a very devout man called Wei went up the mountains to collect firewood and while he was there he saw a tea bush growing between two rocks. It shone so brightly in the sunlight that he dug it up and took it home to plant in his garden. Wei tended it carefully and eventually made oolong tea from it. The flavour and colour were so strong that he called it his 'iron goddess' — *Tieh guan yin*. Tea from this variety of bush is still grown in Fujian and is available in the West under the packet name *Tieh kuan yin* together with another called *Fujian Oolong cha*. Gunpowder is a form of oolong tea specially processed for the Western market. Oolong should always be made with boiling water.

Flower teas are made with either green or oolong tea. They were first invented about six hundred years ago and in the seventeenth century became very popular with the Imperial court. They were originally made in huge jars — first a layer of dry tea leaves, then a layer of flower petals, such as lotus flowers, jasmine, roses or plum blossom, and then more tea — always in the proportion of three of tea to one of flower petals. Flower teas are still very popular among the Chinese and in the West, but they are more suitable for drinking at the end of a meal than with food.

The coarsest tea is black or fermented tea. The leaves are withered in the sun after they are picked until they are limp, then they are rolled, usually by hand, in order to break the leaf cells and free their juices. Then they are left for several hours in baskets under damp cloths to ferment by the action of the natural bacteria on the leaves, before being steamed and dried. The fermentation process turns the leaves black and gives a stronger, but less astringent flavour to the tea. Chinese black teas are rather similar to Ceylon tea and should always be made with boiling water. Many Chinese black teas are available in the West; usually they are known only by their district of origin, as in *Fujian hong cha*. *Puer* from Yunnan is of the highest quality. Strictly speaking, *puer* is a brick tea made by a special steaming and pressing process. It was the original China tea of the eighteenth century. A story is told of the origins of *puer* tea, that in the third century AD when the Chinese General Zhu led his soldiers into Yunnan, many of them developed an eye disease. General Zhu pointed to a stone with his staff and miraculously from it grew a tea bush. The soldiers made tea with its leaves and their blindness was cured. A good story, although *puer* tea bushes pre-date the general's arrival in Yunnan. *Puer* is considered a 'healthy tea' and since it is thought to give protection against oily foods, it is frequently drunk at meal times; in Hong Kong it is the tea most usually drunk with dimsum meals.

Generally speaking, green tea is drunk as a refreshment between meals and with small snacks or cakes, oolong tea or black tea is drunk with food particularly dimsum meals, and flower teas are drunk after food.

Index

Page numbers in *italics* refer illustrations